MORE ADVANCE PRAISE FOR

Evangelical Catholicism:

"This remarkable book offers nothing less than a map and compass for men and women determined to take up the challenge of living the Catholic faith in its fullness under 21st-century conditions. With its bold call for 'deep reform' in every single corner of the Church, *Evangelical Catholicism* is sure to provoke lively discussion. The book's proposals for true renewal are presented with the clarity and verve that have made George Weigel a peerless advocate of the courage to be Catholic."

—Mary Ann Glendon, author of *The Forum and the Tower: How Scholars and Politicians have Imagined the World, from Plato to Eleanor Roosevelt*

"George Weigel has been the leading diarist of authentic Catholic renewal— its progress, detours, personalities, and hopes—for 30 years. In *Evangelical Catholicism* he turns his extraordinary skills to the needs of the Church in the coming decades, calling us back to the missionary vocation we received at baptism and offering us a road map to faithful, vigorous Church reform. Rich in its vision, engaging in style, on target in its counsel, and invaluable for anyone trying to understand the Church and her challenges in the 21st century, this book should not be missed."

—Most. Rev. Charles J. Chaput, O.F.M. Cap., Archbishop of Philadelphia

"A challenging, no-nonsense book that summons the Catholic Church to propose the Gospel without compromise in an ardent, joyful embrace of the new springtime of faith preached by Blessed John Paul II and Benedict XVI."

—Mario Paredes, Presidential Liaison for Roman Catholic Ministries, American Bible Society

"Catholics, especially bishops and priests, who are looking for an insightful and dynamic profile of the Church of the New Evangelization need to read this book soon."

—Most Rev. Philip Tartaglia, Archbishop of Glasgow, Scotland

"A timely, accessible and unusually insightful work."

—Don J. Briel, Koch Chair in Catholic Studies, University of Saint Thomas

EVANGELICAL
CA†HOLICISM

EVANGELICAL CATHOLICISM

DEEP REFORM IN THE 21ST-CENTURY CHURCH

GEORGE WEIGEL

BASIC BOOKS

New York

Published by Basic Books,
A Member of the Perseus Books Group

Books published by Basic Books are available at special discounts for bulk purchases in the United States by corporations, institutions, and other organizations. For more information, please contact the Special Markets Department at the Perseus Books Group, 2300 Chestnut Street, Suite 200, Philadelphia, PA 19103, or call (800) 810-4145, ext. 5000, or e-mail special.markets@perseus books.com.

All Scriptural citations are taken from the
Revised Standard Version of the Holy Bible.

Designed by Pauline Brown
Typeset in 11.5 point Minion Pro by the Perseus Books Group

Library of Congress Cataloging-in-Publication Data

Weigel, George, 1951–
   Evangelical Catholicism : deep reform in the 21st-century church / George Weigel.
      p.   cm.
   Includes bibliographical references and index.
   ISBN 978-0-465-02768-2 (hardcover)—ISBN 978-0-465-03787-2 (e-book)
1. Church renewal—Catholic Church. 2. Catholic Church—History—21st century. 3. Evangelicalism. 4. Catholic Church—Relations—Evangelicalism. 5. Evangelicalism—Relations—Catholic Church. I. Title.
   BX1746.W425 2013
   282.09'051—dc23
                                                           2012037230

10 9 8 7 6 5 4 3 2

For Scott Newman
and Russell Hittinger

Contents

CONTENTS

Where are the tongues of fire talking of God and his love? When do men speak of the "commandments" of God, not as a duty to be painfully observed, but as the glorious liberation of man from the enslavement of mortal fear and frustrating egoism? Where in the Church do men not only pray but also experience prayer as the Pentecostal gift of the Spirit, as glorious grace? . . . We talk too little of God in the Church or we talk about him in a dry, pedantic fashion, without any real vitality. . . . Only when the message of the living God is preached in the churches with all the power of the Spirit, will the impression disappear that the Church is merely an odd relic from the age of a society doomed to die. . . . And in turn profession of faith in Jesus as Christ and Lord, the decisive and final word of God in history, might become more alive, more joyous and spontaneous.

—KARL RAHNER, S.J.
—1974—

. . . Today we seem to be witnessing the birth of a new Catholicism that, without loss of its institutional, sacramental, and social dimensions, is authentically evangelical . . . [Catholicism] at its best has always promoted a deep personal relationship with Christ. In evangelizing we are required to lift our eyes to him and transcend all ecclesiocentrism. The Church is of importance but is not self-enclosed. It is a means of drawing the whole world into union with God through Jesus Christ. . . . The first and highest priority for the Church is to proclaim the good news concerning Jesus Christ as a joyful message to all the world. Only if the Church is faithful to its evangelical mission can it hope to make its distinctive contribution in the social, political, and cultural spheres.

—AVERY CARDINAL DULLES, S.J.
—1991—

The Church is called to a deep and profound rethinking of its mission. . . . It cannot retreat in response to those who see only confusion, dangers, and threats. . . . What is required is confirming, renewing, and revitalizing the newness of the Gospel . . . out of a personal and community encounter with Jesus Christ that raises up disciples and missionaries. . . .

A Catholic faith reduced to mere baggage, to a collection of rules and prohibitions, to fragmented devotional practices, to selective and partial adherence to the truths of faith, to occasional participation in some sacraments, to the repetition of doctrinal principles, to bland or nervous moralizing, that does not convert the life of the baptized would not withstand the trials of time. . . . We must all start again from Christ, recognizing [with Pope Benedict XVI] that "being Christian is . . . the encounter with an event, a person, which gives life a new horizon and a decisive direction."

—FIFTH GENERAL CONFERENCE OF THE BISHOPS
OF LATIN AMERICA AND THE CARIBBEAN
—2007—

Prologue

An Invitation to Evangelical Catholicism and Deep Catholic Reform

---

A S THE CATHOLIC CHURCH MARKED THE FIFTIETH ANNIVERSARY OF THE opening of the Second Vatican Council, demands for the reform of the Church were insistent, widespread, and often cacophonous. But the call for "reform" was usually the end of any agreement among the petitioners.

In the first decades of the twenty-first century, "progressive" Catholics have their reform agenda; so do "traditionalist" Catholics. Hans Küng, who once described Vatican II's task as "reform and reunion," is quite certain that he knows what true "reform" is; so are the publishers of *The Wanderer* and the editors of *The Tablet*, although none of them can agree on the specifics of this reform. The *New York Times* has its idea of what Catholic reform would look like; so does the Vatican newspaper, *L'Osservatore Romano*; so do hundreds of thousands of bloggers and Internet commentators throughout the world. There the resemblance stops. The call for reform is virtually universal, while the terms of reform are comprehensively disputed.

Still, there may be one other point of concord. Among all the contending parties, there is general agreement that 1962–1965—the years of the Second Vatican Council—were the years in which the problems and promise of twenty-first-century Catholicism took shape. More sophisticated observers may drive the analysis back a few decades, to the Catholic intellectual renaissance of the mid-twentieth century, from which they rightly trace many of the themes that shaped the Council's deliberations: a new biblical consciousness; a heightened awareness of the importance for theology of history and different philosophical perspectives; the renewal of the Church's worship; a new engagement with public life. But across the spectrum of opinion, ecclesiastical or secular, it is usually agreed that Vatican II was where twenty-first-century Catholicism began, for good or for ill.

This consensus-within-the-cacophony tends to lose sight of the deeper currents of Church and world cultural history, however. It is as if the debates over Catholic identity that occupied the Council years and the decades that followed simply began *ex nihilo*—or began in the forms into which the debate quickly congealed. This book and the proposals it contains are based on the premise that these familiar analyses, which shed some light on various aspects of the twenty-first-century Catholic reality, are nonetheless analyses on the surface of things. That means that the proposals for "reform" that come out of those analyses are also, in the main, surface proposals that do not cut to the heart of the imperative of deep Catholic reform.

THE DEEP REFORM OF THE CATHOLIC CHURCH HAS IN FACT BEEN UNDERWAY for more than one and a quarter centuries. It began with Pope Leo XIII. It continued in one way through the revitalization of Catholic biblical, liturgical, historical, philosophical, and theological studies in the mid-twentieth century. It continued in another, and at least as important, way in the martyrdom of millions of Catholics at the hands of the mid-twentieth-century totalitarian systems. It was furthered by Pope Pius XII in his teaching on the Church as the "Mystical Body of Christ."[1] It reached a high-water mark of ecclesiastical drama in the Second Vatican Council. It was given new impetus by Pope Paul VI in the 1975 apostolic letter *Evangelii Nuntiandi*, which called the entire Church to a new sense of missionary fervor in proclaiming the Gospel.[2] And it has been brought into sharper focus by the pontificates of two men of genius, Blessed John Paul II and Benedict XVI. Many of Catholicism's twenty-first-century struggles—from the sexual abuse crisis, to the radical secularization of Europe, to the contest with evangelical, Pentecostalist, and fundamentalist Protestantism for the Christian future of Latin America, to the challenge of finding an appropriate "inculturation" of Catholic faith in Africa and Asia—reflect the churning of these deeper currents of reform, the resistance they have encountered, and the slow, difficult emergence of a new way of being Catholic: a new "form" of Catholicism.

This new form is in essential continuity with Catholicism's origins and doctrinal development, for otherwise it would not be a genuinely Catholic "form" of being the Church. But it is also something new. Perhaps better, it is the recovery and redeployment, in twenty-first-century guise, of something quite old, something that goes back to the first centuries of the Christian era.

It is called, here, *Evangelical Catholicism*. Before I unpack that phrase in what follows—both in terms of what Evangelical Catholicism is and in terms of the deep reforms in the Church to which it will lead—it is important to specify what I do *not* mean by Evangelical Catholicism.

EVANGELICAL CATHOLICISM IS NOT A WAY OF BEING CATHOLIC THAT ADAPTS certain catechetical practices and modes of worship from evangelical, fundamentalist, and Pentecostalist Protestantism.

Evangelical Catholicism is not the Catholicism of the future as imagined by either "progressive" Catholics or "traditionalist" Catholics, although Evangelical Catholicism does take from the former the imperative of development and from the latter the imperative of a development—a reform—that follows the essential form of the Church given to it by Christ.

Evangelical Catholicism is not a Catholicism tailored to what appears to be, by contrast to western Europe, the comparatively stronger condition of the Catholic Church in the United States.

Evangelical Catholicism is not simply a response to the sexual abuse crisis that has dominated the world media's coverage of the Catholic Church since 2002.

Evangelical Catholicism is not a movement within Catholicism, or a Catholic sect, or a new kind of Catholic elite.

Evangelical Catholicism is not a substitute for *Roman* Catholicism. Indeed, its evolution is closely linked to the emergence of the modern papacy, even as its further development will place demands on a reformed Office of Peter in the Church.

If this is what Evangelical Catholicism is *not*, then just what is it?

EVANGELICAL CATHOLICISM IS THE CATHOLICISM THAT IS BEING BORN, OFTEN with great difficulty, through the work of the Holy Spirit in prompting deep Catholic reform—a reform that meets the challenges posed to Christian orthodoxy and Christian life by the riptides of change that have reshaped world culture since the nineteenth century. Evangelical Catholicism will be defined in greater detail in the first part of this book, *The Vision of Evangelical Catholicism*. The deep reforms to which that vision, embodied in the Church's life, ought to lead is the subject of the book's second part, *The Reforms of Evangelical Catholicism*.

The Catholic Church believes that it was constituted—that it was given a distinctive *form*—by the will of Christ himself. Thus all true Catholic reform is by reference to that divinely given constitution of the Church, a "constitution" in the British, rather than in the American, sense of the term. Over two millennia of history, authentic, genuine Catholic reform has meant reaching back into that constitution and retrieving aspects of the Christ-given form of the Church. That is what happened in the so-called Dark Ages, with the development of western monasticism. That is what happened in the Gregorian reforms of the eleventh century (which also had an enormous impact on the evolution of political life in the West). That is what happened when the sixteenth-century Council of Trent, having taken a hard look at the corruptions that had been one cause of the Reformation, created a form of Catholicism—Counter-Reformation Catholicism—that endured for centuries. And that is what the Second Vatican Council intended to do, and in some measure achieved.

The challenge today is not only that Catholicism is confronted by hostile cultural forces contending that the Church and its teaching ill serve men and women living in a free, just, and humane society. That is an old story. And, to be candid, such New Atheists as Richard Dawkins, Sam Harris, and the late Christopher Hitchens rather pale in comparison to Nero and Diocletian, Voltaire and Robespierre and Bismarck, Lenin and Mao Zedong. The challenge today is to recognize the distinctive character of that cultural hostility, which was born of an indifference to biblical religion that mutated in the nineteenth century into the claim that the God of the Bible is the enemy of human freedom, human maturity, and progress in the natural sciences. In the twenty-first century, this hostility may lead to new forms of overt persecution directed at believers for the simple reason that they *are* believers. In the first two decades of the new millennium, however, it has been directed primarily to the marginalization of Catholicism and its reduction to a private lifestyle choice of no public consequence. In any case, the challenge of the post-conciliar Church is to preach the Gospel in a new, and perhaps unprecedented, cultural situation.

The Western world, the historic homeland of Christianity, has become "disenchanted," in sociologist Max Weber's famous term. The windows and skylights of the human experience seem to have been nailed shut and painted over. A modernity (and postmodernity) that owes far more to the Christian civilization of the West than many heirs of the continental Enlightenment are prepared to concede has produced an often-toxic public culture that is increasingly Christophobic, to adopt a term used by an Orthodox Jew and distinguished international legal scholar, Joseph H. H. Weiler.[3] All of this poses new challenges to Catholicism. These challenges can only be met by the deep reforms of Evangelical Catholicism: reforms that will reclaim the essential, Christ-given form of the Church while equipping its people and their ordained leaders with the tools to convert a disenchanted and not-infrequently hostile world.

Grasped in its fullness, Evangelical Catholicism invites Catholics (and indeed all who are interested in the Catholic Church) to move beyond the left/right surface arguments of past decades, which were largely about ecclesiastical power, and into a deeper reflection on the missionary heart of the Church—and to consider how that heart might be given expression in the twenty-first century and the third millennium. Evangelical Catholicism is about the future. Grasping its essence, however, means learning a new way of looking at the recent Catholic past. So that is where we shall begin.

PART ONE

The Vision of Evangelical Catholicism

CHAPTER ONE

Ends and Beginnings

A FEW BRIEF YEARS INTO THE PONTIFICATE OF BENEDICT XVI, A SALIENT fact about his successor was already known: the next pope— whoever he might be, wherever he may have been born, or whatever positions he had previously held—would not be a man who had participated in the Second Vatican Council.

Unlike Blessed John Paul II, who, as a young Polish bishop, played a significant role in drafting several of the Council's documents, and unlike Benedict XVI, who as Father Joseph Ratzinger was a key theological adviser at Vatican II, the next Bishop of Rome will not have been present at the most significant Catholic event since the sixteenth-century Council of Trent. Indeed, should Benedict XVI live as long and full a life as the founder of the modern papacy—Leo XIII, who died at age ninety-three in 1903—his successor may not even have been born, or may have been in elementary school, when the Second Vatican Council met from 1962 to 1965. The next pope's entire ecclesiastical life will have been spent in the turbulence of the postconciliar Catholic Church. Unlike his two immediate predecessors, the 265th successor of St. Peter will not have shared in the experience of Vatican II, which was decisive for both John Paul II and Benedict XVI.

When Benedict XVI was elected in 2005, at the age of seventy-eight, it was sometimes said that he would be a "transitional" pope—which was precisely what was said of seventy-seven-year-old John XXIII at his election in 1958. In both cases, the prediction turned out to be true, if not precisely in the way the prognosticators meant. For neither of these popes became the placeholders that predictors of their "transitional" papacies imagined; they became "transitional" in entirely different ways.

By summoning the Second Vatican Council, John XXIII tried to create the ecclesiastical conditions for a new Pentecost, a new and enlivening experience of the Holy Spirit that would enable the Church to enter the third millennium with renewed evangelical energy, engaging the modern world in a dialogue about humanity's future. In the event, however, his Council provoked a crisis in Catholic identity that made the pontificate of Pope John's successor, Paul VI, a longsuffering *Via Crucis*, a papal walking of the way of the Cross. By the time of Pope Paul's death on August 6, 1978, both the papacy and the Catholic Church seemed exhausted and dispirited.

Then, after the brief "September papacy" of John Paul I, came the pope from Poland, John Paul II, who, at his first public Mass as Bishop of Rome, put evangelical heart and courage back into the Catholic Church by his bold summons to a fearlessness that would "open the doors to Christ!" For twenty-six and a half years, with the able assistance of Cardinal Joseph Ratzinger as his principal theological counselor, John Paul II did what had seemed impossible in 1978: he gave the Council an authoritative interpretation; led the Church into the kind of new Pentecost that John XXIII had envisioned, through the experience of the Great Jubilee of 2000; and pointed the Church firmly and confidently into the future, declaring that a "New Evangelization" would be the Catholic Church's grand strategy in the twenty-first century and the third millennium.[1] That grand strategy has been followed by Benedict XVI, whose pontificate has been one of dynamic continuity with that of his predecessor, whose accomplishment may lead history to remember him as Pope St. John Paul the Great.

The turbulence of Catholic life since Vatican II is often thought to have been caused by an ongoing ecclesiastical civil war between "progressives" and "conservatives" (or "traditionalists"), a taxonomy that became fixed in the public (and Catholic) mind during Vatican II and that has proven difficult to dislodge ever since. But dislodged it must be. For the progressive/conservative filter for reading Catholic life since Vatican II obscures far more than it illuminates. And what it most obscures is the deep reform that has been underway in the Church since Cardinal Vincenzo Gioacchino Pecci was elected Bishop of Rome on February 20, 1878, taking the name Leo XIII. Pecci's election, not the opening of Vatican II on October 11, 1962, is the date to which we must trace the birth of the twenty-first-century Church. For Leo XIII set in motion a profound transformation of Catholicism in which the Church slowly moved beyond the catechetical-devotional model that had been dominant since the sixteenth-century Counter-Reformation to a new model—a model that is best described as Evangelical Catholicism.

More than one and a quarter centuries after Leo XIII initiated it, that transformation is not by any means complete. Indeed, its completion will involve the further, deeper reform of the Catholic Church. That reform will reflect a radically regrounded idea of both Christian discipleship and of the Church's task—an idea of discipleship and mission that synthesizes the growth of Catholic self-understanding from Leo XIII through Benedict XVI; that recognizes that the challenges of this unique moment in the history of world culture require a new and dynamic way of being Catholic that is in continuity with the authentic heritage of the Catholic past; and that calls the Church out of the stagnant shallows of institutional maintenance and points Catholicism into what John Paul II called "the deep" of a new millennium.[2]

Benedict XVI is, then, a "transitional pope," in that, with his pontificate, the Catholic Church is indeed at the end of an era. But the end that is at hand carries within itself the fertile seed of the future. In that future, a deeply Catholic reform—a reform built on the twin foundation stones of Word and Sacrament—will enable the Church to respond with renewed energy to its Master's Great Commission: "Go therefore and make disciples of all nations, baptizing them in the name of the Father, and of the Son, and of the Holy Spirit" [Matthew 28.19].

The End of the Counter-Reformation

When Pope Pius IX died in 1878, many European statesmen and intellectuals imagined the papacy—and, by extension, the Catholic Church—to be finished as a force in human affairs. Having lost the Papal States, the pope was the "prisoner of the Vatican." The rapidly expanding working class of an industrializing Europe was leaving the Church in large numbers, and European high culture was becoming increasingly secularized—indeed, hostile to biblical religion.[3] And, while many remembered Pius IX as an admirable man who had been badly abused by his contemporaries (in reaction to which Pius IX was the first pope to become a figure of mass popular adulation), the image of "Pio No-No" hung heavily over the Church; for this, after all, was the pope who had said a resounding "No" to his times with his 1864 *Syllabus of Errors*, which condemned the notion that "the Roman Pontiff can and should reconcile himself with progress, liberalism, and modern civilization." On Pius IX's death, the general atmospherics did little to suggest that Catholicism could recover from the beating it had taken since the French Revolution, which, along with its cultural and political offspring, had overthrown the old European regimes, shattered traditional ideas of authority, and severed the bond between Church and state that had defined crucial aspects of Catholic life since the Roman emperor Constantine.

Given the anticlerical passions that had shaped the *Risorgimento* (the unification of Italy in the nineteenth century), the cardinals who met to elect Pius's successor were not even certain that they could conduct their business safely in Rome. Cardinal Henry Edward Manning of England even suggested moving the conclave of 1878 to Malta, so that it could meet under the protective guns of the Royal Navy.[4] The cardinals eventually decided to stay in Rome, but they likely thought they were electing a placeholder when they chose the sixty-eight-year-old Vincenzo Gioacchino Pecci as pope. In fact, what they did was set in motion the end of Counter-Reformation Catholicism, a process that has continued into the twenty-first century.

Pope Leo XIII enjoyed the third longest pontificate in reliably recorded history. And during a reign that lasted over a quarter of a century, he quietly, steadily, and doggedly set about creating the conditions for a new Catholic engagement with modern cultural, political, economic, and social life. He reformed the Church's philosophical and theological mind by mandating a close reading of Thomas Aquinas's original texts, which were to become the foundation from which to build a distinctive Catholic intellectual engagement with modernity.[5] He was the papal father of modern Catholic biblical studies, which he thought necessary to meet the deconstructive aspect of the challenge posed by the historical-critical method of reading ancient texts.[6] He fostered serious historical scholarship in an effort to determine what was truly enduring and constitutive—and what was transient—in the life of the Church.[7] He also drew on the thinking of men such as the German Wilhelm Emmanuel von Ketteler and Britain's Manning to forge a new Catholic encounter with modern political and economic life, launching modern Catholic social doctrine with the 1891 encyclical *Rerum Novarum*; its very title suggested an engagement with the "new things" of modernity, and thus a striking move beyond the blanket, antimodern rejectionism of Pius IX (which Leo understood to be the product of Pius's unique circumstances and personality).[8] His tacit approval of the American constitutional arrangement on church and state began the process by which the Catholic Church would embrace religious freedom at Vatican II as a fundamental human right. That, in turn, created the platform from which John Paul II, the man who bested Leo's papal longevity record, would change the history of the twentieth century.[9]

Leo's tomb in the Roman basilica of St. John Lateran neatly captures his epic achievement. The marble image of the deceased pontiff is not recumbent. Rather, the statue of Leo XIII depicts the Pope standing upright, right arm extended and foot thrust forward, as if inviting the world into a serious conversation about the human prospect—as if leading the Church out of the past and into a new, confident, evangelical future.

Viewed through this Leonine lens, Catholic history since Vatican II comes into a clearer focus than is possible when the viewing is done through the "progressive/conservative" prism that got set in analytic concrete during the Council. It is certainly true that, in the fifty-nine years between Leo's death in 1903 and the opening of Vatican II in 1962, various forces contended within the Church over the path into the future; some of those forces wanted to shore up the crumbling ramparts of Counter-Reformation Catholicism, while others were more sympathetic to the basic thrust of the Leonine renewal. But if one understands just how much of Vatican II's teaching was made possible because of the ground broken by Leo XIII, then it becomes possible to "see" beneath the surface confusions and contentions of contemporary Catholic history. And at that deeper level of perception, it becomes clear that what happened at Vatican II, and in the Church's efforts to implement its teaching faithfully, cannot be understood simplistically as a struggle for ecclesiastical power between a party of the Left and a party of the Right. More was happening and more was at stake—much more.

If Leo XIII, the last pope of the nineteenth century and the first of the twentieth, is the starting point for understanding the deeper currents at work in late twentieth-century and early twenty-first-century Catholicism, then Vatican II and what has happened since can be properly understood, and in depth. The Second Vatican Council brought to a moment of high drama the dynamic process begun by Leo's reforms: the process of moving Catholicism beyond the Counter-Reformation. The pontificates of John Paul II and Benedict XVI put an authoritative interpretation on Vatican II by treating the Council as one of reform through retrieval, renewal, and development, in which lost elements of the Church's life that had been forgotten or marginalized during the Counter-Reformation were recovered and made into instruments of evangelical renewal. The interpretive framework created by the teaching of John Paul II and Benedict XVI has, in turn, effectively put an end to two inadequate readings of Vatican II: the idea of the Council-as-rupture-with-the-past (typically advanced by the progressive camp), and the idea of the Council-as-terribly-mistaken-concession-to-modernity (the preferred trope of traditionalists).

In all of this, to repeat, something of far greater consequence than can be perceived through the distortions of the progressive/conservative filter was afoot. That *something* was nothing less than the end of an era—the era of Counter-Reformation Catholicism—and the birth of a new moment in Catholic history: the era of Evangelical Catholicism.

The Counter-Reformation Church, which sought to preserve Catholicism through simple, straightforward catechetical instruction and devotional piety, may well have been a necessity in the centuries between the fracturing of Western Christianity in the mid-sixteenth century and the cultural triumph of modernity during the nineteenth century. Counter-Reformation Catholicism gave birth to innumerable saints as the priesthood and consecrated religious life were reformed. It was the form of Catholicism that evangelized the New World; that sent great missionaries like Francis Xavier to India, Japan, and China, and Peter Chanel to Oceania; and that inspired Charles Martial Lavigerie to found the White Fathers, the Missionaries of Africa. It was the form of Catholicism that restored some measure of Catholic life to Great Britain, that survived the French Revolution, that held firm against Bismarck's anti-Catholic *Kulturkampf*, and that stood fast against anticlerical persecutors in Mexico. It was the form of Catholicism that, under unprecedented conditions of religious freedom, planted the Church firmly in the new United States against the opposition of both Protestant bigots and Deist skeptics. It was the Catholicism in which a rich, populist devotion to the Blessed Virgin Mary accelerated. And it was, in the main, the Catholicism that resisted the communist persecution of the Church, the worst such persecution in history.

But it was not a form of Catholicism that could successfully meet the full challenge of modernity, the response to which required more of Catholics than (to take American reference points) memorizing the *Baltimore Catechism* and wearing the Miraculous Medal. John Henry Newman knew this in mid-nineteenth-century Great Britain—as he knew that the answer to the challenge of modernity was not to be found in what he dismissed as "liberalism" in religion: religion as mere sentiment.[10] Leo XIII knew this from his days as a nuncio in Belgium and a diocesan bishop in Perugia. And as Bishop of Rome, he began the process by which Counter-Reformation Catholicism would be supplanted.

Counter-Reformation Catholicism created Catholic cultures (or microcultures) that transmitted the faith as if by osmosis. But when the acids of modernity hit those Catholic cultures with full force—especially in the turbulence of the 1960s—those Catholic microcultures crumbled: in the urban-ethnic Catholic centers of the United States, in Québec, in Ireland, in Spain, in Portugal, in the Netherlands, in Bavaria, in France, and indeed throughout the North Atlantic Catholic world. Some hint of what might be necessary as an alternative to the Counter-Reformation model was emerging at the same time—a deeply biblical and sacramental Catholicism that displayed enormous growth in Africa. But the evangelical alternative to Counter-Reformation Catholicism remains to be fully described for the Church in the West, where, for cultural reasons that have now become clear, the Counter-Reformation model ran aground and shattered.

In his 2011 intellectual memoir, *Adventures of an Accidental Sociologist*, Peter L. Berger distilled a lifetime of reflection on the relationship between religion and modernity in these terms: Modernity breaks down traditional cultures through a process of pluralization. Under the conditions of modernity (urbanization, markets, mass education, post–*ancien régime* politics, natural science as the dominant metaphor for knowledge), competing explanations of the world and the human prospect inevitably emerge. As Berger wrote, "modernity . . . relativizes all worldviews and value systems, including the religious ones. This relativization is intrinsic to modernity, just about impossible to avoid. It presents a deep challenge to all religious traditions and to their truth claims."[11] In these circumstances, religious certainty is not, and cannot be, transmitted through osmosis by the ambient culture (or microculture). Religious faith, commitment to a religious community, and a religiously informed morality can no longer be taken for granted.

Progressive Catholicism accepts this relativization of religious truth and sees Catholicism as one possible story—one possible truth—in a pluralistic world of truths and "narratives," none of which can claim the mantle of certainty. Traditionalist Catholicism imagines that modernity can be rolled back and that the old, culturally transmitted certainties can be restored. But what Hegel called the "butcher's board of history" has determined that the latter option is not in fact an option. At the same time, the infertility of progressive Catholicism—its inability to transmit the faith to successor generations, which has a lot to do with its watering down of Catholic truths claims, or doctrines—has now been amply demonstrated throughout the religious wasteland of Western Europe, the part of the world Church that adopted the progressive project most enthusiastically. History, not argument, has shown the implausibility of progressive Catholicism as a strategy to empower the Church for mission in the third millennium.

Catholic traditionalism is also an implausible, indeed impossible, model for living Catholicism. It denies the reality of the conditions under which the Gospel must be proclaimed in the twenty-first century—and thus renders itself evangelically sterile, sounding the retreat into bunkers and catacombs rather than issuing a call for witness and mission. The variant on liberal Protestantism that is progressive Catholicism has no demographic traction in the world Church (although it is sustained in academic life by the tenure system); neither does traditionalist Catholicism, especially that schismatic variant of traditionalism that was founded by the late French archbishop Marcel Lefebvre. Both of these options turn out, on closer examination, to be variants of the same Counter-Reformation, rule-based, catechetical-devotional Catholicism: the traditionalist camp wants to tighten up and ratchet down the rules, the catechism answers, and the devotions, while the progressives want to loosen the bolts in the name of openness or compassion. Like fossils in amber, both remain stuck within the Counter-Reformation model.

Both are dying, and in the first decades of the twenty-first century, their demise is another sign pointing toward the emergence of Evangelical

Catholicism: a Catholicism born from a new Pentecost, a new outpouring of missionary energy for a new historical and cultural moment.

Pentecost, Again

Blessed John XXIII wanted the Second Vatican Council to be a new Pentecost. Blessed John Paul II wanted the Great Jubilee of 2000 to be a pentecostal experience of the Holy Spirit for the entire world Church, empowering Catholicism for a "New Evangelization" in the third millennium. To wish for a new Pentecost, however, is to wish for no easy thing. To wish for a new Pentecost is to play with fire.

As Joseph Ratzinger once wrote in a meditation on the Solemnity of Pentecost (the annual celebration of the first outpouring of the Holy Spirit that is often described as the birth of the Church), "the Holy Spirit is fire; whoever does not want to be burned should not come near him." Ratzinger went on to recall a nonbiblical saying of Jesus transmitted by the third-century Alexandrian theologian Origen: "Whoever is near to me," Jesus says in Origen's account, "is near to the fire"—a dominical maxim that closely parallels Luke 12.49: "I came to cast fire upon the earth; and would that it were already kindled!" This fire, Ratzinger continued, is an "inimitable" part of "the relationship between Christ, Holy Spirit, and Church."

That relationship and its connection to mission is nicely caught, Ratzinger wrote, in a commentary by St. John Chrysostom, the learned fourth-century patriarch of Constantinople, on the passage in the Acts of the Apostles in which the excitable people of Lystra imagine Paul and Barnabas to be incarnations of the Greek gods Zeus and Hermes. Their popular acclamation as deities stuns the two apostles, who quickly respond, "We also are men, of like nature with you, and bring you good news" [cf. Acts 14.8–18]. Chrysostom, explicating this text, noted that, yes, they were indeed human beings like the frenzied men and women of Lystra. But they were also something more, something different, for they had been touched by fire—and they now spoke in a purified and powerful way, having been touched by the tongues of fire that came upon the Church through the outpouring of the Holy Spirit at Pentecost.

The fire of the Holy Spirit purifies, inspires, and fuses men and women together into a new human community, the Church. Through each of its members, and in them as a whole, the Church is the Body of Christ on earth. Paul, Barnabas, and all who have been truly converted to Christ—such that friendship with Christ and extension of the possibility of friendship with Christ to others has become the basic dynamic of their lives—have become something different. Radically converted Christians have become men and women marked by tongues of fire, animated by the Spirit, whose abiding presence they recognize in the liturgy by their common prayer, their exchange of the peace of Christ, and their common reception of the Lord's body and blood.

Closing his meditation on Pentecost, Joseph Ratzinger readily conceded that one must ask of many Christians today, "Where is the tongue of fire?" And then he issued a challenge that captures the drama of Evangelical Catholicism: "Faith is a tongue of fire that burns us and melts us so that ever more it is true: I am no longer I. . . . When we yield to the burning fire of the Holy Spirit, being Christian becomes comfortable only at first glance. . . . Only when we do not fear the tongue of fire and the storm it brings with it does the Church become the icon of the Holy Spirit. And only then does she open the world to the light of God."[12]

As these reflections on Pentecost suggest, there is nothing easy, simple, or comfortable about Evangelical Catholicism. The cultural Catholicism of the past was "comfortable" because it fit neatly within the ambient public culture, causing little chafing between one's life "in the Church" and one's life "in the world." Evangelical Catholicism, by contrast, is a counterculture that seeks to convert the ambient public culture by proclaiming certain truths, by worshipping in spirit and in truth, and by modeling a more humane way of life. Evangelical Catholicism does not seek to "get along"; it seeks to convert.

No one should doubt that this is hard. Counter-Reformation Catholicism was not easy, in that the abiding restlessness of the human heart and the ancient turmoils of the human passions still had to be calmed. But in a premodern world where authority was taken for granted, the religious authority of the Church to discipline human waywardness was, well, taken for granted. In Peter Berger's sociological terminology, the Church's authority was an unchallenged "plausibility structure" for ordering one's life, and adherence to it was typically absorbed from the ambient public culture. At the very least, adherence to this mode of life was not frontally attacked by the ambient public culture.

That is no longer the case throughout the developed world in the twenty-first century. Catholics cannot walk down New York City's Madison Avenue or its equivalents in Toronto, Buenos Aires, Paris, Berlin, London, Rome, or Sydney without having their "plausibility structure," their Christian way of understanding How Things Are and How Things Ought To Be, sensorily assaulted at every turn. To profess the truths of the Creed as true—and not just as "true for me," but as the truth of the world, revealed as such by the Son of God who became man—is to risk being thought an imbecile. To uphold biblical morality as a way of ordering human relationships that is both revealed truth and rationally knowable truth is to court being called a bigot.

Under these circumstances, lukewarm Catholicism has no future: submitting to the transforming fire of the Holy Spirit is no longer optional.

Evangelical Catholicism is in many respects far more demanding than Counter-Reformational, catechetical-devotional Catholicism. It requires more effort by priests and bishops, consecrated religious, and laity; no one gets a pass on the tongues of fire. It requires a deeper religious culture: to take one counterexample, Evangelical Catholicism is nourished not by the simple formulas of the *Baltimore Catechism*, but by the mystagogical reflections of the ancient *Jerusalem Catecheses*, which invited Christians to immerse themselves deeply into "the mysteries" that are the sacraments, and to have the entirety of one's life formed by them.[13] Evangelical Catholicism requires a generosity about time from the laity, who must make time amid the rush of postmodern life for a deeper encounter with Christ than that permitted by an hour's worth of weekly worship. Evangelical Catholicism also requires a greater measure of stability from pastors and bishops, because building vibrantly evangelical Catholic parishes and dioceses takes time, just as it takes time to foster the relationships necessary for what St. Paul called a "more excellent way" [1 Corinthians 12.31]—which has always been a harder way—to form and bear fruit in mission.

The Evangelical Catholicism that is being born as a result of the Catholic renewal of Leo XIII and his successors will require more attention to sacramental preparation and sacramental discipline, for it will be nourished by the sacraments in the way imagined by the classic mid-twentieth-century liturgical movement, which linked liturgy and worship to Christian formation, Christian mission, and Christian work for justice in the world. Evangelical Catholicism will require far more attention to preaching than is found throughout most of the Church in the developed world, for mission is nourished by the Word of God in Scripture just as it is by the sacraments. And that, in turn, will require a deeper reform of recruitment to the ordained ministry and a deeper reform of seminary formation.

Evangelical Catholicism will also require bishops to reimagine their roles as instruments of unity in the Church: bishops of the Catholic future must recognize that they can only be instruments of unity when they are helping to unite souls to the liberating truth of the Gospel, which in turn requires those souls to let go of falsehood and sin. Thus Evangelical Catholicism will sometimes require the Church, in its interface with public life, to say a firm and unambiguous "No"—as the German bishops had to do during the Bismarckian *Kulturkampf* (which saw half of them imprisoned); as the bishops of Poland did in 1953 when they said "No" to the efforts of Polish communism to turn the Church into a subsidiary of the party (another bold defense of the Gospel that led to imprisonment for some successors of the apostles); as bishops throughout the Western world of the twenty-first century have to do when the state declares its authority to alter the nature of marriage or to declare entire classes of human beings outside the community of common protection and concern.

Evangelical Catholicism builds up the community of the faithful not for the sake of the community but for the sake of a common reception of the mysteries of the faith, which in turn become the fonts of grace from which the community sets about the conversion of the world. The tongues of fire from which the Church is formed thus become the fire of mission by which the world is set ablaze.

Evangelical Catholicism calls the entire Church to holiness for the sake of mission.[14]

Growing Through Deepening

It will be objected that this is simply too hard—that such a vision of deeply converted, thoroughly catechized, sacramentally enriched, and evangelically impassioned Catholics being launched "into the deep" of the postmodern world simply asks too much and is thus a prescription for a new kind of Catholic sectarianism: a Church that is purer, but smaller. Evangelical Catholicism certainly asks a lot. But it is precisely by calls to Christian greatness based on the grace of God lifting up our hearts, and the fire of the Holy Spirit infusing our efforts, that the Catholic faith has always grown.

It was this kind of faith that conquered the pagan world and sustained the proto-martyrs in their trials.

It was this kind of faith, nurtured by a mystagogical approach to the sacraments, that led fishmongers and bakers in Constantinople to debate the relationship of the divine to the human in Jesus Christ. And if Byzantine tradesmen could debate the hypostatic union, then surely the most educated Catholics in the history of the Church can, when led by pastors who are masters of preaching, probe the depths of their weekly Sunday confession that the Lord Jesus is "consubstantial with the Father," and draw from that reflection new insight, energy, and passion for mission.

It is this kind of faith—deeply biblical and richly sacramental, a faith in which the divine Presence is a palpable reality of everyday life—that has led to the tremendous growth of Catholicism in twentieth- and twenty-first-century Africa, as millions of Africans have been drawn from a world of spirits and powers into the truth of the one true God, his Son, and their Holy Spirit.

And it is Evangelical Catholicism that undergirds the growth that is possible amid what often seem the ruins of the once-substantial Catholic world in the West.

Catholic parishes in the unlikeliest places (Soho, in London's West End; Greenville, South Carolina, in the heart of the American Bible Belt; midtown Manhattan) and Catholic campus ministries around the world (at Texas A&M University, at Princeton, and at a Catholic university in L'viv organized by the formerly illegal and underground Ukrainian Greek Catholic Church) are flourishing because pastors are preaching the Gospel without compromise, celebrating the sacramental mysteries with dignity and grace, serving the marginalized, and thereby "equipping the saints" for mission. It is no accident that these and similar parishes, campus ministries, and Catholic institutions of higher learning give birth to large numbers of priestly and religious vocations in an otherwise dry season.

From Yonkers, New York, to Alma, Michigan, to Nashville, Tennessee, and from Pluscarden Abbey in the Scottish highlands to Our Lady of the Annunciation Monastery in Clear Creek, Oklahoma, religious congregations of women and men who live the consecrated life according to the model of Evangelical Catholicism are growing—and growing at a time when other religious orders are shriveling into nothingness because of their inherent implausibility.

Renewal movements and new Catholic communities that have grasped the evangelical essence of Vatican II, and are living missionary discipleship, are the liveliest sectors of the Church in such once-solidly-Catholic countries as France and Argentina.

Seminaries that are forming twenty-first-century priests for Evangelical Catholicism are growing (and in a few rare cases, full), while seminaries that are still stuck in the grooves of either progressive or traditionalist Catholicism are stagnant or slowly dying.

Throughout the Western Catholic world, Evangelical Catholicism inspires genuine creativity in the intellectual life. And it does so in no small part because the faith is understood from the outset as a precious, revealed gift to be appreciated through the arts of reason, rather than an object to be dissected according to postmodern canons of skepticism and incoherence.

One can even see the beginnings of an evangelical Catholic renaissance in the arts—in the work, for example, of British composer James MacMillan, American architect Duncan Stroik, Russian-born painter Natalia Tsarkova, Irish sculptor Dony MacManus and Dutch sculptor Daphne Du Barry, and the Rome-based critic Elizabeth Lev.

In these circumstances, it may be tempting to cite G. K. Chesterton's famous observation that "the Christian ideal has not been tried and found wanting; it has been found difficult and left untried." But that would be unfair to those who have never had Evangelical Catholicism proposed to them—the poorly catechized, the liturgically bored, the morally confused. In the first decades of the twenty-first century, Evangelical Catholicism is just coming into its first maturity after more than a century of struggle to define this reformed mode of being Catholic in the world—a struggle whose origins can be traced to Pope Leo XIII. When Evangelical Catholicism is proposed, it is more often embraced enthusiastically than rejected as impossible to accept. That is the experience of the parishes, campus ministries, religious orders, seminaries, renewal movements, and intellectual centers just noted.

But it must be proposed. Sketching that proposal in far more detail is the next order of business.

CHAPTER TWO

Truths with Consequences

D ID THE SECOND VATICAN COUNCIL MANDATE A FUNDAMENTAL CHANGE in Catholic self-understanding that amounted to a rupture with the past? Was the Council a terrible mistake that let loose a host of demons that might otherwise have been contained? Was Vatican II a triumph subsequently hijacked by men determined to return the Church to the certainties and security of the 1950s? Did the Council break faith with settled Catholic teaching on questions such as the right relationship of church and state, the relationship of the Church to living Judaism, the quest for Christian unity, the interreligious dialogue, and religious freedom?

For decades, the Catholic Church debated these and other basic questions of how to correctly interpret what all the contestants acknowledged as a watershed moment in Catholic life: Vatican II. Those debates produced some interesting historical scholarship and some serious theology—as well as mutual anathemas (usually tacit rather than explicit), more than a few hard feelings, one formal schism on the right (the small Lefebvrist break), and a much more consequential psychological schism on the left (in which large numbers of Catholics have long ceased to believe and profess what the Catholic Church believes and professes, but have remained formally, or canonically, within the Church's boundaries). These debates have not been worthless.

They have, however, tended to obscure the truly radical intention of the Second Vatican Council and its program of deep Catholic reform.

That intention was to put the Gospel at the center of Catholic life and to build out from that center a reformed Catholicism: an Evangelical Catholicism that had the capacity to propose the good news of Jesus Christ to a disenchanted world, and thus fulfill the Master's Great Commission in the distinctive cultural circumstances of the third millennium of Christian history.

Not "Spirituality"

One of the oddities of late-modern and postmodern culture has been the proliferation of any number of "spiritualities." Their wares can be examined on shelf after shelf in the "spirituality" sections of bookstores: artifacts that bear testimony to the fact that, although the twenty-first-century West may indeed be Max Weber's "disenchanted world," the ancient hungers of *Homo religiosus* remain to be satisfied. In the main, these "spiritualities" represent a vast number of variations on the theme of the human search for God, to the point where the word "seekers" has entered the world's vocabulary (and even the Church's vocabulary) to designate those looking for some contact with the divine.

This anthropocentric and deeply subjective searching for the divine is precisely the opposite of what the Second Vatican Council taught and what Evangelical Catholicism proposes. That proposal is neatly summarized in the Council's central theological document, *Dei Verbum*, the Dogmatic Constitution on Divine Revelation:

> It pleased God, in his goodness and wisdom, to reveal himself and to make known the mystery of his will [cf. Ephesians 1.9]. His will was that men should have access to the Father, through Christ, the Word made flesh, in the Holy Spirit, and thus become sharers in the divine nature [cf. Ephesians 2.18; 2 Peter 1.4]. By this revelation, then, the invisible God [cf. Colossians 1.15; 1 Timothy 1.17], from the fullness of his love, addresses men as his friends [cf. Exodus 33.11; John 15.14–

15] and moves among them [cf. Baruch 3.38], in order to invite and receive them into his own company. This economy of revelation is realized by deeds and words, which are intrinsically bound up with each other. As a result, the works performed by God in the history of salvation show forth and bear out the doctrine and realities signified by the words; the words, for their part, proclaim the works, and bring to light the mystery they contain. The most intimate truth which this revelation gives us about God and the salvation of man shines forth in Christ, who is himself both the mediator and the sum total of Revelation.[1]

"Spirituality," as the postmodern world understands it, is the human search for the divine. Christianity, by contrast, is about God's search for us, and our learning to take the same path through history that God is taking. That is the understanding of Christianity that animates Evangelical Catholicism, in full agreement with Christian orthodoxy through the centuries—which itself mirrors the dynamics of God's revelation to Abraham and his descendants, the Jewish people.

Moreover, as the Dogmatic Constitution on Divine Revelation also teaches, this search of God for us, and our response in faith, is a truth with the most weighty of consequences. The Fathers of the Second Vatican Council wanted to make those consequences unmistakably clear at the very beginning of the Constitution:

Hearing the word of God with reverence, and proclaiming it with faith, [this Council] assents to the words of St. John: "We announce to you the eternal life which dwelt with the Father and was made visible to us. What we have seen and heard we announce to you, so that you may have fellowship with us and our common fellowship be with the Father and his Son, Jesus Christ" [1 John 1.2–3]. Following, then, in the steps of the Councils of Trent and Vatican I, this [Council] wishes to set forth the true doctrine on divine Revelation and its transmission. For it wants the whole world to hear the summons to salvation, so that through hearing it may believe, through belief it may hope, through hope it may come to love.[2]

Postmodern "spirituality" is for seekers. Evangelical Catholicism is for finders. And the point of being a finder—better, the point of being found by grace and accepting that "being-found"—is to convert the world—and to do so in the challenging cultural circumstances of this historical moment.[3]

A Challenge Accepted

In placing the Gospel—all that God has revealed for our salvation in Holy Scripture and in apostolic tradition—at the center of the Church, the Second Vatican Council accepted the gauntlet laid down by modernity and whatever would come after modernity. Modernity and postmodernity deny that there is any such thing as "revelation." Evangelical Catholicism accepts that challenge and agrees that, if Christianity is not a revealed religion, then it is a false religion. It then insists that Christianity is not of our making, but of God's.

The conviction that Christianity is a revealed religion is thus the conviction on which Evangelical Catholicism rests: the supernatural gift of divine revelation (i.e., God coming in search of us) is given to men and women so that, by an act of faith that is itself made possible by supernatural grace, they may be set on the path of salvation, which is the glorification of the human person within the light and life of God the Holy Trinity (i.e., our responding to God's search for us by learning to take the same path through history that God is taking).

It is, so to speak, all supernatural, all the time. Evangelical Catholicism's response to the "disenchantment of the world" is not virtuous stoicism and honorable resignation, along the lines proposed by honest modern nonbelievers like Albert Camus. Rather, Evangelical Catholicism, following the Second Vatican Council's radical reorientation of the Church to the Gospel, believes that modern anxiety and postmodern malaise alike are best met by the proclamation of the good news of biblical revelation: that this is a creation in which the windows, doors, and skylights have been opened to transcendent light by God himself, who enters history for the redemption of the creation he brought into being. And through that light of divine revelation, the darkness of here-and-now, which is in part a reflection of the human propensity for evil and in part a recognition of the inevitability of death, is illuminated with the deepest truth of the human condition: that we are made by God and destined for God by acts of divine love that precede time, define time, and will extend beyond time.

In his 1847 novel, *Loss and Gain*, John Henry Newman captured the essential, radical quality of the evangelical Catholic conviction about the act of faith being ordered to divine revelation. In a chastened reflection on the difference between tepid, culturally transmitted religiosity and genuine Christian faith, offered by one of the novel's characters, Newman the novelist sheds as much light on the twenty-first century as he did on the Victorian Age:

> Individuals may display a touching gentleness, or a conscientiousness which demands our reverence; still, till they have faith, they have not the foundation, and their superstructure will fall. They will not be blessed, they will effect nothing in religious matters, till they begin by an unreserved act of faith in the word of God . . . ; till they go out of themselves; till they cease to make something within them their standard; till they oblige their will to perfect what reason leaves sufficient, indeed, but incomplete . . . 4

The Church of the twenty-first century cannot, however, invite men and women to faith on the basis of authority. It must deploy a bolder, more evangelical appeal. It must change the game.

Changing the Terms of Reference

Fifty years after Vatican II, the invocation of ecclesiastical authority carries little weight. The phrase "The Church teaches . . ." means nothing outside the Church. It also means much less than it should inside the

Church—as is clear from the endless examples of Catholics who live a kind of do-it-yourself Catholicism, in which Catholic teaching may be a reference point, but is hardly life-defining. As Americans have come to learn in the debates over issues such as the right to life and the meaning of marriage, however, these teachings are life-defining by their very nature; and thus the resolution of these debates will have specific consequences in what the world calls "the real world." Yet the hard fact is that "The Church teaches . . ." is language destined to fall upon deaf ears in twenty-first-century cultures of radical subjectivity, in which the highest authority is the imperial autonomous Self.

"The Gospel reveals . . ." is a different matter. "The Gospel reveals . . ." is a challenge in answer to the critique of the very idea of "revelation" mounted for the past two centuries by the high culture of the West. "The Gospel reveals . . ." is a challenge not unlike the challenge posed by Jesus to his disciples on the road to Caesarea Philippi: "Who do you say that I am?" [Mark 8.29]. By throwing down a gauntlet in the form of a proposal, "The Gospel reveals . . ." demands a response. That response may, initially, be skepticism, even hostility. But it will likely not be indifference. Moreover, if the truth, proclaimed clearly and fearlessly enough, has its own power—as two millennia of Christian history have shown—"The Gospel reveals . . ." may, at the very least, be a conversation starter—unlike "The Church teaches . . . ," which sets off every modern and postmodern and antiauthoritarian alarm bell in minds and hearts formed by the ambient culture of the twenty-first-century West.

Evangelical Catholicism understands that there is an inherent connection between divine revelation and the Church: "The Gospel reveals . . ." eventually leads to "The Church teaches . . ." But it gets to the latter from a distinctive starting point. Evangelical Catholicism begins from an unapologetic confession of Christian faith as revealed faith—"the eternal life which was with the Father *and was made manifest to us*" [1 John 1.2].[5] That eternal life, that Word of God that has come into history in search of us, is "what we have seen and heard" [1 John 1.3].

That, and nothing less or other than that, is the starting-point of Evangelical Catholicism, its proclamation, and the reforms of the Church it will undertake.

An admittedly dramatic, but perhaps not completely implausible, example might help drive home the point. If a certain diocese was reduced, by scandal, desertion, and bankruptcy, to its local bishop sitting in a public park after saying his daily Mass and saying to passers-by, "Hello, I'm Bishop _____. May I tell you about Jesus Christ?" the Gospel, and the essential nature and mission of the Catholic Church, would still be there, despite what would seem to be utter institutional collapse.

For friendship with Jesus Christ is at the center of Evangelical Catholicism.

Friendship with Christ

On May 25, 1899, at the end of a century widely regarded as having set the stage for an era of boundless human progress, Pope Leo XIII issued the encyclical *Annum Sacrum*. There, he commanded the Church's bishops to consecrate the world to the Sacred Heart of Jesus—"the image of the infinite love of Jesus Christ which moves us to love one another"[6]— during three special days of prayer the following month.

A decade and a half later, and irrespective of the dictates of the calendar, the nineteenth century as an era ended and the twentieth-century era began with the guns of August 1914: the opening salvos in what would become a seventy-seven-year civilizational emergency that ended with the collapse of the Soviet Union on August 15, 1991 (when, in terms of epochs, the twentieth century ended). During those intervening eight decades, more human beings were slaughtered for political reasons than in any other comparable period—and by orders of magnitude. Whatever the horrors of the Thirty Years' War—and they were truly horrible—the Seventy-Seven Years' War was worse.[7] This was the era of the trenches of Flanders, No Man's Land, and unrestricted submarine warfare; the Gulag camps; the Ukrainian terror famine; Auschwitz-Birkenau, Majdanek, and Sobibor; the bombing of Rotterdam and London, Hamburg and Dresden, Tokyo and Hiroshima and Nagasaki; the deliberate starvation of hundreds of thousands of prisoners of war; a Cold War that threatened global catastrophe; and the greatest persecution of the Church in history.[8] While the medium- and long-term impacts of that emergency remain to be seen, the short-term impact was the end of Europe as the center of world civilizational initiative. Indeed, the demographic winter into which Europe has seemingly consigned itself in the twenty-first century, by its willful failure to produce future generations, can be read as the result of a malaise that hung over much of the West, like a thick, choking fog, at the end of an era that was supposed to have produced a matured humanity, tutored by reason and science.[9]

On April 30, 2000, almost nine years after the epoch of the twentieth century ended, Pope John Paul II canonized Sister Mary Faustina Kowalska, a Polish nun who had received visions, during the 1930s, of the Divine Mercy radiating from the heart of Christ. In the year of the Great Jubilee, April 30 happened to be the Octave of Easter; so the last pope of the twentieth century and the first pontiff of the twenty-first proclaimed that the Church would henceforth celebrate the Octave of Easter as Divine Mercy Sunday. For it was the divine mercy, John Paul preached in his canonization homily, that was the face of God the postmodern world most needed to see, given everything that had happened since Leo XIII had lifted up the Sacred Heart of Jesus as the answer to secular modernity's imagined self-sufficiency.

That hubris had turned the twentieth century into an abattoir. God had provided a response to the crushing burden of guilt that humanity had brought upon itself in the visions of St. Faustina. Those visions were a reiteration in modern guise of the truths taught in the parable of the Prodigal Son, which (as Rembrandt made clear in his depiction of its climax) is more properly called the parable of the Merciful Father.[10]

Christ, John Paul believed, was beckoning to the world, inviting postmodern humanity to a new understanding of its grief and calling the Church to a new proclamation of his Gospel. In this, too, John Paul was completing a reform initiated by Leo XIII.

Leo XIII, At the Point

The Sacred Heart devotion so cherished by Leo XIII was in one sense a populist answer to the ongoing problem that theology calls "monophysitism"—the tendency to stress the divinity of Christ to the point that his humanity becomes a mere disguise, as Clark Kent's horn-rimmed glasses disguised Superman. Monophysitism has plagued Christianity for more than a millennium and a half and was a recurring theological and catechetical problem for Counter-Reformation Catholicism.[11] In emphasizing this devotion, and by consecrating the world to the Sacred Heart in 1899, Leo XIII set three interesting developments in motion.

First, he sent a shot across the bow of modernity's ultramundane politics. The Sacred Heart had long been a symbol of resistance to post-Jacobin radical secularism and the legally enforced privatization of religious belief and practice. Consecrating the world to the Sacred Heart was thus a tacit but unmistakable warning about the risks run by a public life that excluded from the public square the truths contained in this image of compassion and fraternity. Whatever the reaction in Leo's time, his warning seems remarkably prescient, given the West's twentieth century self-cannibalization: an act of cultural vandalism and auto-genocide that Aleksandr Solzhenitsyn famously said was the by-product of men having "forgotten God."[12]

Second, by consecrating the world to the Sacred Heart of Jesus, Leo was extolling a form of popular piety that expressed important themes in the thinking of St. Thomas Aquinas, whose work Leo saw as the intellectual fulcrum for the Church's new engagement with a disenchanted world. The Sacred Heart, Leo wrote in *Annum Sacrum*, reminded the Church that Christ, who on the day of his death had told Pontius Pilate that he was indeed a king [John 18.37], exercised his unique sovereignty by "truth, justice, and above all, by charity," not by coercion.[13] In his *Summa Theologiae*, Leo noted, Thomas Aquinas had highlighted this unique form of sovereign power, thus helping cement into the cultural foundations of the West a nobler notion of sovereignty and authority than the mere will-to-power that unhappily characterized many expressions of political modernity (in Leo's time and our own).

Third, Leo was placing a papal seal of approval on a process of development in Catholic self-understanding that would lead to the Second Vatican Council's restoration of the Gospel to the center of the Catholic Church's life. For to recenter the Church on the Gospel is to restore Jesus Christ, and friendship with the Christ who displays in his humanity the merciful face of God the Father, to the center of the Church—a point underscored by John Paul II in the historical bookend to *Annum Sacrum*, the designation of the Octave of Easter as Divine Mercy Sunday.

Christ, Gospel, Church

In this line of thinking, Evangelical Catholicism offers friendship with Jesus Christ and acceptance of his sovereign but gentle yoke as the answer to the question that is every human life. Evangelical Catholicism proclaims that Jesus is both the teacher *par excellence* and the Gospel that is taught, even as he is the preacher *par excellence* and the Good News that is preached. His Gospel, which is at the heart of the evangelical Catholic proclamation, is a call to "repent and believe." It is a call to recognize that the Kingdom of God is at hand, here and now, among us. It is an invitation to enter that Kingdom, here and now, through ongoing conversion of heart and way of life.[14]

Because the Gospel is the starting point, Evangelical Catholicism insists that no one is born a Catholic and that "becoming a Catholic" is a lifelong process: a matter of living out the promises and grace of one's Baptism in radical discipleship, according to the teaching of Christ as transmitted by Holy Scripture and the apostolic tradition of the Church. You are not a Catholic in the full sense of the term because your grandmother was born in County Cork or Palermo or Guadalajara and your parents submitted you to a certain religious ritual when you were an infant. You are a Catholic because you have met the Lord Jesus and entered into a mature friendship with him—which is to say, in evangelically

Catholic language, that the sacramental grace of your Baptism, should you have been baptized as an infant, has been made manifest in the pattern of your life as you have grown into human maturity.

Evangelical Catholicism, therefore, preaches no generic truth-about-God. Rather, Evangelical Catholicism, born from the Old and New Testaments, proclaims that the God of Abraham, Isaac, and Jacob, who is also the God of Moses and Sinai and the abiding covenant with the People of Israel, finally and definitively revealed himself in Jesus of Nazareth, Son of God and son of Mary. His Incarnation, one of the two central mysteries of Christian faith, reveals the second of those great mysteries: that God is an eternal communion, a Holy Trinity, of self-giving and receptive love. The affirmation of those two truths, made possible by friendship with Jesus Christ, is the bottom of the bottom line of the life of Christian faith. No one comes to the Father except through friendship with Jesus Christ. And it is by adhering to him that one receives the gift of the Holy Spirit, sent by the Father and the Son to bring tongues of fire to earth.

One of the great themes of the pontificate of Pope Benedict XVI has been that friendship with Jesus Christ is the *raison d'être* of the Church. The Church exists to offer the possibility of personal friendship with the Lord Jesus, the acceptance of which leads both to the truth about God and to the richest imaginable human life. And where does one find this Church through which we become friends of Christ? We find it where Chapter 2 of the Acts of the Apostles tells us to look: where the apostolic teaching is transmitted and where the bread of fellowship in the Body of Christ is broken and shared.[15] In that community, men and women are empowered to live lives in conformity to the ways in which the Lord Jesus himself tells us that friendship with him is lived: in giving bread to the hungry, drink to the thirsty, clothes to the naked, and freedom to prisoners.[16]

This way of living is deeply, and, to some, alarmingly, countercultural. The mode of life Evangelical Catholicism proposes, however, is vastly—indeed infinitely and eternally—more humane than living according to the insatiable demands of the imperial autonomous Self, its worship of worldly prestige, and its indifference to humility. As modeled by evangelical Catholic communities in mission and service, this way of living is the Catholic Church's twenty-first-century answer to the colossal human suffering caused by the politics of the will-to-power. The worlds of pagan antiquity were converted in no small part by the self-evident superiority of the Christian way of life. The postmodern world of the twenty-first century and the third millennium will be converted in the same way: through humane modes of living that are grounded in Gospel truth and that offer the possibility of being seized by that truth.

Which is, Evangelical Catholicism proclaims, the truth of the world: a truth that forms a mission-centered community of disciples with a clear sense of identity and purpose.

The Evangelical Importance of Doctrine

This recentering of the Church's life on the Gospel, and on friendship with Jesus Christ who *is* the Gospel as well as the Anointed One of God who proclaims it, is the reason why doctrinal clarity and purity are important. Amid the doctrinal turmoil of the decades since Vatican II, some of the combatants within the Church may have forgotten the stakes in these debates.

What is at stake in the demand for doctrinal clarity (and for the clarity of Catholic identity that follows from doctrinal clarity) is not a matter of winning an intellectual argument, which is how self-absorbed intellectuals often understand it. Rather, doctrinal clarity is a matter of equipping "the saints," the men and women who have entered into friendship with the Lord Jesus, to become his witnesses in the world and the servants of those who most need to see the face of the Father of Mercies. Doctrinal clarity and conviction foster the process of lifelong conversion. Doctrinal clarity and conviction deepen one's friendship with Christ. Thus there is no "doctrinal Catholicism" *here* and "social justice Catholicism" *there*. The truth of the Gospel, conveyed through the apostolic preaching as preserved and proclaimed by the ordained teachers of the Church and celebrated in the Church's sacraments, is what makes authentic Christian service possible.

This Gospel-centered approach to the Christian life, which is the central feature and distinctive "marker" of Evangelical Catholicism, sheds light on certain controversies that have plagued the Catholic Church for decades.

If the Gospel—all that God has revealed for our salvation in Holy Scripture and apostolic tradition—is the center of the Church, such that adherence to that Gospel brings one into full communion with the Church, then it becomes clear, if sadly clear, that there are many Catholics in name and canonical (legal) status who are, in existential fact, adherents of another religion. One thinks of members of communities of consecrated life, priests and religious sisters, who deny certain settled matters of doctrine. These are men and women who, while canonically Catholic (in the sense that they have not incurred excommunication, either imposed or self-imposed), in fact cleave to another gospel and another savior. Their connection to the Church of Jesus Christ has become attenuated; their communion with the Catholic Church has become strained; their link to the Church in the early twenty-first century too often involves the legal possession of property given by donors who imagined that they were making gifts to the Catholic Church.

One also thinks of Catholic political leaders whose Catholicism seems, at best, ethnic and vestigial. To deny that what the Church teaches to be true is true is to declare oneself in a defective state of communion with the Church, irrespective of one's legal status under canon law. To deny that those truths, in matters of public moral order (such as the defense of the inalienable right to life or the nature of marriage), ought to be embodied in law and public policy (*not* because "my religion demands it" but because these are rationally defensible moral truths that society ignores at its peril) suggests that one's understanding of public life is gravely incoherent. To work to embody in law and public policy the *opposite* of the truths to which the Church witnesses is to place oneself in such a state of opposition to the Gospel—*not* in the first instance to "Church authority," but to the Gospel—that one's own integrity would seem to demand either finding an alternative religious home or being converted in full.

Thus evangelical Catholics who adhere to the Gospel—once again, the truths that God has revealed for our salvation in Holy Scripture and the apostolic tradition—are in fuller communion with evangelical Protestants who affirm classic Christian orthodoxy than they are with prominent Catholic theologians such as Hans Küng, Roger Haight, and Elizabeth Johnson, despite being, canonically, in the same Church with the latter.

Viewed through the same evangelical Catholic lens, the life of Katharine Jefferts Schori, who left the Catholic Church of her youth for the Episcopal Church and became its presiding bishop in the United States in 2006, has more coherence than the lives of those who, while remaining legally inside the boundaries of the Catholic Church, live in a state of psychological schism from it. Jefferts Schori left the Catholic Church with her parents and, evidently, later came to understand that she did not believe the Gospel proclaimed by the Catholic Church—so she remained an Episcopalian, in a community with clear and radically different understandings of the Gospel than those taught by the Catholic Church. Hers is a more coherent and more honest position than that of those who reject the Gospel proclaimed by the Catholic Church while retaining their "legal residence," as it were, within it.

And whatever their intentions, the latter are, objectively, impeding the evangelical mission of the Catholic Church, which can only be undertaken on the conviction that it is rooted in the Word of God.[17]

The Key to Vatican II and All the Rest

The Second Vatican Council's Dogmatic Constitution on Divine Revelation took more than four years to develop. Originally intended to settle the question of the Catholic Church's relationship to modern biblical scholarship and to resolve a long-standing dispute within Catholic theology over the "sources of revelation" (hence its Latin title, "The Word of God"), *Dei Verbum* underwent a lengthy gestation that involved sharp debates and much redrafting. Overwhelmingly adopted by the Council Fathers and promulgated by Pope Paul VI on November 18, 1965 (just three weeks before the Council closed), *Dei Verbum*, for all the travails of its birth, is in many respects *the* key Vatican II text—the prism through which the developments of Catholic self-understanding set in motion by Leo XIII were refracted into the sharp, clear light of Evangelical Catholicism. And in that crucial sense, *Dei Verbum* is *the* key Vatican II document for the deep reform of the Catholic Church.

Everything discussed just above is present in *Dei Verbum*. In *Dei Verbum*, the Catholic Church unambiguously affirms that Divine Revelation is a fact, not a pious myth. And in that unfolding process of revelation, God chose to reveal not merely propositions about himself, but *himself*. God did this through words and deeds, both of which are recorded in the Old Testament, which will always remain a sacred text for the Catholic Church, as well as in the New Testament, which, like its Hebrew predecessor, is a trustworthy witness to all those truths that God wished to reveal for the salvation of humanity.[18] This process of divine self-disclosure reached its definitive moment in the life, death, and resurrection of Jesus of Nazareth, the Anointed One of God, whose Paschal Mystery (which the Church relives every year, from Holy Thursday through Easter Sunday) is the perfection and seal of divine revelation.

That Paschal Mystery reveals the truth of the world, not just truth-for-Christians. To be brought into contact with that truth is to be offered the possibility of what St. Paul called the "obedience of faith" [Romans 1.5, 16.26], which is itself made possible by the grace of God poured into the world by the Holy Spirit. Rather than being a burden, this obedience is a joyful liberation into the truth about one's own humanity, a liberation made possible by a sure knowledge of God, and of God's love.

The apostles of Christ, *Dei Verbum* continues, were commissioned by the Lord Jesus himself "to preach the Gospel, which had been promised beforehand by the prophets, and which he fulfilled in his own person and promulgated with his own lips." Thus the apostles were to "communicate the gifts of God to all men," for the Gospel was "the source of all saving truth and moral discipline." In fulfilling that commission, the apostles and their successors "committed the message of salvation to writing," and thus produced the New Testament.[19] Those successors continued the apostolic preaching with the same authority that Christ had given to the apostles; they created, under the guidance of the Holy Spirit, the unified, evangelical witness of the Catholic Church.

One Witness

Throughout the generations of the Church, then, Scripture, apostolic tradition, and the teaching authority of the Church (as manifest in those bishops who are the apostles' successors) form one witness to the Gospel. That witness is "like a mirror in which the Church, during its pilgrim journey here on earth, contemplates God, from whom she receives everything, until such time as she is brought to see him face to face as he really is [cf. 1 John 3.2]."[20] Thus Scripture and the Church's tradition form "a single sacred deposit of the word of God," which is "entrusted to the Church" not as some sort of prize to be grasped, but as a gift to be gratefully received and then given away in proclamation and witness.[21] The primary task of the teaching authority of the Church, therefore, is to maintain the integrity of that proclamation while empowering the entire Church for the work of evangelization and service.

Evangelical Catholicism is built on the firm conviction that all of this is *true* and makes that affirmation without getting lost in the technical weeds of discussion about the "inerrancy" of the Bible. What is taught in Scripture and the authentic apostolic tradition is truth, not metaphor or "narrative." The Bible, from the perspective of Evangelical Catholicism, is a complex but unified narrative tradition in which metaphorical language is sometimes used because no other form of human language is possible to convey the truths that God revealed for our salvation.

This conviction that what the Church teaches is true by no means obviates the need for theology. It does ask theologians to see, as *Dei Verbum* put it, that theology "relies on the written word of God," together with apostolic tradition, "as on a permanent foundation."[22] Which is to say that theology, as Evangelical Catholicism understands it, is not a matter of human cleverness alone, or even primarily. Theology is the business—the *privileged* business—of reflecting through the arts of human intelligence on the truths that God has revealed, truths of which the Church's teaching authority is the custodian.

Dei Verbum thus suggests one important criterion for the deep reform of the Catholic Church. In their teaching on divine revelation (which enjoyed the highest authority as a "dogmatic constitution"), the Fathers of the Second Vatican Council offered the Church and the world a great act of faith in the fact of revelation. This act of faith contains within itself an implicit criterion of deep and authentic Catholic reform: *the criterion of truth.* That criterion can be applied in a blunt question: Do you—whether you are deacon, priest, or bishop, member of a seminary faculty or certified Catholic intellectual, consecrated religious man or woman under vows, or layperson living and working "in the world"— *believe* that the Gospel (understood as all that God has revealed for our salvation in Holy Scripture and apostolic tradition) is a supernatural gift of divine revelation that measures your life, rather than your life measuring it? Do you *believe* that the Gospel measures the enthusiasms of the moment, rather than those enthusiasms measuring it?

As the entire experience of the Church for two millennia testifies, the Gospel is always a sign of contradiction. The contradictions can be severe, which can lead to martyrdom, or they can be mild, depending on the ambient public culture. But in every age, including this age of the "New Evangelization" called forth by Blessed John Paul II and Benedict XVI in response to the Second Vatican Council, the Gospel is a matter of conviction, not convention. Thus Evangelical Catholicism, with the Gospel at the center of its life, is not a sect within Catholicism, nor a movement of Catholics, but a way of understanding the vocation of every

Christian to be a true disciple and faithful missionary witness to the Lord Jesus, who is the Gospel preached and the primordial Sacrament of the human encounter with God.

Word and *Sacrament, Gospel* and *Vocation*

One of the more important books shaping the deliberations of the Second Vatican Council was *Christ the Sacrament of the Encounter with God* by the Flemish Dominican Edward Schillebeeckx.[23] Father Schillebeeckx's later tangles with the teaching authority of the Church should not impair anyone's appreciation of the keen insight displayed in this earlier work: that the fundamental "sacrament," or *ur*-Sacrament, is Jesus Christ. For the life, teaching, ministry, suffering, death, and resurrection of Jesus Christ, taken as a whole, is the definitive "outward sign" (as the *Baltimore Catechism* might put it) through which Christians see both the truth about God and the truth about themselves as loved by God and redeemed by God's Son. The sacraments of the Church are far more than seven rituals by which the Church acknowledges various key moments in life. The seven sacraments—Baptism, Confirmation, Penance (Reconciliation), the Eucharist, Holy Orders, Matrimony, and the Anointing of the Sick—are seven privileged encounters with the Christ who is himself *the* sacramental expression of the living God in the world and in history.

Jesus is not an "eighth sacrament." The Lord Jesus, met in the Gospel, is the sacramental reality of God who reveals himself to his creation. And through his filial "sacramentality" as the incarnate Son of God, Christ makes the encounter with God through the sacraments of the Church possible. "He who has seen me has seen the Father," Jesus told the apostle Philip at the Last Supper [John 14.9]. Whoever meets the Lord Jesus in the saving waters of Baptism has been given the gift of Christian sight, by which we see the Father through the Son. Whoever meets the Lord Jesus in the gift of the Spirit in Confirmation, or in the words of absolution in the confessional, or in the oils and prayers of

Holy Orders, or in the exchange of vows and the gift of mutual love in Holy Matrimony, has seen the Father through the Son. So do those who receive spiritual healing, and sometimes physical healing, through the Anointing of the Sick. Preeminently, whoever obeys the Son and feeds on his body and blood in the Holy Eucharist is united to the Father in the power of the Spirit, who is called down upon bread and wine prior to their consecration.[24]

Evangelical Catholicism is thus a reality of Word *and* Sacrament, in several senses. The Gospel word preached is also the Word of God, the Lord Jesus, the Sacrament who is present to the Church through the seven sacraments. The Word of God found in Holy Scripture is encountered in the sacraments, which are never celebrated without reference to the Scriptures. Growth in faith, hope, and love—growth in friendship with Christ—is nurtured through a regular and frequent reception of the sacraments, and that growth in turn breaks open aspects of the Word of God in the Old and New Testaments that may have been previously obscure, unclear, or entirely hidden. It is all one package, one evangelical Catholic reality. Word and Sacrament are no more separable than Gospel and Church, Scripture and apostolic tradition, mission and service.

Evangelical Catholics who are fed by both Word and Sacrament—by a daily reading of the Bible and a regular reception of the Eucharist and the sacrament of Penance—are men and women being formed by the obedience of faith into a genuine freedom.[25] That genuine freedom is freedom *for* and *in* the truth of friendship with Christ and freedom *from* one's disordered self-love, which is everywhere and always the chief obstacle to the encounter with God. Thus the obedience of faith, rather than leading to oppression, is the path to radical freedom: the freedom to freely choose the good, the true, and the beautiful, and to do so as a matter of moral habit.[26]

This, of course, is a profoundly countercultural way of life, based on what is, in the twenty-first century, a deeply countercultural apprehension of reality.

Confronting the Spirit of the Age

Evangelical Catholicism affirms that the humanity of Jesus, son of Mary, is the vessel of the Incarnation of the Son of God. Similarly, Evangelical Catholicism affirms that it is through the ordinary materials of life—the materials of the seven sacraments, such as bread, wine, oil, and water—that the extraordinary grace of God enters history, nourishes the friends of Jesus, and empowers them in their missionary discipleship. This Catholic sacramentality, this sacramental imagination about the world, is one of the distinctive cultural markers of Evangelical Catholicism in the twenty-first century and defines one of the sharpest challenges that the Church poses to the spirit of the age—a "spirit" to which the simple catechetical formulas and devotional practices of Counter-Reformation Catholicism could not effectively respond.

That "spirit" is, in two technical words, Gnostic and antimetaphysical.

Late modernity and postmodernity have seen a powerful cultural revival of Gnosticism, the most ancient of heresies, which denied the goodness of creation and sought redemption not in history and the fulfillment of history, but outside history and materiality. In its twenty-first-century form, Gnosticism teaches the utter plasticity of the human condition: there is nothing *given* in men and women, not even their gender; all is malleable; all can be changed to fulfill the desires (or, as it is usually phrased, to meet the "needs") of the imperial autonomous Self. Nor are there any *givens* in society. There is nothing given about marriage, for example; "marriage" can mean anything we want it to mean, and so, of course, can "family."

Late modernity and postmodernity have also been marked by a collapse of any culturally received notion that there are deep truths built into the world and into human beings, truths that we can grasp (incompletely but surely) through the arts of reason. That collapse was set in motion by the eighteenth-century critique of classical and medieval metaphysics by David Hume and Immanuel Kant: a critique that, over time (and whatever Hume's and Kant's intentions), eroded the Western world's convictions about the purposefulness of life, and indeed the purposefulness of history. The world became a virtual cornucopia of means; but those means were not ordered to any ends. Individual freedom, therefore, must mean the maximizing of possible means; but, again, those means were not attached to ends. And if the end—the good to be sought by societies and individuals—does not justify the means, what does? Absent any notion of "ends"—those goods we ought to seek because we can know them to be good—means are trumps. Technique and utility are all.

The effects of all this on the dignity of the human person and on society was brilliantly anticipated by Aldous Huxley in *Brave New World*. Somehow, decades before the unraveling of the DNA double-helix made Huxley's dystopian vision of the human future scientifically plausible, Huxley seems to have intuited that the ancient Gnostic doctrine of the plasticity of the human condition, married to modern technology and set loose in a culture that had abandoned any notion that the deep truths of things could be read off the givens of human nature, would produce a world where the Promethean temptation would prove irresistible. Aldous Huxley was no great literary stylist. But he caught the gravity of the cultural challenge that Counter-Reformation Catholicism could not meet, and to which Evangelical Catholicism must respond, in a passage midway through his novel, when he described the reflections of one of the all-powerful World Controllers on an academic paper submitted for publication by a thinker who had rediscovered some old truths:

> "A New Theory of Biology" was the title of the paper which Mustapha Mond had just finished reading. He sat for some time, meditatively frowning, then picked up his pen and wrote across the title-page: "The author's mathematical treatment of the conception of purpose is novel and highly ingenious, but heretical and, so far as the present social order is concerned, dangerous and potentially subversive. *Not to be published.*" He underlined the words. "The author will be kept under supervision. His transference to the Marine Biological Station at St. Helena may become necessary." A pity, he thought, as he signed his

name. It was a masterly piece of work. But once you began admitting explanations in terms of purpose—well, you didn't know what the result might be. It was the sort of idea that might easily decondition the more unsettled minds among the higher castes—make them lose their faith in happiness as the Sovereign Good and take to believing, instead, that the goal was somewhere beyond, somewhere outside the present human sphere; that the purpose of life was not the maintenance of well-being, but some intensification and refining of consciousness, some enlargement of knowledge. Which was, the Controller reflected, quite possibly true. But not, in the present circumstances, admissible. He picked up his pen again, and under the words "*Not to be published*" drew a second line, thicker and blacker than the first.[27]

In the brave new world of Huxley's dystopia, what classical and medieval theology called the *anima naturaliter Christiana*—the natural inclination of the human spirit toward the truths of Christian faith—atrophied under the pressure of the pleasure principle, an ultramundane substitute for the life of virtue. The brave new world of Huxley's imagination is largely a soulless world, or perhaps better, a world of souls without longing (which is not to be confused with either "desire" or "need"). It may seem a fictional future so extreme as to be virtually impossible; but we ignore or deny its possibility at our peril.

The American writer Flannery O'Connor warned of the same cultural undercurrents and their dehumanizing effects when she criticized the nihilism of late modernity for having produced the human equivalent of "wingless chickens": men and women who had lost what O'Connor called the "habit of being." And they had lost that essential, human quality because they had forgotten the givens of a life they imagined to be utterly plastic and malleable; they had lost their humanity because the sacramental sensibility that Christianity had first taught Western civilization, that intuition of the extraordinary that is revealed through the materials of the ordinary, had been culturally bred out of them.

In these dire cultural circumstances, the social and political effects of which are sometimes masked by material prosperity, it was providential indeed that the deep reform of Catholicism initiated in the late nineteenth century by Leo XIII should have passed through a recovery of Word and Sacrament as the two pillars of the life of Christian discipleship. The life-transforming power of the Word of God in the words of the Bible is the Church's countercultural riposte to the postmodern deprecation of the human capacity to know the deep truths of the human condition. The sacraments are Evangelical Catholicism's countercultural antidote to the regnant Gnosticism of later modernity and postmodernity, because the Church's sacramental system takes the stuff of the world and of human relationships with utmost seriousness, seeing in them the vehicles of divine grace.

The Qualities of an Engaged Faith

Word and Sacrament nourish a deepening of one's personal friendship with the Lord Jesus, which is essential to the full-time Catholicism required to live faith, hope, and love amid the spirit of the age—and to set about the world's conversion. Immersion in Word and Sacrament thus nurture that lifelong process of conversion that leads to the four distinguishing qualities of evangelical Catholics.

Radical conversion

Evangelical Catholicism calls the people of the Church, laity and clergy, to a life in which friendship with the Lord Jesus is at the center of everything: personal identity, relationships, activity. The statement "I believe in the Gospel" is the defining commitment of an evangelically Catholic life. Everything else flows from that. Evangelical Catholicism is thus not a lifestyle choice: it is a life-changing process of lifelong conversion to the truth of the Gospel. The character of this conversion, its power, and its demands were well caught in the dialogue between Margaret More and her father, Sir Thomas More, in the Tower of London toward the end of *A Man for All Seasons*. Margaret asks More, who has given up position, wealth, and freedom, whether God could reasonably ask any more. To which Sir Thomas replies, "Well . . . finally . . . it isn't a question of matter of reason; finally it's a matter of love."[28] In a radically converted, evangelically Catholic life, the love of Christ has transformed the disciple and brought him or her into an earthly experience of the love shared by the Holy Trinity—an experience of atonement, of being "at one" with God, made possible by the Paschal Mystery and the gift of the Holy Spirit.[29] That experience changes everything. It is the driving force behind the deep reform of the Church.

Deep fidelity

The radically converted evangelical Catholic remains a poor sinner. Yet the radically converted evangelical Catholic knows that he or she, in whatever state of life, can and must strive for fidelity despite the wounds of sin. Commitment to living from the love of Christ poured into our hearts, even amid temptation and sin, leads to the pursuit of Christian perfection—never achieved, to be sure, but always there as a horizon of aspiration to which grace calls the disciple. For the evangelical Catholic, the journey toward sanctity is nurtured daily by reading the Word of God in the Bible and by frequent reception of the sacraments, especially the Holy Eucharist and the sacrament of Reconciliation, or Penance. One cannot be an evangelical Catholic, as this form of radical conversion was imagined by the Second Vatican Council, absent a daily encounter with the Word in the Word of God, and a regular embrace of Christ the Sacrament of the human encounter with God in the sacraments of the Church. The evangelical Catholic reads the Word of God as a treasury of truth expressed in a variety of literary forms, just as he or she receives the sacraments as genuine encounters with the God of Abraham, Isaac, Jacob, and Jesus. The Bible and the sacraments measure our discipleship. Evangelical Catholic disciples do not stand in a position of skeptical judgment on the Church's twin foundations of Word and Sacrament.

Joyful discipleship

The evangelical Catholic's joyful embrace of life is an expression of the gratitude that the radically converted and deeply faithful disciple feels for the friendship of the Lord Jesus, who redeemed us from the burden of sin and guilt at a great price. Evangelical Catholics are not absolved from spiritual aridity, desolation, even dark nights of the soul. Evangelical Catholics can live *through* those experiences (in the sense of plumbing their depths) because of their friendship with the Lord Jesus, whose redemptive work was cruciform. The joyful discipleship of the evangelical Catholic is thus not a matter of self-assertion, but of self-giving. Having been redeemed by the Christ who demonstrates in his own passion, death, and resurrection the cruciform shape of salvation, and having entered into friendship with that same Christ through encountering him in Word and Sacrament, the evangelical Catholic comes through aridity, desolation, and dark nights strengthened by the power of the Risen One: Christ, who took all human fear upon himself at Calvary and, by burning that fear in the fires of self-sacrificial love, made it possible for all those who adhere to him in faith to live not *without* fear, but *beyond* fear.[30] Thus the characteristic courage of a radically converted, deeply faithful evangelical Catholic is a courage that comes on the far side of fear—which is to say, on the far side of the Cross. And that courage gives birth to a unique and impregnable joy that suffuses one's entire life.

Courageous evangelism

Evangelical Catholics measure the impact of their discipleship, and the degree to which they have truly opened themselves to "the power of God for salvation to everyone who has faith" [Romans 1.16], by the measure to which they give away to others the gift they have been given—by the degree to which they bring others into friendship with Christ, or deepen the already-baptized's experience of the love of Christ. Evangelical Catholicism is thus unapologetically missionary Catholicism. The evangelical Catholic—lay disciple, priest or bishop, consecrated religious—sees every venue of his or her life as an evangelical opportunity. That evangelical commitment is lived out, in the first instance, through charity: through an encounter with others that helps heal what is broken, that sustains what is weak, that comforts what is bereaved, that enlightens what is confused. Having been empowered to live beyond fear by an embrace of the Cross of the Lord Jesus, the evangelical Catholic seeks to inspire others to live with a similar courage. That example (which is a form of what catechists call "pre-evangelization") opens the possibility of then offering an encounter with the Word of God in the Bible, and with the Word of God incarnate through the sacraments of the Church. Evangelical Catholicism models the "more excellent way" [1 Corinthians 12.31] of Christian love before it teaches it; but it is indefatigable in teaching that "God is love, and he who abides in love abides in God, and God in him" [1 John 4.16].

Thus evangelically Catholic parishes (and pastors), and evangelically Catholic dioceses (and bishops), will measure their conversion, their fidelity, and their discipleship by a different set of criteria than those prevalent in institutional-maintenance Catholicism. How many potential converts the parish or diocese has invited, and how many of those potential converts have decided to follow the way of the Lord Jesus, is understood to be a better measure of "how we're doing," in Evangelical Catholicism, than the annual count of Catholics-at-Mass-on-Sunday-X (the standard measure of "Catholic practice" in much of the Church), precisely because it is a more evangelical measure. And in an evangelically Catholic parish or diocese, those questions will be asked, and the answers pondered, by lay disciples as much as by clergy.

The response of Peter to the Transfiguration of Jesus—that it is "well that we are here" with the Lord in his glory [Matthew 17.4]—is a Gospel summary of the characteristics of evangelical Catholics. The joy of being in the presence of the Lord is the sustaining dynamic of the communion, the unique form of human community, that is the Church. That very same joy impels those who share that *communio*, that communion, to offer it to others in evangelical mission.

Living this mission effectively means recognizing why the Church in so much of the Western world has been in a dry season—which brings us back to the matter of truth.

The Consequences of Infidelity

If a robust Evangelical Catholicism, formed by Word and Sacrament to take the Gospel of truth and love "into the deep" of the modern and postmodern world, is the deeply reformed Church to which the entire trajectory of Catholic development from Leo XIII to Benedict XVI points, and which the Second Vatican Council envisioned, then the great postconciliar failure of Catholicism—the collapse of the Church in Christianity's historical heartland, Western Europe—comes into sharper focus.

Western European Catholicism's demise was not, it becomes clear, the result of an internal civil war between Catholic progressives and Catholic traditionalists. Nor are the prescriptions of either of these exhausted camps likely to lead to revival and reform in the future. The Church in Europe has been in free fall throughout the postconciliar years because too many of its people ceased to believe that the Gospel is true. The crisis of Catholicism in Europe did not come about because the institutional Church faltered and its people subsequently bailed out. The crisis came because the people of the Church (including the clergy) ceased to believe with passion and conviction, ceased to find joy in the presence of the Lord—and sought their happiness elsewhere. Because of *that*, the institution (which in some countries, such as Germany and Italy, remains extremely wealthy) faltered—and seems to be collapsing in the first quarter of the twenty-first century. The Catholic future in Europe lies not in managerial reforms (although those are needed), but in a renaissance of faith, which will likely come (as such things often do) from outside the formal structures of Catholic life (i.e., parishes and dioceses) and from within renewal movements and new forms of Catholic community. There, the vision of Evangelical Catholicism is alive. And if that vision attains critical mass, following the authentic promptings of the Holy Spirit, it may eventually reform—and transform—the institutional Church.

That same evangelical Catholic prism also sheds light on the faltering pace of deep Catholic reform in the United States, where the situation, in the first decades of the twenty-first century, seems rather better than in Europe, but with notable signs of trouble. In the United States, too, the core problem is one of belief. Deep Catholic reform in the United States is impeded by bishops, priests, consecrated men and women in religious life, intellectuals, and laity who are in a diminished state of communion with the Church—existentially if not canonically—because they deny to be true what the Catholic Church "believes, teaches, and proclaims to be revealed by God," as the profession of faith for those being received into full communion with the Church puts it. How many Catholics in the United States—again, bishops, priests, consecrated men and women in religious life, intellectuals, and laity—can say, without mental reservation, "I believe and profess all that the holy Catholic Church believes, teaches, and proclaims to be revealed by God"? To the degree that the answer to that question is negative, or ambiguous, then to precisely that degree is the deep reform of the Church envisioned by Vatican II being imperiled.

A quarter-century ago, Richard John Neuhaus, then a Lutheran pastor, proposed that the Catholic Church was fitted to be the "lead Church" among world Christian communities in proclaiming the Gospel thanks to the pattern of development that had run from Leo XIII through Vatican II to John Paul II. In *The Catholic Moment*, Neuhaus criticized those Catholics who thought that John Paul II was overly concerned with dissent in the Church. John Paul, Neuhaus argued, was far more concerned with a deeper, more evangelical question, one first posed by the Lord Jesus himself: "When the Son of Man comes, will he find faith on earth?" [Luke 18.8]. *That* was the question, Neuhaus suggested, that anyone, pope or layperson, would understand to be most urgent, had he or she truly understood the Catholic possibility created by the Council of reform and reunion.[31]

That remains the question for anyone truly concerned with the deep reform of the Catholic Church today.

CHAPTER THREE

Evangelical Catholicism
in Profile

T HE NICENE-CONSTANTINOPOLITAN CREED, RECITED BY CHRISTIANS throughout the world, lists four "marks" of the Church of Jesus Christ: the Church, Christians profess, is *one, holy, catholic*, and *apostolic*. Different Christian communities understand these four ecclesiastical marks in different ways. The Catholic Church believes that it bears these four marks with a fullness that cannot be attributed to any other ecclesial community. At the same time, the Catholic Church affirms that elements of grace and sanctification can be found (if in varying degrees) wherever communities of faith profess Jesus as Lord and Savior.[1]

As the Catholic Church understands them, the four marks of the Church cited in the Creed identify four essential attributes of the community called into being by the outpouring of the Holy Spirit on the first believers in the Risen Lord Jesus.

By professing that the Church is *one*, the Catholic Church declares its belief that there is only one Church of Christ, for the Church is the Body of Christ and Christ is one. The means of incorporation into that one Body is baptism administered in the name of the Father, the Son, and the Holy Spirit. Thus there is "one Lord, one faith, one baptism, one God and Father of all, who is above all and through all and in all" [Ephesians 4.5].[2]

By professing that the Church is *holy*, the Catholic Church declares its belief that Christ has kept his promise to send the Spirit upon his disciples and continues to do so throughout history. Despite the sinfulness of the Church's members, the Church itself, the Bride of the Lamb as depicted by St. John in the Book of Revelation, is holy, sharing in the immortal and ineffable holiness of the Bridegroom, the Lord Jesus Christ.[3]

By professing that the Church is *catholic*, the Catholic Church declares its belief that the Gospel is intended for all of humanity, that the Church is called to bring the Gospel to the entire world, and that everyone is capable of conversion to Christ. The catholicity or universality of the Church, as the Fathers of Vatican II taught, is "a sign and instrument . . . of communion with God and of unity among all men."[4] For in the Body of Christ that is the Church, there is "neither Jew nor Greek, male nor female, slave nor free" [Galatians 3.28].[5]

By professing that the Church is *apostolic*, the Catholic Church declares its belief that the Gospel is transmitted in its integrity through the apostles and their successors, the bishops in full communion with the Bishop of Rome. Thus the Church also declares its belief that it is founded on the witness of men whose lives were transformed by their friendship with the Lord Jesus, who empowered them to bring others into that saving fellowship.[6]

The Characteristics of Counter-Reformation Catholicism

Counter-Reformation Catholicism, of the catechetical-devotional sort that shaped Catholic life from the mid-sixteenth century to the mid-twentieth century, expressed these four marks through distinctive characteristics or qualities.

Through a process of historical and theological evolution, the Catholicism of the Counter-Reformation came to understand the Church, and relationships within the Church, by analogy to a pyramid. The pope reigned at the apex of the structure; bishops, priests, and vowed religious occupied the pyramid's middle tiers; the lay faithful manned the bottom. Authority flowed down the pyramid—and so, most of the time, did discussion. Thus Counter-Reformation Catholicism came to conceive the Bishop of Rome as the chief executive of a global enterprise whose local leaders (the bishops) were, in effect, papal delegates (or branch managers) for their respective areas; this, it was thought, was the appropriate embodiment of Catholic unity and apostolicity for the early modern age.

There was, to be sure, a certain clarity here. Yet this distinctive theology of the Church, the papacy, and the episcopate tended to crowd out the rich array of images that earlier embodiments of the Church had drawn from the Bible: the Johannine images of the Church as sheepfold, flock, and spotless spouse of the Lamb; or the Pauline images of the Church as the household of God and the Jerusalem from above. This displacement of biblical imagery reinforced the tendency to imagine the Church by analogy to the state and thus to think of the Church in predominantly legal-juridical terms. It also led to a kind of clerical caste system in which those in Holy Orders were understood to be "the Church" in a way that others were not.

Counter-Reformation Catholicism expressed the holiness of the Church by emphasizing a rich devotional life centered on Mary, the saints, and the Sacred Heart. But it did not lay much stress on sanctification through a regular encounter with the Bible and frequent reception of holy communion (a lacuna that eventually had to be addressed by legislating the annual reception of communion during the Easter season). As it did in conceiving the Church, Counter-Reformation Catholicism thought of the moral life in legal-juridical terms: to grow in the moral life was a matter of training the will to obey a prescribed set of moral rules. The biblical, patristic, and medieval idea of the moral life as a life of growth in the virtues (a growth ordered to beatitude, or happiness) tended to get lost amid this heavy emphasis on rules. The Counter-Reformation Church expressed catholicity by enforcing a marked uniformity in liturgical and educational practice and in patterns of Church governance: an expression of universality that often relegated the eastern Catholic Churches (Byzantine in liturgy and Church polity but in full communion with the Bishop of Rome) to second-class citizenship.

These expressions or characteristics of the four enduring marks of Counter-Reformation Catholicism were frequently ridiculed in the post–Vatican II period, and, in truth, some aspects of this form of being Catholic were not invulnerable to satire. In their time, however, they played an important role in safeguarding the symphony of Catholic truth, in transmitting it to future generations, and in inspiring great missionary efforts. Yet like other time-bound expressions of the fourfold constitution of the Church willed by Christ, their time eventually passed. The cultural circumstances changed dramatically, and the evangelical carrying capacity of this way of being Church consequently diminished—and in some instances disappeared.

The Characteristics of Evangelical Catholicism

Evangelical Catholicism is an expression of the four fundamental realities of Christian ecclesial life—unity, holiness, catholicity, and apostolicity—as mediated through the deep reform of the Catholic Church that has been underway since Pope Leo XIII. Evangelical Catholicism, which will displace Counter-Reformation Catholicism so that the Church can fulfill its mission under the new cultural circumstances of the twenty-first century and the third millennium, displays ten distinctive characteristics that, taken together, provide a profile of the Catholic Church of the future and suggest standards for achieving deep reform in the Church.[7]

1. Evangelical Catholicism is friendship with the Lord Jesus Christ.

In the catechetical-devotional Catholicism of the Counter-Reformation Church, Catholics learned *about* Jesus Christ, through brief catechism formulas that aptly summed up the Church's doctrine about the Son of

God who becomes the son of Mary.[8] Evangelical Catholicism begins not with *knowing about* Jesus, but with *knowing* Jesus.

Evangelical Catholicism affirms that the brief and easily memorized formulas of faith in the catechisms of the Counter-Reformation Church convey Gospel truths; they are, in fact, simplified but doctrinally sound answers to the question, "Who do you say that I am?" [Mark 8.29]. For Evangelical Catholicism, however, these brief doctrinal formulas are expressions of what is fundamentally a personal encounter: a personal meeting with and knowledge of the Lord Jesus Christ, whom the believer has met in faith and with whom the believer has entered into friendship. The Catholicism of the Counter-Reformation asked the people of the Church to know who Jesus Christ was, and through that knowledge *about* him to meet him. Evangelical Catholicism *begins* with meeting and knowing the Lord himself, the primordial Sacrament of the human encounter with God.

As Evangelical Catholicism understands it, this friendship with the Lord Jesus teaches us two things necessary for salvation and for living a life of human fulfillment this side of death.

First, in friendship with Jesus Christ, we come to know the face of the merciful Father, for whoever sees the Son sees the Father. Whoever experiences the Son's power to forgive sins and restore the human dignity lost by self-love sees the merciful Father, who welcomes home the prodigals and reclothes them with the garments of integrity, while pouring into their hearts the Spirit, the bond of love between the Father and the Son.

Second, in friendship with Jesus Christ, which opens us up to the life of the Holy Trinity, we come to know the full truth about our humanity. For friendship with the Lord Jesus—conforming our lives to the pattern of his life of self-giving love—enables us to live our lives as the gift to others that life itself is to each of us. Thus friendship with Jesus Christ enables us to gain a glimpse, here and now, of life within the light and life of the Trinity, a communion of radical self-giving and receptivity.[9]

Evangelical Catholicism proclaims the great gift of friendship with Jesus Christ not as one attractive possibility in a supermarket of spiritualities, but as the God-given and unique means of salvation for everyone. Everyone who is saved is saved in some fashion because of Jesus Christ, the truth of whose life and mission as universal savior is revealed in a definitive way by his passion, death, and resurrection. Further, Evangelical Catholicism affirms as true, not as pious myth, that Jesus was the Son of God born of the Virgin Mary through the power of the Holy Spirit; that Jesus, who was born into time and history, is the true Son of God, not the son of any human progenitor; that this Jesus understood himself to embody, in a unique way, the world's hope for salvation, as it was first borne in history by the Jewish people; that this Jesus embraced his death as the divinely ordered means of making salvation possible to all; and that he was vindicated in this act of obedience to God's will by being raised from the dead, after which he was seen as the Risen Lord by those who knew him during his public ministry of teaching and healing.[10] All of this, Evangelical Catholicism proclaims, is *true*.

The Christ proclaimed by Evangelical Catholicism is no mere moral paragon, no mere teacher of noble truths about righteous living who comes to a sad end because of human wickedness. He is Son of the Most High God, incarnate in the flesh and in history, for, as C.S. Lewis provocatively suggested, there are only two other possibilities: that Jesus of Nazareth was a madman, or that he was history's greatest liar. There are no other options.[11] Evangelical Catholicism begins with the confession of faith that Jesus is indeed Lord, as the Great Tradition of Christianity has always understood him. And Evangelical Catholicism affirms that that basic confession of faith measures all theological efforts to explain just how this could be, or what it might mean.

Evangelical Catholicism fully recognizes that, in proclaiming the lordship of Jesus Christ and the possibility of life-transforming friendship with him, it is making a profoundly countercultural proposal. Evangelical Catholics also know that it has ever been thus: for the proclamation of a crucified and risen savior was, from the outset, a "stumbling block" to some and a "folly" to others, as St. Paul told the rowdy paleo-Christians of Corinth [1 Corinthians 1.2]. That is how it was; that is how it is; and that is how it will be. Yet Evangelical Catholicism also confesses, with St. Paul, that for those who accept the invitation of friendship with him, he is "Christ the power of God and the wisdom of God" [1 Corinthians 1.24]. Through that power and wisdom, the deepest questions of the human condition receive answers and the deepest longings of the human heart are satisfied.

At the same time, Evangelical Catholicism recognizes that, in offering everyone the possibility of friendship with the Lord Jesus, it is offering the postmodern world something postmodernity badly needs: an encounter with the divine mercy. As the God of the Bible came into the ancient world as One who liberates humanity from the whims and fancies of the Olympian gods or the terrors of fearsome Moloch, the Gospel of Jesus Christ and friendship with him liberate postmodern humanity from its burden of guilt, born of a tacit (if often intuitive and inarticulate) understanding of the awfulness that humanity visited upon itself throughout the twentieth century. By whom can that burden of guilt be expiated? To whom can that wickedness be confessed, and from whom can forgiveness be received? In offering friendship with Jesus Christ, Evangelical Catholicism offers postmodern humanity a path to a more humane future, absolved of the guilt of the recent past.[12]

And where is this friendship with Jesus to be found? According to the evangelical Catholic proposal, this friendship is found in the Church, in the Word of God recognized as such by the Church in the Bible, in the sacraments celebrated by the Church, in the works of charity and service, and in the fellowship of those who have been "born of water and the Spirit" [John 3.5]. Despite the sinfulness of its members and their failure to live fully the meaning of friendship with the Lord Jesus, the Church is always the privileged place of encounter with the living God, who continually forms his people into the community in which the full truth about humanity is grasped.

The truth about God and humanity the Church bears, and to which it must give witness in mission, evangelism, and service, is the principal criterion for the ongoing reform of the Church. All genuinely Catholic reform begins from this truth, just as all genuinely Catholic reform enhances the possibility of men and women entering into friendship with Jesus Christ.

2. Evangelical Catholicism affirms divine revelation and embraces its authority, which continues through history in the teaching authority of the Church.

There are parts of the world in which transparency to the divine remains obvious in everyday life, and traditional forms of authority remain self-evident. Yet in the twenty-first-century West, the Gospel of friendship with the Lord Jesus must be proclaimed to a world that has become largely "disenchanted"—or, perhaps more to the point, a world that has convinced itself that it is "disenchanted" and that this disenchantment is a good thing. In these cultural circumstances, skepticism about authority is born from skepticism about the human capacity to know the truth (for how can anyone know the truth of things in such a way as to be authoritative?). And that skepticism frequently leads to moral relativism (for if we can't know the truth of things with certainty, why should we think there are absolute moral truths binding on everyone?). The entire enterprise—disenchantment that becomes postmodernism—too often leads into the quicksand of cynicism about the human prospect.

In this cultural environment, Evangelical Catholicism is inevitably countercultural, for it lives by faith in the dramatic claim of the Lord Jesus with whom evangelical Catholics have entered into friendship: "All authority in heaven and on earth has been given to me. . . . And lo, I am with you always, to the close of the age" [Matthew 28.18, 20]. In a culture of competing truth claims in which the most cherished "truth" is that there is no such thing as *the* truth, the obedience of faith that is an integral part of friendship with Jesus the Lord can seem a bit odd, a bit needy—a bit immature. For surely a true human maturity is marked by skepticism toward authority and a settled conviction that authentic living means doing things "my way."

Evangelical Catholicism proposes a radically different notion of truth and of the relationship of mature and free human beings to the truth. Embracing Jesus as what he says he is—"the way, and the truth, and the life" [John 14.6]—is essential to entering into friendship with him. If that is true of the most deeply counterintuitive aspect of the Gospel—the claim that it is through the unjust death of a just man that the world is redeemed—it is also true of his claim to *be* the truth that is the way to authentic human life, and to eternal life. Having embraced him who is truth as *the* truth because they have entered into friendship with him, however, evangelical Catholics are freed from skepticism and enabled to embrace the authority that Jesus represents and incarnates: the authority of the living God, who reveals himself in deed and word to the people of Israel, and who finally and definitively reveals himself in his Son. That divine authority is what gives Scripture its authority as the written form of those truths that God wished to reveal for the world's salvation. That divine authority is also what gives the Church its authority.

If Jesus Christ is indeed "the truth," and if that truth is liberating truth, then the Lord Jesus would wish to preserve his followers in the truth. That, evangelical Catholics believe, is why the Lord empowered the apostles, those twelve followers who were closest to him in his public ministry and who were witnesses to his Resurrection, to remain in the truth through the gift of the Holy Spirit. That Spirit, who never ceases to enliven the Church from within the very inner life of the Holy Trinity, creates a succession of true teachers throughout time and history, teachers who teach authoritatively. Those authoritative teachers, evangelical Catholics profess, are the college of bishops who are in full communion with the Bishop of Rome, for these bishops are the true successors of the apostles and the heirs of the authority that the Risen Lord first conferred on the apostles and their head, Peter [see John 20.21–24; Matthew 16.18–19].

And that, Evangelical Catholicism affirms, is why the Second Vatican Council lifted up the ministry and mission of the local bishop: as the

Church prepared to enter its third millennium, the Council rightly wished to emphasize that the office of bishop is, in its essence, a *teaching* office.[13]

The local bishop thus stands as the first witness to the truth of the Gospel in his local church—and thus the first challenger to the skepticism and cynicism of postmodernity. As Evangelical Catholicism understands the relationship of the episcopacy to the countercultural truth of the Gospel, a man is not called to the office of bishop as a reward for services rendered; nor is the episcopate to which the bishop is joined a caste: bishops form an *order*, the highest of Holy Orders, whose primary function is the guardianship and proclamation of the truth of the Gospel. Thus an evangelically centered Church will choose its bishops from among those men who have demonstrated a capacity to mount that kind of countercultural witness by inviting people into friendship with the Lord Jesus—and it will do so in the full knowledge that it is calling these men to various forms of martyrdom, of which opprobrium and ridicule are often the least of what may be expected.

If entering into friendship with Jesus Christ is embracing the One who is the truth, and if that friendship means incorporation into Christ's Body, the Church, for which the Lord himself has provided an episcopally governed structure, then the evangelical Catholic will, of necessity, "believe and profess all that the holy Catholic Church believes, teaches, and proclaims to be revealed by God." Further, the evangelical Catholic will know what "all that" is by reference to what is taught by the bishops of the Church in full communion with the Bishop of Rome, who is the vital center of the Church's unity and who bears a special responsibility for preserving the integrity of the truth that Christ left to his Church. The truth of what is taught by the pope and the college of bishops is not a matter for debate (although the terms in which that truth should be understood and explained can be legitimately debated).[14] There is no "private judgment" in Evangelical Catholicism, which considers that those who deny to be true what the Catholic Church teaches to be true are in a defective condition of communion with the Body of Christ.

To accept this is not to surrender one's maturity. It is to recognize that the embrace of the Lord Jesus in friendship is an embrace of the truth that he is and that he teaches, and that that truth measures my life and calls me to the fullness of human dignity, which is incorporation into the light and love of the Holy Trinity. Moreover, to accept that the Church teaches authoritatively is not a violation of the rights of conscience, for conscience, rightly understood, is ordered to the truth and is not a mere organ of personal opinion.

Is there a kind of surrender here? Yes, for ultimately the evangelical Catholic must let go of the imperial autonomous Self and be forged into a true member of the living Body of Christ. But that, as Blessed John Henry Newman knew, is a surrender that takes us *ex umbris et imaginibus in veritatem*—"out of shadows and phantasms into the truth," from unreality to reality.[15]

3. Evangelical Catholicism celebrates the seven sacraments as divinely given means of sanctifying life.

Friendship with Jesus Christ is not lived in isolation; nor is it a matter of a one-time "conversion experience." As Evangelical Catholicism understands it, friendship with the Lord Jesus is lived within the Church and is nourished by the seven sacraments of the New Covenant, which are seven privileged ways in which we deepen our encounter with Jesus the primordial Sacrament, the Holy One who makes God present to us.

The catechetical-devotional Catholicism of the Counter-Reformation era defined a sacrament as an "outward sign instituted by Christ to give grace."[16] Evangelical Catholicism accepts that definition as a brief summary formula, but defines the "grace" in question as a deepening of one's friendship with God in Christ. And it understands those "outward signs" as the ordinary things—water, salt, and oil; bread and wine; marital love and fidelity; words of forgiveness—that disclose the extraordinary that lies just on the far side of the ordinary: incorporation into the life of God himself through Baptism into the Church of Jesus Christ; the Body and

Blood of the Son of God, given as real food and drink for the nourishment of Christ's brothers and sisters; the power to act in the person of Christ in the priesthood of the New Covenant; the genuine forgiveness of sins; marriage as an icon of Christ's relationship to the Church.

While all seven sacraments are encounters with Christ and channels of grace, Evangelical Catholicism lays particular stress on Baptism and the Holy Eucharist.

As the Church has understood from its inception, the Evangelical Catholicism of the twenty-first century recognizes that the baptism of infants and its pastoral implications can only be understood by reference to adult baptism. An adult is baptized because a man or woman has met the Lord, has been converted to friendship with him, and seeks incorporation into his Body and the forgiveness of sins through this first of the sacraments. That is the baptismal paradigm, as the Church makes liturgically clear through the baptism of adults at the Easter Vigil, the center and apex of the liturgical year. Thus in infant baptism the faith of the Church, embodied in the faith of parents and godparents, is crucial. Once, that faith could be taken for granted. Today, it can no longer be assumed. Evangelical Catholicism therefore sees in the prebaptismal preparation of parents and godparents the opportunity for a deeper evangelization that can no longer be imagined to have taken place through the ambient culture, as it often was in Counter-Reformation Catholicism.

The Holy Eucharist stands at the very center of evangelical Catholic life. It is the sacrament that links the disciples most intimately to the Lord, who commanded us to feed on him in memory of him. As Douglas Farrow wrote, it is the sacrament that is left behind as a permanent witness in the world of what actually happened in the Paschal Mystery of Christ's death, Resurrection, and Ascension: "The entire cosmos [was] fundamentally reordered to God in Christ." Through the Eucharist, the Church has been given, by the Lord himself, "the means of participation in the offering that Christ in his Ascension presents to the Father— himself and the people whose redemption he has won—and in all the benefits that flow from the Father's reception of that offering."[17] And through that, the Church is made participant in the divine life.

Thus the Holy Eucharist is the sacrament in which the Church is most truly what she is, the People of God being formed into the Body of Christ through the gift of the Lord's Body and Blood. It is the sacrament through which the Church most fittingly offers worship to God, and in which all of the people of the Church exercise the priestly gift—the gift of being able to approach the Lord God in prayer—that was conferred in Baptism (although the ordained priests of the Church and the people of the Church exercise this gift in distinct ways). The Holy Eucharist is the sacrament "for the journey"—*viaticum*—not only as death approaches, but throughout life. For the Eucharist is the sacrifice that "allows us to participate in the divine nature, which is one of [sacrificial] giving and receiving."[18] And through that sacramental participation in the divine life, the people of the Church are empowered for charity and service, and above all for mission and evangelization. In the Holy Eucharist, the twin foundations of Word and Sacrament on which Evangelical Catholicism rests are most powerfully evident.

In the weekly celebration of the Eucharist on the Lord's Day—Sunday, the Sabbath of the New Covenant—the Church lives out its obedience to the divine command to keep the seventh day holy. At the same time, and through the Eucharist, the Church returns to the Father the gift of the Son the Father has lent us so that we might not come before him empty in hand and heart.[19] Participation in the weekly worship of the entire parish community is thus of the essence of being an evangelical Catholic, for on this day, the Day of Resurrection, the Church celebrates the definitive revelation of Jesus as Lord and Redeemer that took place at the first Easter. In an evangelical Catholic perspective, every Sunday is Easter. Every Sunday is thus an opportunity for evangelical Catholics to be reminded that they are not "following a character from past history, but the living Christ, present in the today and the now of their lives."[20] Every Sunday is an opportunity to meet the Risen One in the Upper Rooms and on the Emmaus roads of the twenty-first century—and that opportunity is embraced as a great gift, not a burdensome obligation. Sunday worship is the evangelical Catholic's participation in the divine rest with which creation was completed, and thus Sunday worship is a privileged means by which Christ perfects his people in their humanity.

The Eucharist shapes the life and mission of evangelical Catholics throughout the week, both by their participation in daily Mass and through Eucharistic adoration (i.e., prayer before the Blessed Sacrament exposed on the altar). A daily participation in the Eucharist enables evangelical Catholics to enter more fully into the cycle of saints in glory whose witness is celebrated throughout the Church year—and thus to enter more fully into the circle of communion in which the saints and the people of the Church here-and-now both participate. Daily Mass also enables the evangelical Catholic to plumb more deeply the riches of the Word of God, through cycles of readings that bring virtually all of the Bible to the people of the Church on a biennial basis.

For evangelical Catholics, Eucharistic adoration, liturgically celebrated or silent, is another way to meet the Lord Jesus in the sacrament of his Body and Blood and thus to deepen our knowledge of him and our friendship with him. In Eucharistic adoration, the friends of the Lord look on him, and he looks upon them. That encounter is perhaps most powerfully lived where the local community's prayer before the Blessed Sacrament is linked to prayer requests that come from Catholics and non-Catholics alike.[21]

4. Evangelical Catholicism is a call to constant conversion of life, which involves both the rejection of evil, and active participation in the works of service and charity.

During the first decades of the twenty-first century, the Catholic Church in the United States and elsewhere was deeply engaged in a debate over Catholic identity, which was, more often than not, framed in canonical terms: When and how did a Catholic put himself or herself outside of the Church's legal boundaries? When ought the local bishop (or the

Bishop of Rome) declare someone outside the boundaries of the Church? The entire discussion of Catholic identity often reflected the rules-oriented Catholicism of the Counter-Reformation, with one party arguing for a looser interpretation of the rules and another party for a more strict interpretation, while both agreed that this was, at bottom, about rules.

Evangelical Catholicism affirms the need for rules—for canon law— but suggests that too close a focus on canonical boundaries obscures both real problems and their possible solutions. One real problem is that there are some, and perhaps many, Catholics who remain within the legal boundaries of the Church as defined by the Code of Canon Law, but who are not Catholics in any other meaningful sense.[22] This phenomenon of the baptized Catholic pagan is a serious one: a breakdown of interior communion and internal discipline in the Church impedes the Church's evangelical mission, for it suggests that the Church is not serious about the truths it proposes, or the consequences of living (or not living) by those truths. The problem is further complicated by another truth, namely, that the Church is a Church of sinners, constantly in need of reform, and a failure to recognize and deal with *that* fact of Catholic life is also an impediment to mission.

Evangelical Catholicism reframes this entire discussion by emphasizing that friendship with the Lord Jesus is a matter of constant conversion of life; that this conversion involves both the rejection of evil and sacramental reconciliation with Christ and the Church when we fail; and that there are degrees of communion with the Church that are not identical with the canonical boundaries of the Church.

Conversion—*metanoia*, in the New Testament Greek—is a lifelong matter for evangelical Catholics. Whether one is baptized as an infant or an adult, and no matter how old one is upon first meeting the Lord Jesus in a personal way, the Christian life as proposed by Evangelical Catholicism is one of constant conversion. That process continues until the moment of death, which the Christian should approach as the moment in which the gift of life is offered to the Creator: with gratitude for that gift having been redeemed by the Son, and with confidence that death is, in the power of the Spirit, the moment of transition and purification into a fuller encounter with the Holy Trinity. Living toward death in that way requires a lifetime of preparation, a lifetime of deepening one's friendship with the Lord Jesus, the conqueror of death.

That lifelong journey, Evangelical Catholicism teaches, is a life of growth in *beatitude*, or goodness. Thus Evangelical Catholicism's understanding of the moral life is built out from the gospel story of the rich young man who asks Jesus what good he must do to have eternal life [Matthew 19.16]. The Lord's response—that he must give himself away in discipleship and mission, making both what he owns and who he is into a gift for others—sets the pattern for all Christian morality, which is a matter of growing into goodness. The moral law is important, but it is important because the rules it lays down are boundaries that guide the evangelical Catholic's growth into beatitude.

Thus Evangelical Catholicism challenges the proscription-centered understanding of the moral life—an understanding traditionally accepted by both Catholic traditionalists, who insist on hard-and-fast rules, and lots of them, and Catholic progressives, who want to loosen "the rules," to the point where they often disappear. Both of these forms of Counter-Reformation Catholicism think of the moral life as primarily engaging the will, whereas Evangelical Catholicism understands the moral life to be a matter of training both minds and hearts, the reason and the will, to make the choices that truly contribute to goodness, human flourishing, and the beatitude that enables the friends of Jesus to live forever within the light and love of the Most Holy Trinity.

That growth in the capacity to choose the good—to choose for beatitude—continues throughout a lifetime, and along the way, even the most deeply converted evangelical Catholic will fall, and fail. Those failures, Evangelical Catholicism teaches, are no reason to lower the bar of expectation, or to foreshorten our aspirations to the goodness needed for eternal life. Rather, Evangelical Catholicism invites all who fail—which is to say, every Catholic—to get up, seek reconciliation, and continue on the journey into the life of blessedness that the Holy Spirit, "the

Counselor" who brings consolation [John 16.7], makes possible for the sons and daughters of the Church.

For evangelical Catholics, Lent is the privileged moment in the liturgical year for reflecting on these matters. Lent is the last stage of preparation for the adult catechumens who will seek Baptism at the Easter Vigil. It is also the period of the Church year in which all Catholics are invited to reenter the catechumenate metaphorically by reflecting in a deeper way on the truths of the Gospel, through works of penance, and in acts of charity. Lent is the annual liturgical reminder that conversion to Christ is never finished on this side of the Kingdom of God.[23]

Lifelong conversion requires of evangelical Catholics regular examinations of conscience—regular, even daily reflections on our failures to live out the meaning of friendship with the Lord Jesus, coupled with a renewed commitment to reject what is contrary to the Gospel and to live in fidelity to Gospel truth. Thus Evangelical Catholicism sees the sacrament of Penance, or Reconciliation, as an integral part of a life of constant conversion and encourages frequent confession of sins as an important way to meet the merciful Father through the mercy of the Son, embodied in the priest-confessor. Regular confession is not, therefore, just a matter of taking a weekly or monthly spiritual shower, although its effects in relieving burdens of guilt are an important part of the lifelong journey of conversion. Regular confession of sins is also a matter of growth in holiness of life, which is one effect of the sacramental encounter with the Lord of mercies in the sacrament of the divine mercy that the Risen Lord entrusted to the Church on the first Easter evening, when he gave the apostles the healing salutation "Peace be with you," and the gift of the Holy Spirit for the forgiveness of sins: "Receive the Holy Spirit. If you forgive the sins of any, they are forgiven" [John 20.19–23].

In light of all this, Evangelical Catholicism approaches the question of Catholic identity not primarily through the legal question of canonical boundaries, but through the theological reality of different degrees of communion with the Church. In its Decree on Ecumenism, the Second Vatican Council used this image to describe the relationship of other

Christian communities to the Catholic Church: Christian communities that had maintained the apostolic succession of bishops but had broken off full communion with the Bishop of Rome were in a fuller degree of communion with the Catholic Church than Christian communities that had not maintained apostolic succession but had retained the sacramental system. And those communities were in a fuller degree of communion with the Catholic Church than the Christian communities that had reduced the sacramental system to Baptism and the Lord's Supper.[24]

This image of "degrees of communion," drawn from ecumenical theology, can be analogously applied inside the Catholic Church. Catholics who deny certain truths taught as certainly true by the Church are, obviously, in a different degree of communion with the Church and with their fellow Catholics than Catholics who affirm those truths to be true. Catholics who undertake or support actions that the Church authoritatively teaches to be immoral, on the basis of reason as well as revelation, are just as obviously in a defective state of communion with the Church. Catholics who deny the truths the Church teaches, and Catholics who act in ways that contradict the Church's settled understanding of good and evil, may remain Catholics, in a formal canonical sense. But those Catholics are leading lives of such spiritual incoherence that their own integrity ought to compel them to seek reconciliation through the sacrament of Penance, and to do so before affirming a fuller communion with the Church than they in fact enjoy by receiving holy communion during Mass.

As Evangelical Catholicism understands these matters, it is a primary duty of the bishops, as the chief guardians of Catholic truth in their local churches, to call Catholics in a defective state of communion to a fuller communion with the Church. Doing so is not, in this perspective, so much a matter of "enforcing the rules" or "showing who's in charge" as it is a pastoral imperative: the shepherds issuing a call to conversion of life. Pastors share in that responsibility of the bishops in the parishes given to their care. That responsibility, to repeat, is spiritual before it is judicial: it is the responsibility conferred by Holy Orders to tend the flock, which includes the good shepherd calling back the straying sheep, no matter who those sheep may be.

Constant conversion is a work of grace, and both the people of the Church and their ordained ministers cooperate in this work of conversion through grace. It is Christ the Lord who calls each Catholic to conversion, and it is Christ the Lord who, through the agency of his priests, forgives sins and restores communion with his Body, the Church. This constant conversion is an essential foundation for works of charity and service, even as those works themselves deepen the evangelical Catholic's friendship with the Lord Jesus, who commands us to give a cup of water in his name and identifies himself with those whom his people serve.

5. Evangelical Catholicism is a liturgically centered form of Catholic life that embraces both the ancient traditions of Catholic worship and the authentic renewal of the liturgy according to the teaching of the Second Vatican Council.

The catechetical-devotional Catholicism of the Counter-Reformation inspired great religious art: Mozart's *Ave Verum*, Caravaggio's *Entombment of Christ*, Rome's Church of the Gesù. Yet catechetical-devotional Catholicism, while emphasizing truth (doctrine) and goodness (the moral law), paid relatively little attention to beauty as one of the "transcendentals" that point us toward God. One of the signs of the emergence of Evangelical Catholicism over the past six or seven decades has been a renewal of theological interest in beauty as a means of apprehending the divine. In a disenchanted world, the enchantment of the beautiful is a rumor of angels, a hint of the transcendent—a pathway to God.[25]

Evangelical Catholicism embraces this rediscovery of beauty as a primary category for understanding God and his ways and applies it to the Church's liturgy. Its approach to church architecture, church decoration, liturgical music, liturgical vesture, and all the other tangibles of the Church's liturgical life proceeds from the question, "Is this beautiful in such a way that it helps disclose the living God in Word and Sacrament?"

In that respect, Evangelical Catholicism's approach to liturgy is not somewhere "between" the approaches favored by liturgical traditionalists and liturgical progressives, but ahead of the curve of the now-tiresome Liturgy Wars.

Although it would be unfair to say that the liturgical reform mandated by the Second Vatican Council has been a failure, it would also be inaccurate to say that the fruits of that reform anticipated by the leaders of the mid-twentieth-century liturgical renewal have been realized. These hoped-for fruits included a deeper understanding of "the mysteries" revealed in a privileged way in the liturgy; a more extensive reception of the sacraments on a regular basis; a more widespread praying of the Liturgy of the Hours—the Church's official daily prayer—beyond the boundaries of those obliged to do so by Holy Orders, vows, and canon law; and a close linkage between the liturgical renewal, on the one hand, and work for justice, on the other. There are many reasons why the liturgical renewal has not had the effects that the reformers of the mid-twentieth century and the Fathers of Vatican II anticipated. But rather than dissect what went wrong, it will be more useful to sketch here how Evangelical Catholicism understands the liturgy, for that understanding intends to be in continuity with the great traditions of Christian worship through the centuries while being fully faithful to the intentions of twentieth-century liturgical reform.

To begin: Evangelical Catholicism understands the liturgy to be fundamentally God's work, not ours. To celebrate the Church's liturgy, especially Holy Mass, is our privileged participation in the liturgy of angels and saints around the Throne of Grace of the thrice-holy God. When the liturgy becomes something we create, rather than an act of sacramental worship in which we participate, it risks imitating the Israelites in their worship of the golden calf at the base of Mt. Sinai—which is to say, it risks becoming self-worship, the worship of the self-gathered and self-affirming community.[26] That is why Evangelical Catholicism takes the liturgical laws and rubrics of the Church seriously: these boundaries are barriers against the deterioration of the liturgy into a communal celebration of ourselves.

Evangelical Catholicism seeks to celebrate the *Novus Ordo* Mass of Pope Paul VI, inaugurated in 1970, in such a way as to incorporate within that rite the richness of the ancient liturgical tradition of the Church. Thus Evangelical Catholicism welcomes the availability of the Extraordinary Form of the Mass according to the Missal of 1962—the form of the Mass that emerged in the Counter-Reformation—because an experience of that older form of the one Roman Rite will accelerate a reform of the reform of the liturgy, bringing the post–Vatican II *Novus Ordo* to its proper splendor and furthering the noble aims of authentic liturgical renewal. Evangelical Catholicism does not regard the Extraordinary Form as a substitute for the *Novus Ordo*, the "Old Mass" gradually replacing the misbegotten "New Mass." Rather, Evangelical Catholicism sees the Extraordinary Form as a kind of liturgical magnet, the experience of which will eventually extract from the *Novus Ordo* (which is the normal form of the Roman Rite) the accumulated shrapnel of decades of liturgical detritus.

Evangelical Catholicism measures the tangibles of the liturgy— liturgical vessels and vestments, church decorations, ecclesiastical architecture—by the standard of beauty, and while recognizing that beauty takes many forms, it is cautious about the capacity of starkly modernist architecture, art, and design to convey rumors of angels to a disenchanted world. Conversely, evangelical Catholic liturgy is not antiquarian, and it does not regard patterns of liturgical vesture popular in the 1940s and 1950s as an aesthetic norm. Evangelical Catholic liturgy can and does accommodate various musical forms, although, following the teaching of the Second Vatican Council, it takes seriously Gregorian chant as a kind of universal Catholic musical grammar; at the same time, it welcomes more modern chant forms and seeks to incorporate into Catholic worship the great hymn traditions of other Christian communities.

The Church worships God not to make itself feel better, but because God has commanded that he be given the worship due him—and fulfilling that commandment is a privilege, not an onerous duty. In that light, evangelical Catholic liturgy is "high" liturgy, because evangelical Catholics are convinced that beauty is a pathway to the divine, a remedy for the dulling of Christian and human sensibilities, a motivator of Christian mission and service—and a reminder that the disciples of the Lord are ambassadors of the King of Glory, who, in their embassy to the world, remind the world that the present things are passing away in light of the radical reordering of history and the cosmos by the Paschal Mystery [see Revelation 21.1–4].[27]

This emphasis on beauty in the liturgical life of the Church is another reason why Evangelical Catholicism takes sacramental preparation and adult catechesis so seriously. Absent a true understanding of what the liturgy is, grounded in a firm grasp of what the Gospel is, those who "come to church" do not grow in living faith. Liturgy without Gospel is superstition, or self-worship, or both. Thus evangelical Catholic parishes take care to provide ongoing liturgical catechesis; this is primarily done through preaching, but it is also done through the various other means by which pastors communicate with their people. Pastors who understand that liturgical catechesis is a matter of empowering their people to exercise the priestly gift that is theirs by reason of Baptism will be likely to be effective in building worshipping communities that celebrate the sacred liturgy nobly, according to the teaching of the Second Vatican Council.

Evangelical Catholic liturgy is, finally, mission-driving. Having been lifted up to the threshold of the Throne of Grace through the dignified celebration of the Church's liturgy, evangelical Catholics leave Sunday Mass with a new charge of missionary energy. Thus they are always ready to welcome non-Catholic Christians and nonbelievers to the Church's worship as a means to meet Jesus Christ and enter into friendship with him.

6. Evangelical Catholicism is a biblically centered form of Catholic life that reads the Bible as the Word of God for the salvation of souls.

Counter-Reformation Catholicism revered the Bible, but at a distance. Beginning with Leo XIII in the 1893 encyclical *Providentissimus Deus,* the deep reform of the Catholic Church, wherever it has taken hold, has involved a return of the Church's book to the people of the Church as part of a grand strategy of recentering the Church on *Word* and Sacrament. This was the pastoral motive driving the development of Catholic biblical studies, which Leo XIII accelerated with the establishment of the Pontifical Biblical Commission in 1902: returning the Bible to the people of the Church meant offering the people of the Church another, and special, means of encounter with the living God, who speaks through Holy Scripture. The line of development that unfolded after *Providentissimus Deus*—not without difficulty—reached its summit at the Second Vatican Council in *Dei Verbum*, the Dogmatic Constitution on Divine Revelation.[28] There, the Catholic Church affirmed its self-understanding as the bearer of a Gospel that is divine revelation, a Gospel that is found in Word and Sacrament, both of which lead to, and then enhance, friendship with Jesus Christ. This entire movement from *Providentissimus Deus* to *Dei Verbum* was a reformist reaffirmation of St. Jerome's axiom that ignorance of the Scriptures is ignorance of Christ, who is the living center of the Word of God read and the Word of God preached.

Yet the biblical renaissance imagined before and during Vatican II has not, in the main, taken place. It is true that more Catholics read the Bible today than in the mid-1950s. It is true that the Bible is at the center of the explosion of Catholic life in Africa, where the life of the people of biblical times, including the liberation of the children of God from demonic powers, remains intensely and immediately real. And it is also true that educated Catholics and Catholic intellectuals trained in biblical studies know far more about the history, literary forms, and editorial evolution of biblical texts than they did in the mid-1950s. But all that learning has not led to the biblical renaissance that was eagerly anticipated in the wake of Vatican II.

For what many Catholics in the West have learned from modern biblical scholarship is a profound distrust of the Bible: this didn't happen; that's just a metaphor; this is a myth. The Bible that was to have been loved, and that was to become a means for encountering the living

God and his Son, has become in too many instances an artifact to be dissected, leaving unlovely and even repellant remains on the dissecting-room floor.

With Pope Benedict XVI, Evangelical Catholicism recognizes that the essential fruits of a modern, post-nineteenth-century historical-critical reading of the Bible have been harvested, and that the Church's task in the twenty-first century is to learn to read the Bible once again through theological lenses—lenses ground in part by the machinery of historical-critical studies, but further polished with a mature, theologically informed faith.[29] This means that Evangelical Catholicism reads the Bible as a whole, not as a collection of independent books of various literary forms: in an evangelical Catholic reading of Scripture, the parts form a coherent whole, and the center of that whole is Jesus Christ, to whom the Old Testament points and with whom the New Testament invites its readers to friendship. Evangelical Catholicism is thus formed by such modern critical tools as canon criticism, which analyzes books and texts of the Bible in their relationship to what the Church defined as the authentic "canon" of Scripture.[30] Twenty-first-century Evangelical Catholicism also reads with new appreciation the allegorical explication of the Scriptures by Church Fathers of the first millennium and the theological explication of the Bible by medieval commentators. Thus Evangelical Catholicism practices the ecumenism of time in its reading of the Bible.

Moreover, Evangelical Catholicism understands that a truly ecclesial biblical scholarship is intended to support the Church's evangelical mission by giving new power to Catholic preaching, Catholic catechesis, and Catholic evangelism. Forms of exegesis or biblical interpretation that do not support the homiletic, evangelical, and educational missions of the Church may have their place in the academy, but they are subsets of religious studies, not theology, and they should be understood as such. No serious evangelical Catholic homilist preaches out of the historical-critical notebook; his preaching is informed by historical-critical study of the Bible, but the substance preached is theological, and the focus is always on the encounter with Jesus Christ through the words of the written Word of God. Thus the formulas at the end of biblical readings at Mass—"The word of *the Lord*" and "The Gospel of *the Lord*"—take on the meaning intended by the Second Vatican Council.

Evangelical Catholicism takes with utmost seriousness the reformist claim that the Bible is the people's book. Thus evangelical Catholic parishes and dioceses call their people to meet the Lord daily in biblical reading and prayer and to build their programs around the Word of God (asking, in their planning, "What does the Word of God suggest about? . . .").[31] In the first decades of the twenty-first century, this call to biblical literacy and biblical spirituality necessarily involves a measure of historical-critical deprogramming, for both Church and world, having mistakenly assumed that a dissecting approach to the Bible is the only intellectually mature approach, have fostered a suspicion of Scripture that must be addressed before the encounter with the Word made flesh can take place through the Word of God in written form.

7. Evangelical Catholicism is a hierarchically ordered Catholicism in which a variety of vocations is respected.

If the proclamation of the Lord Jesus Christ as the unique savior of the world is the deepest point of countercultural conflict between the Catholic Church and the disenchanted worlds of the twenty-first century, the Church's claim that its hierarchical structure is the embodiment of the will of Christ, and not the result of historical accidents and ancient social conventions, is perhaps the next most countercultural of Catholic convictions. In a cultural environment where all authority is suspect and the notion of divine authority is thought to be a psychological hangover from the premodern world, the claim that that divine authority is transmitted in an unbroken chain of apostolic succession through the bishops of the Church in communion with the Bishop of Rome seems literally incredible.

Yet that is what the Catholic Church believes, and that is what Evangelical Catholicism must proclaim, explain, and live. It does so by locating the Church's hierarchical "constitution" within the ambit of God's call of each Christian to a unique vocation—a unique way of living one's membership in the Body of Christ. "Vocation," as Evangelical Catholicism understands the term, is not something that only the Church's ordained ministers and its consecrated religious men and women "have." *Vocation* is a reality of every individual Catholic life, each of which is "vocational" in a unique way.

Thus Evangelical Catholicism thinks of vocation, the constitutional hierarchy of the Church, and the variety of Spirit-given gifts in the Church as Blessed John Henry Newman did:

> God has created me to do him some definite service. He has committed some work to me which he has not committed to another. I have my mission. I may never know it in this life, but I shall be told it in the next. I am a link in a chain, a bond of connection between persons. He has not created me for naught. I shall do good; I shall do his work. I shall be an angel of peace, a preacher of truth in my own place, while not intending it if I do but keep his commandments. Therefore, I will trust him, whatever I am, I can never be thrown away.
>
> If I am in sickness, my sickness may serve him, in perplexity, my perplexity may serve him. If I am in sorrow, my sorrow may serve him. He does nothing in vain. He knows what he is about. He may take away my friends. He may throw me among strangers. He may make me feel desolate, make my spirits sink, hide my future from me. Still, he knows what he is about.[32]

The vocation of bishop has been emphasized throughout the reform of the Catholic Church that began with Pope Leo XIII, and in several ways. From the mid-nineteenth century on, the Church gradually regained control over its internal life by reclaiming the appointment of its bishops from public authorities and from local Church bodies, such as cathedral chapters. In the early twenty-first century, the Catholic Church has complete freedom to appoint the bishops it chooses to appoint, with rare exceptions, such as in China and Vietnam. Thus the Church is legally positioned to give effect to the reform of the episcopate envisioned by Vatican II, which described the local bishop as a true teacher, governor, and sanctifier in his local Church, and not just a branch manager of Catholic Church, Inc.

The Council emphasized the role of the local bishop as teacher, preacher, and catechist. Thus the reform of the episcopate envisioned by Vatican II will be realized in bishops who follow the model of the great teacher-bishops of the past, many of whom also left a deep impress on their cultures and societies: Clement, Leo the Great, and Gregory the Great; Ambrose and Augustine; Athanasius and John Chrysostom; Charles Borromeo and Francis de Sales; Clemens von Galen and Ildefonso Schuster; Andrey Sheptytsky and Karol Wojtyła. In their various ways and under different cultural circumstances, von Galen, Schuster, and Sheptytsky anticipated Evangelical Catholicism, while Wojtyła defined the evangelical Catholic reform at the end of the twentieth century and the beginning of the twenty-first through his witness and work as archbishop of Kraków and Bishop of Rome.

In catechetical-devotional Catholicism, the priesthood was often understood in largely functional terms. True, the catechisms of the preconciliar Church taught that ordination to the priesthood conferred a special sacramental character on a man, configuring him to Christ in a unique way such that he became an *alter Christus*, another Christ. The theology was sound, but the reality was that priests were primarily thought of as men who had been licensed to conduct certain types of ecclesiastical business: baptizing infants, hearing confessions, celebrating Mass, presiding at weddings and funerals.[33] This functionalist understanding of the priesthood easily extended into the management of parish affairs, and priests became a kind of clerical caste, separated from the people of the Church. In the theological confusions of the postconciliar decades, this functionalist understanding of priesthood took on a new and darker guise, with seminarians talking about learning "priestcraft," and the clerical caste system sometimes functioning as a protection racket hiding sexual predators.

Evangelical Catholicism understands the priesthood in iconic terms: the Catholic priest is a man whose ordination makes him into an icon, a living re-presentation (or "making present") of the Lord Jesus. Thus the priest, like the bishop, is first a preacher, teacher, catechist, and sanctifier before he is an administrator. Priests are leaders of their parishes, as bishops are of their dioceses. But in a fully embodied Evangelical Catholicism, deacons and other qualified lay members of the Church will handle more and more of the routine business of parish and diocesan administration. The pastors—bishops who are true successors of the apostles, and priests who form a presbyteral college with and under the bishop (as the bishops form an episcopal college with and under the Bishop of Rome, the pope)—have more urgent matters to which they must attend.

Yet the lay vocation, as understood by Evangelical Catholicism, is not primarily one of Church management, in which only a small minority of laity will be involved. The lay vocation is evangelism: of the family, the workplace, and the neighborhood, and thus of culture, economics, and politics. As Evangelical Catholicism rejects the clericalism by which the lay members of the Church were simply to pray, pay, and obey (or, as a nineteenth-century aristocratic English variant had it, to hunt, shoot, and entertain), so it rejects a clericalized notion of lay vocation as primarily having to do with working in the parish office or diocesan chancery.[34] There is important work to be done in those venues, and lay Catholics can and ought to do more of it, thus freeing priests and bishops for the work they were ordained to do. But the primary lay vocation, as John Paul II taught in the 1990 encyclical *Redemptoris Missio*, is to bring the Gospel into all of those parts of "the world" to which the laity has greater access than those who are ordained: the family, the mass media, the business community, the worlds of culture, and the political arena, for example.[35]

Evangelical Catholics are men and women who, having shared the great grace of Baptism, and having been appropriately catechized into "the mysteries," understand, appreciate, and live the biblical truth of Christian vocation as given by St. Paul: "Now there are varieties of gifts, but the same Spirit; and there are varieties of service, but the same Lord; and there are varieties of working, but it is the same God who inspires them all in every one. To each is given a manifestation of the Spirit for the common good" [1 Corinthians 12.4–7].

8. Evangelical Catholicism is both culture-forming and countercultural.

Evangelical Catholicism creates its own culture. Because friendship with the Lord Jesus shapes every aspect of a Christian's life, that friendship is culture-forming: those who are living in friendship with the Risen Lord in the communion of the Church speak a distinctive language (in which, to take two examples, "obedience" and "forgiveness" have richer and deeper meanings than in postmodern culture). They live according to a distinctive temporal rhythm (in which, to take but one example, Sunday is not simply a day on which the shopping malls close earlier). They celebrate unique rituals, observe a unique set of laws, cherish and tell a unique set of stories, and perceive life (and death) against a unique horizon. The culture of Evangelical Catholicism orders the way evangelical Catholics think, choose, and behave. Evangelical Catholics know that friendship with the Lord Jesus and the communion that arises from that friendship is an anticipation of the City of God in the city of this world. Thus evangelical Catholics have a kind of dual citizenship, in that they acknowledge the sovereignty of Christ the King as well as the sovereignty of the political community within which they live.[36]

In the waning decades of Counter-Reformation Catholicism, which coincided with the post–World War II period, Catholics experienced a relatively comfortable fit between the culture of the Church and the ambient public culture throughout the regions in which Christianity had been long established (with the exception of those Christian lands under communist rule). The public culture of the West was still recognizably Christian, in many respects; to be a Christian in the "free world" was not to experience the Church as a counterculture. This was the circumstance that seems to have shaped the rather optimistic view of the Catholic

Church's dialogue with modern culture found in Vatican II's Pastoral Constitution on the Church in the Modern World.[37]

Yet in less than a decade after the Council, the high culture of the West took a sharp turn toward an aggressive and hegemonic secularism that, in the twenty-first century, manifests itself as Christophobia: a deep hostility to Gospel truth (especially moral truth) and a determination to drive Christians who affirm those truths out of the public square and into a privatized existence on the margins of society.[38] In these circumstances, the preaching of the Gospel and the living-out of Gospel truths in activities ranging from health care to foster care to education are profoundly countercultural. They put the believer at risk in terms of psychological comfort and social status. When the ambient public culture is dominated by nihilism and relativism and conscripts public authority to impose that nihilism and relativism on others through the coercive use of state power, the Church faces a challenge that is somewhat similar, at least structurally, to the challenge it faced in communist lands during the Cold War years.

That challenge cannot be met by timid or lukewarm Catholicism. It can only be met by a robust Evangelical Catholicism that proposes the Gospel in a compelling and courageous way, and that insists that public authorities allow the Church the free space in which to be itself, make its proposal, and offer the service of charity to others. Thus the culture that is Evangelical Catholicism seeks to be a culture-forming counter-culture for the sake of the world, its healing, and its conversion.

Christianity is Christ, and thus it is Christ, not some abstract cluster of "Christian" ideas, who shaped the culture of the West for centuries. It was Christ, working through the people of the Church who are his Body, who converted the classical world and who saved that world's intellectual and cultural heritage through the Christian microcultures of Benedictine monasticism.[39] It was Christ, through the Church, who shaped the Christendom of the Middle Ages, where the foundations of modern science and democracy were laid.[40] It was Christ in his Church who brought Europe—its peoples and their cultures—to the Western

Hemisphere, shaping the New World's social, cultural, and political life for over five centuries. It was Christ whom Jacobin politics, in a line from Robespierre to Stalin, sought to drive out of the future of the West by the brutal suppression of the Church. It is Christ whom the twenty-first-century Christophobes fear.

And if the West is to recover from the crisis of civilizational morale in which it has been immolating itself in the last decades of the twentieth century and the first decades of the twenty-first, it is Christ, through Evangelical Catholicism, who will help humanize the earthly city through the agency of the City of God, present in an anticipatory way in the counter-culture that is the Church.

9. Evangelical Catholicism enters the public square with the voice of reason, grounded in Gospel conviction.

Because it lives under two sovereigns, Evangelical Catholicism is bilingual.

The Gospel cannot be preached in any other language than its own, which means a language deeply shaped by the sacred Scriptures. The same is true for catechesis, or Christian education and formation within the Church: it must take place within a biblical and sacramental, even "mystagogical," vocabulary. Because of this, Evangelical Catholicism understands that there can be no substitutes for certain biblical words and images. As patristics scholar Robert Louis Wilken wrote, "there are some words and phrases in Christian culture that are simply irreplaceable. Words and phrases such as 'obedience,' 'grace,' 'long-suffering' (the biblical form of patience), 'image of God,' 'suffering servant,' 'adoption,' 'will of God'—when used again and again—form our imagination and channel our affections."[41]

Working this language and its rich theological meaning into the texture of Catholic lives and imaginations is likely kneading yeast into flour. That is why Evangelical Catholicism insists on biblical literacy, meaning regular reading of the Bible and praying with the Bible. To pray the Psalms regularly is to apprehend the world in a new way—an evangelical way. To read the gospels so that they become entirely familiar (even as they continually surprise us with new patterns of meaning) is to acquire the vocabulary and the "grammar" that allows every Christian to be an evangelist.

Moreover, to speak the language of the Church is to speak a language that has been revealed and received, a language that is not to be recast whenever the ambient culture suggests that the Church do so. In its preaching, catechesis, worship, and evangelism, Evangelical Catholicism cherishes and uses the vocabulary that names "Father," "Son," and "Holy Spirit," and it is not shy about countercultural words like "Lord," and "sin," because these are the words it has received as part of the patrimony of the Gospel. In some cases, it has received these words from Jesus himself, and understands in humility that it has no authority to change them. The concreteness of the received sacral vocabulary of Christianity—in particular, the Trinitarian vocabulary of "Father, Son, and Holy Spirit"— is also a rebuff to the regnant Gnosticism of postmodern culture, in which everything is malleable and functional. To name "Creator, Redeemer, and Sanctifier" rather than "Father, Son, and Holy Spirit" is to declare oneself a believer in a religion other than Christianity, even if one is canonically a member of the Catholic Church.[42]

In addressing issues of public policy in pluralistic and typically secular societies, however, Evangelical Catholicism speaks its second language, which is the language of reason. The ordained leaders of the Church, and the laity who are Christ's principal witnesses in the public square, do not enter public life proclaiming "The Church teaches . . ." as the first move in their efforts to defend the inalienable right to life from conception until natural death, or to defend the integrity of marriage. When the question at issue is an immoral practice, the leaders and people of the Church enter the debates saying, "This is wicked; it cannot be sanctioned by the law and here is why, as reasonable people will grasp." When the issue at hand is the promotion of some good, the first things the leaders of the Church and its people say is, "This is good; it's a requirement of justice that the law acknowledge it; and here is why it's both good and just."

This use of the language of reason in pluralistic democracies is justified on several grounds. It is a matter of good democratic manners: serious debate is the lifeblood of democracy, and those committed to the democratic project take care to observe its grammatical protocols, which ask us to speak in such a way that our arguments can be engaged by our fellow citizens. It is also a matter of political common sense: if you want an argument to be heard, engaged, and accepted, you make it in a language that those you are seeking to persuade can understand. It is, furthermore, a matter of calling the bluff of those who insist that the Catholic Church's teachings on such issues as abortion, euthanasia, and marriage are "sectarian" teachings that cannot be "imposed" on a pluralistic society. To the contrary, the arguments that evangelical Catholics make on these issues in the public square are arguments drawn from the grammar of reason, which is (or should be) accessible to all, whatever their theological location (and even, indeed, when they lack any religious conviction).

Evangelical Catholicism draws the will, the energy, the strength, and, if necessary, the stubbornness to continue defending and promoting the dignity of the human person in twenty-first-century society from the power of the Gospel. It speaks publicly in secular, pluralistic democracies in such a way that its words can be heard, so that the truths it bears can be engaged by everyone. Only religious and secular sectarians will find a contradiction here.

10. Evangelical Catholicism awaits with eager anticipation the coming of the Lord Jesus in glory, and until that time, Evangelical Catholicism is ordered to mission—to the proclamation of the Gospel for the world's salvation.

In the encyclical *Redemptoris Missio*, Pope John Paul II, summing up a line of development that had begun with Leo XIII's new engagement with modernity, taught that the Church does not *have* a mission, as if "mission" were one among a dozen things the Church does; rather, the Church *is* a mission, and everything the Church does is ordered to that mission, which is the proclamation of the Gospel and the conversion of the world to Christ.[43] Evangelical Catholicism is that form of twenty-first-century Catholicism that has fully embraced John Paul's teaching on the nature of the Church-as-mission and that declares itself and its people to be in permanent mission.[44] And as such, it is the form of Catholicism that will complete the deep reform of the Catholic Church that has been underway since 1878.

In an evangelical Catholic perspective, mission measures *everything*; or, in the language of management theory, Evangelical Catholicism is *mission-driven*. Even in the sacred liturgy—that part of the Church's life that seems to be a step back from the world, or better, a step into the real world that is the Kingdom of God in the Wedding Feast of the Lamb— the Church is being equipped by sacramental grace for mission. Even contemplative vocations that really are cloistered, from both the world and the rest of the Church, are mission-oriented. For the consecrated life, as John Paul II taught in the 1996 apostolic exhortation *Vita Consecrata,* is the spiritual engine of the Church. Here the energies of evangelism are refined and shared in a great exchange of gifts by which the entire Church, as the Bride of Christ, strives for union with her divine Spouse.[45] Thus the mission of the Church in-the-world is ordered to the coming of the Lord in glory and the New Life of the New Jerusalem.

If mission measures everything in Evangelical Catholicism, it also measures *everyone*, for as the Fathers of the Second Vatican Council taught, "each disciple of Christ has the obligation of spreading the faith."[46] In an evangelical Catholic perspective, every Catholic is a missionary, an evangelist, a baptized disciple commissioned by the Lord to take the Gospel to every nation, calling all to be baptized in the name of the Most Holy Trinity. Thus does Evangelical Catholicism respond to the challenges posed by evangelical Protestantism (in which sharing the friendship of the Lord Jesus is understood to be everyone's responsibility) and clericalized Catholicism (in which mission is something reserved for the ordained).

Furthermore, mission measures the deep reform of the Church. Those things that need to be changed in the Church, and that can be changed, must be changed for the sake of the mission. Those things in the Church that cannot be changed, because they are of the divinely ordered constitution of the Church, must be reformed when necessary so that they contribute as they ought to the mission. The notion of a Church always in need of purification and reform is drawn not from the Reformation slogan *ecclesia semper reformanda* [the Church must always be reformed], but from within the Church's deepest inner dynamics: its longing to be joined to its spousal Head, Christ the Lord, and its passion to share his love with those to whom it has been commissioned to bring the Gospel—that is, everyone.

Thus the Church draws the criteria of its deep reform from within itself: the *criterion of truth* and the *criterion of mission*.

Evangelical Catholics know that the Gospel and the sacraments have been given to them so that they in turn may give them to others. The timidity (or selfishness) that precludes offering others the possibility of friendship with the Lord Jesus is unworthy of those whom he calls to be his witnesses. Thus all the baptized must be constantly formed and educated for mission. Some will do this by the quality of their lives, which, lived openly in fidelity to Christ, will inspire in others the hope for a similar faith and charity. Others will do it by proposing the Gospel, in and out of season, in the knowledge that the word, if it truly be formed by the Word of God, does not go forth without effect. But however the mission is lived, all evangelical Catholics are called to mission—and to live the mission in the joy, the confidence, and the firm faith that the Lord who has conquered sin and death will complete his victory in the Wedding Feast of the Lamb in the New Jerusalem, where every tear will be wiped away "and death shall be no more, neither shall there be mourning nor crying nor pain anymore, for the former things have passed away" [Revelation 21.4].

THE LATE FRENCH JOURNALIST ANDRÉ FROSSARD WAS A CONVERT TO Catholicism from the fashionable atheism of his class, an atheism that was once a Parisian intellectual fad but that has taken on a much harder, Christophobic edge across the twenty-first-century Western world.

When Frossard saw John Paul II at the Mass marking the beginning of the Pope's public ministry on October 22, 1978, he wired back to his Paris newspaper, "This is not a pope from Poland; this is a pope from Galilee." It was a brilliant metaphor that illustrates in one rich biblical image the nature and task of Evangelical Catholicism.

The Leonine revival that reached its fulfillment in John Paul II and Benedict XVI, heirs and authentic interpreters of the Second Vatican Council, is inviting the Catholic Church to Galilee, and then beyond Galilee. The Catholic Church is being invited to meet the Risen Lord in the Scripture, the sacraments, and prayer, and to make friendship with him the center of Catholic life. Every Catholic has received this invitation in Baptism: the invitation to accept the Great Commission, to act as evangelists, and to measure the truth of Catholic life by the way in which Catholics give expression to the human decency and solidarity that flows from friendship with Christ the Lord.

In the first decades of the twenty-first century, Evangelical Catholicism challenges all of the people of the Church, lay, consecrated religious, or ordained, to have the courage to be Catholic: to have the courage to take the Gospel in its fullness beyond Galilee and out to the nations. Meeting that challenge requires the continuation of the deep reform of the Catholic Church that began with Pope Leo XIII, guided by the twin criteria of *truth* and *mission*.

CHAPTER FOUR

True Reform in the Church

Then he made the disciples get into the boat and go before him to the other side, while he dismissed the crowds. And after he had dismissed the crowds, he went up the mountain by himself to pray. When evening came, he was there alone, but the boat by this time was many furlongs distant from the land, beaten by the waves; for the wind was against them. And in the fourth watch of the night he came to them, walking on the sea. But when the disciples saw him walking on the sea, they were terrified, saying, "It is a ghost!" and they cried out for fear. But immediately he spoke to them, saying, "Take heart, it is I; have no fear."

And Peter answered him, "Lord, if it is you, bid me come to you on the water." He said, "Come." So Peter got out of the boat and walked on the water and came to Jesus, but when he saw the wind he was afraid, and beginning to sink he cried out, "Lord, save me." Jesus immediately reached out his hand and caught him, saying, "O man of little faith, why did you doubt?" And when they had got into the boat, the wind ceased. And those in the boat worshipped him, saying, "Truly you are the Son of God."

—MATTHEW 14.22–33

THIS FAMILIAR EPISODE, WHICH OCCURS AT THE MIDPOINT OF MATTHEW'S gospel, offers a rich menu of reflection for those who would deepen the reform of the Catholic Church in the twenty-first century so that Evangelical Catholicism comes to full maturity.

Biblical scholar Gianfranco Ravasi has pointed out that this story has the same literary structure as the paschal appearances of the Risen Lord during the forty days between Easter and the Ascension. "Be not afraid; it is I," the admonition by which Jesus seeks to calm the fears of his storm-tossed disciples, is also the reassurance the Risen One often gives after the Resurrection when identifying himself to his followers and friends, who frequently cannot at first recognize him. In this story, Peter twice addresses Jesus with the paschal title "Lord," as John does when he sees the Risen One on the shore while he and Peter are fishing [John 21.7].

The disciples, huddled in the boat in fear, frightened by the storm and their inability to quell its effects, remind us of the disciples hiding in the Upper Room, terrified by the horrific events of Good Friday and unable to imagine a future; yet these same disciples, who may stand for the Church of all times and places, come to recognize the Risen One and worship him, both in the boat and at the Easter appearances. The acclamation of these pious Jews on the Sea of Galilee, "Truly you are the Son of God," is a precise parallel to the first act of faith by gentiles, the Roman cohort at the foot of the cross ("When the centurion and those who were with him, keeping watch over Jesus, saw the earthquake and what took place, they were filled with awe and said, 'Truly this was the Son of God!'" [Matthew 27.54]). Thus at the very midpoint of Matthew's account, the evangelist offers a tacit anticipation of a Church in which the "wild olive shoot" of the gentiles will be grafted onto the tree of Israel, so that God's universal saving will may be accomplished [Romans 11.17].

Ravasi's commentary points out several other features of the story that give it enduring power and contemporary relevance. Throughout its history, the Church has frequently been in difficulty; those difficulties often come because of that "little faith" or lack of faith for which Jesus chides Peter. A Church in difficulty or crisis is, typically, a frightened Church: a Church that has lost sight of the Lord, that has fixed its gaze on another horizon, and that is awash in troubles because it is no longer looking as closely or intently as it should at the Risen One who comes to his people in ways they often do not expect. Then the situation is rectified and the disciples' fears are relieved (as Catholic crises through the centuries will be rectified and Catholic fears for the future relieved) by the Lord's initiative: the Risen One, the Son of God, gets into the boat of the Church, on the Sea of Galilee and throughout the millennia, and puts things right.

Through this story, Matthew's gospel constantly reminds the Church that, for all our cleverness and skill, we are impotent in matters of salvation—that we are the saved, not the saviors, and that all attempts at self-justification come to naught. Put another way, the Church is Christ's Church, not ours, and we start sinking when we try to make it ours.[1]

Courage "in the Boat"

In bringing Evangelical Catholicism to full maturity in the twenty-first century—thus accelerating the process of deep Catholic reform that began in 1878 with the election of Pope Leo XIII—all Catholics are, as it were, in the same boat: the "boat" whose prototype was that fishing smack trying to cross the Sea of Galilee on a stormy night in the third or fourth decade of the first century A.D. As it was then, so it is now: the Church—all of those "in the boat"—must depend completely on the Christ of the outstretched hand in order to come safely to shore and get on with the mission of the Redeemer, the preaching of the Gospel. The Church of the twenty-first century must reach out and be grasped by the outstretched and pierced hand of the Risen Lord if all of the people of the Church are to live lives of radical fidelity and supernatural charity, help effect genuinely Catholic reform, and be the witnesses "to all nations" that the Risen One has commanded us to be [Matthew 28.20].

The "boat" that is the Catholic Church has been severely rocked in the first decades of the twenty-first century by a seemingly endless series of scandals, many of them involving its priests and bishops. Thus the Lord's call across the water—"Do not be afraid!"—has a particular resonance at the beginning of the third millennium of the Church's history. As it happens, of course, that call to courage—"Be not afraid!"—was the signature phrase of the pontificate of Blessed John Paul II for twenty-six and a half years. That challenge to fearlessness—to a time when "hearts are brave, again, and arms are strong"[2]—is evangelically ordered. It is not a call to feel better, or safer, or more secure, although we are safer and more secure in the embrace of the Holy One of God, who calls us to fearlessness, than we can ever be elsewhere. No, the call to courage and fearlessness is a call to take heart precisely so that the Great Commission can be fulfilled. That is why, at John Paul II's first public Mass as Bishop of Rome on October 22, 1978, the thrice-repeated challenge, "Be not afraid!," was linked to mission: "Open the doors to Christ!"

In grasping the outstretched hand of Christ, the Church of the twenty-first century, and of all time, finds the remedy for its fear. It also finds the criteria of authentic Catholic reform: the *criterion of truth*—for it is the truth of Christ that measures all in the boat that is the Church—and the *criterion of mission*—for it is by Christ overcoming our fear that the Church finds the courage to *be* the mission it is.

The Criteria of Catholic Reform

The first criterion of authentic Catholic reform reflects the promise of the Lord to his first disciples: that through him, they would "know the truth, and the truth will make you free" [John 8.32]. This is the criterion of truth: *all true Catholic reform is built out from the truth that* is *Christ and reflects the truths that have been entrusted to the Church* by *Christ.*

It is his truth that sets us free, because it is he, the Truth incarnate, whose obedient sacrifice on the cross has set us free in the deepest meaning of freedom: by winning our redemption, which is the conquest of that which we most fear—death and oblivion.

It is his truth that sets us free, because it is his Resurrection and Ascension that reveal the final truth about the human condition: that *in* our human nature, not fetched out of it, the redeemed who were made for God and have been given the pledge of the Spirit are marked for eternal life within the light and life of the Holy Trinity.

It is his truth that empowers the Church for evangelism and witness, for the truth about humanity and its destiny that he commands his followers to carry to the ends of the earth is of such overpowering magnificence that it demands to be proclaimed and shared. This is both the truth that speaks *to* power and the truth that *is* power, a power that proposes rather than imposes, a power that is both sweet and overwhelming.

And it is his truth that gives the Church the courage to be Catholic—to undertake genuinely Catholic reform that enables, empowers, and advances the mission of the Church.

Thus the second criterion of all authentic Catholic reform, the criterion of mission, emerges from and is inseparable from the first criterion: *all true Catholic reform is reform ordered to mission, to the proclamation of the Gospel, to building up the Body of Christ for the healing and salvation of the world.* True Catholic reform is not a matter of settling ecclesiastical scores, or of declaring winners and losers in various arguments over ideas or power. True Catholic reform does not mean conforming the Church to the spirit of the age; nor does it mean fossilizing the Church by declaring one historical expression of its essential form to be unchangeable and definitive. By constant reference to the essential "form" that Christ bequeathed to his Church, true Catholic reform is a "re-formation" that empowers all those "in the boat" to become the extension of that outstretched hand of the Lord, so that others may be grasped by him, know him, love him—and be safe in him.

That "re-formation" of the Church draws from the Church's roots in the People of Israel, and in the stories the Old Testament tells of their struggle to live out their covenant with God faithfully.

The Prophetic Pattern of Reform

Thus the pattern of authentic Catholic reform begins in the prophetic literature of the Hebrew Bible: those remarkable Old Testament texts by and about astonishing figures who emerge from a variety of circumstances (tending sycamores, shepherding flocks, offering priestly service), typically in times of crisis, to announce without ambiguity or apology, "*Thus says the* LORD . . ."

The crises these prophets were called to address were crises of fidelity. For, although they were settled in the Land of the Promise, the Chosen People were nonetheless beset by temptations to imitate the false worship of their neighbors. This ongoing drama of false worship, on the one hand, and the prophetic witness to the truth that God called forth to counter infidelity, on the other, finds its prototype in the epic battle between the prophet Elijah and the priests of Baal, who enjoyed the protection of Jezebel, wife of Ahab, king of Israel—a battle settled when the LORD God, who gave his name to Moses as "I AM," intervened with power to resolve the question of "Who is God?" [see 1 Kings 16.29–22.40; Exodus 3.14]. The perversity of false worship among God's Chosen People would culminate in the grotesque practice of fiery child-sacrifice to the pagan horror-god known as Moloch. Here was the depth of depravity, which two of the classic prophets, Jeremiah and Ezekiel, described in unsparing terms as they called down the uncompromising condemnation of the God of Abraham, Isaac, and Jacob:

> So you shall . . . say to them, "This is the nation that did not obey the voice of the LORD their God, and did not accept discipline; truth has perished, it is cut off from their lips. . . . For the sons of Judah have done evil in my sight, says the LORD. . . . They have built the high place of Topheth, which is in the valley of the son of Hinnom, to burn their sons and daughters in the fire." [Jeremiah 7.27–28, 30–31]

> Again the word of the LORD came to me: "Son of man, make known to Jerusalem her abominations. . . . You trusted in your beauty, and played the harlot because of your renown, and lavished your harlotries on any passers-by. . . . You also took your fair jewels of my gold and of my silver, which I had given you, and made yourselves images of men, and with them played the harlot. . . . And you took your sons and

your daughters, whom you had born to me, and these you sacrificed to them to be devoured. Were your harlotries so small a matter that you slaughtered my children and delivered them up as an offering of fire to them?" [Ezekiel 16.1–2, 15, 17, 20–21]

In the face of such depravity, rooted in a collapse of faith in the truth of what God had revealed in the Exodus and at Mt. Sinai, the only answer was a reconstitution of the Chosen in the truth: a reform that was built out from the "form" that had been given these ragtag former slaves at Sinai, where they had entered into covenant with the liberator God of the Exodus. And that meant reform by reference to the truth contained in the gift of the Law, given by God so that the newly liberated people of Israel would not fall back into slavish habits. Thus the prophets insisted, often at their grave peril, that the answer to an infidelity so depraved that it could countenance the slaughter of children was not Idolatry Lite (the more subtle, less gruesome worship of false gods) or Syncretism Lite (finding more clever ways to cover one's theological bets). No, the only reform that was true reform among the Chosen People, according to the prophets, was radical fidelity to the one true God and to the things he had commanded at Sinai. The only true reform was radical reconversion to the LORD whose holy presence had traveled with the people of Israel in the desert and was now housed in the Holy of Holies in the Temple in Jerusalem.

This prophetic pattern of authentic reform continues in the Church, the Israel of the New Covenant. And if one were to draw a deliberately disturbing analogy between the infidelity displayed in horrible ways by Israel's whoring after false gods through child-sacrifice and the twenty-first-century revelation of the abuse of the young by churchmen, then the analogy should be drawn fully: the latter, too, was primarily a matter of radical infidelity, which can only be remedied by radical fidelity. True Catholic reform, like true Israelite reform, is neither Idolatry Lite (in which we take it upon ourselves to reimagine and rename the Triune God who has already been revealed to us and named for us by the Son of God) nor Syncretism Lite (in which the truths of Catholic faith are exchanged for the "truths" of the ambient public culture). True Catholic reform, in other words, is not Catholic Lite.

True Catholic reform is to be found in the maturation of Evangelical Catholicism: in radical fidelity to what God has revealed in Scripture and apostolic tradition, in the proposal of those truths to the world, and in the Church's works of supernatural charity. What the Church *does* cannot be separated from what the Church *believes*. Theology would express this in technical terms: there is no orthopraxis (in terms of either mission or service) without orthodoxy. Pope Benedict XVI has said the same thing in more biblical language: there is no charity that is not charity in truth, *caritas in veritate*.[3]

Boundary Markers of Reform

These biblical patterns of authentic reform cast light on the two criteria of authentic Catholic reform. Reflecting on those criteria in light of the witness of the prophets helps identify several other boundary markers for determining what is true reform in the Church and what is false.

The criterion of truth—which is another way of saying "the criterion of Christ"—suggests that, in the final analysis, the truths the Church bears, while susceptible of doctrinal development (meaning deeper understanding on our part), stand in judgment on the "truths" of the world or the intellectual fashions of any given historical moment, not the other way around. In this sense, the global collapse of mainline Protestantism ought to have been foreseen when the World Council of Churches, in the second half of the twentieth century, adopted the slogan, "The world sets the agenda for the Church." For when "the world" sets the agenda for the Church, the people of the Church, to return to the Sea of Galilee, have leaped out of the boat into stormy waters, where they are likely to drown. (An analogous criticism could be made of some forms of late twentieth-century Catholic liberation theology, in which the requirements of the revolution, typically understood in Marxist categories, so distorted classic Catholic understandings of the Bible, the Church, the Eucharist, the priesthood, the Church's mission, and the Church's social doctrine as to reduce the Church to another regiment in a revolutionary vanguard.)

This does not mean that the Catholic Church has nothing to learn from "the world." It does mean that the way in which the Church learns from the world must be a distinctively *ecclesial* way of learning, if it is to be authentically Catholic. Perhaps the clearest recent example of this genuinely ecclesial kind of learning (which was also an important moment in the evolution of Evangelical Catholicism) involves the development of Catholic doctrine on church and state, in which the key issue was the question of religious freedom.

In the early nineteenth century, it seemed a settled matter of Catholic self-understanding that the preferred arrangement between civil authority and the Catholic Church was one in which the Church was "established," i.e., the Catholic Church was the Church *of* the state, enjoying particular benefits that were not extended to other Christian communities or religious bodies, whose members might, depending on the stringency of the regime, suffer civil penalties for their different religious "location." It was also understood that, in this preferred relationship, the civil authority (which usually meant the monarch) would have a privileged say in the selection of bishops. About a century and a half later, the Second Vatican Council issued its Declaration on Religious Freedom, *Dignitatis Humane*, in which the Catholic Church declared religious freedom a fundamental human right that could be known by both reason and revelation, and taught that any just state was obliged to acknowledge and protect that right in law.

Vatican II's Pastoral Constitution on the Church in the Modern World followed the lead of *Dignitatis Humanae* by casting a critical eye on church-state establishments and seeming to suggest a settled Catholic preference for constitutional democracy and limited government. The Council's Decree on the Pastoral Office of Bishops in the Church [*Christus Dominus*] declined to give any rights to state authorities in the appointment of bishops, a teaching given legal force by the 1983 Code of Canon Law. What happened? How did this development occur? Was it a matter of pragmatic accommodation to twentieth-century political reality? Or did it involve, rather, a genuinely *ecclesial* development of Catholic self-understanding?

The Church certainly learned some things from "the world" between, say, Pope Pius VII (who was kidnapped by Napoleon) and the Second Vatican Council. From the experience of the United States, the Catholic Church learned that a society in which there was no established church could be good for Catholicism and its evangelical mission. From its experience of the French Revolution and the French Third Republic, from the German *Kulturkampf* and the Italian *Risorgimento*, the Catholic Church learned that there was a totalitarian temptation—an ultramundane and radically secularist variant on royal absolutism—built into a lot of political modernity, and that this was very bad for the Church's evangelical mission. From its experience of the missions, especially in Asia and Africa, the Catholic Church began to intuit that, if its basic character was kerygmatic (or Gospel-centered), and its basic mission was evangelical, the fulfillment of that mission and the living-out of that character could be compromised by too close an identification between the Church and state power (meaning colonial power). Wittingly or not (and usually the latter), "the world" taught the Church a lot in the nineteenth and early twentieth centuries.

The Catholic Church dealt with what it learned in the hard school of nineteenth- and twentieth-century Western politics through a distinctively ecclesial method of reflection and development, however. No small part of that development was made possible by the intellectual work of an American Jesuit theologian, John Courtney Murray. With Leo XIII's encyclicals on political modernity as his primary texts, Murray began to argue in the 1950s that the oldest, deepest, and most authentic Catholic tradition had made a clear distinction between religious and political authority. It had done so on the basis of the Lord's juxtaposition of what was variously owed to Caesar and God in Matthew 22.21. That dominical injunction had been given theological formulation by Pope St. Gelasius I's fifth-century distinction between "royal" and "priestly" power in governing the world, and it was given worldly effect by Pope Gregory VII's refusal to concede essential elements of the Church's authority to the Holy Roman emperor Henry IV in the eleventh-century investiture controversy.

This "dualism" of authorities, Murray proposed, was the authentic Catholic tradition, the authentic "form" of the Church's relationship to worldly power. That meant that the use of political authority to buttress the Church's truth claims (which had reached a high-water mark in the period of royal absolutism, when the established Church became virtually a department of the state) was the aberration. Thus the legal "establishment" of the Church was not the settled, doctrinal matter it was often thought to be, and a genuine development of doctrine—a reform of the Church's teaching and practice in matters of Church and state—could therefore be effected: not as a concession to the claims of contemporary politics, but as a genuine "re-forming" of the Church according to the truths it bore.[4]

Thus the retrieval of a forgotten deep truth of Catholic self-understanding was the historical fulcrum from which Murray could leverage a reform of the Church's understanding of religious freedom and of the right relationship of church and state, which was ratified at the Second Vatican Council. That process was certainly influenced by the historical events of the nineteenth and early twentieth centuries, not least the experience of hard totalitarianism before, during, and after World War II. At the same time, the process was distinctively and authentically Catholic because *reform* was based not on accommodation to current fashions, but on the *retrieval* of something important and true—something of Christ, and something that was important for the Church's mission—that Catholicism had misplaced and forgotten. Reform was based on retrieval, and renewal followed.

Impediments to Reform

The biblical pattern of prophetic reform and the two criteria of authentic Catholic reform, truth and mission, should also inoculate the Church of the twenty-first century against two temptations: Catholic Antiquarianism and Catholic Presentitis, neither of which has to do with Evangelical Catholicism and its deep reform of the Church.

Catholic Antiquarianism is the temptation to imagine a Catholic Golden Age, usually pre–Vatican II, the return to which is thought to be the path to Catholic vitality in the future. This temptation is often found lurking in debates over the liturgy, over the relationship of the Church to political modernity (especially democracy), and in arguments over ecumenical and interreligious relations. In its most extreme form, Catholic Antiquarianism produced the only formal post–Vatican II schism, that of the followers of the late French archbishop Marcel Lefebvre: a man who, when the moment of decision came, seems to have hated modernity more than he loved the obedience of faith.[5]

The Lefebvrists are, however, a small and marginal extreme. And their inability to acknowledge that the Second Vatican Council taught the truth on matters of church and state, on the relationship of the Church to living Judaism, and on ecumenism has made the accommodation of their liturgical concerns, which some orthodox Catholics share, something rather less than the opening to reconciliation that many (perhaps including Pope Benedict XVI) hoped it would be.[6] The deeper problem for the full maturation of Evangelical Catholicism is that Catholic Antiquarianism that lives inside the household of faith: an antiquarianism that finds expression in everything from liturgical vesture to theological method. That something is antique in the Church, however, does not mean that it is necessarily good, or true, or an aid to mission.

Twenty-first-century Catholic Antiquarianism in the Western world seems to have missed many elements of the true, the good, and the beautiful in the ongoing reform of the Church's life that began with Leo XIII in 1878.

Catholic Antiquarianism correctly mourns the catechetical wreckage in much of the post–Vatican II Church, but it imagines that the remedy for chaos and confusion (not to mention heterodoxy) in religious education is a return to the *Baltimore Catechism* style of catechesis. Thus it does not recognize that the cultural circumstances in which simplified question-and-answer catechesis could be effective no longer obtain. Nor does it recognize the genuine achievements of mid-twentieth-century kerygmatic theology and the recovery of patristic forms of mystagogical catechesis, both of which give the Church better methods of introducing the young and the mature to friendship with Jesus Christ in the twenty-first century.[7]

Catholic Antiquarianism correctly laments the vulgarization of the Church's worship in many quarters after Vatican II, seeing in this dumbing-down a betrayal of the Council's insight and intention; but Catholic antiquarians seem to think that the remedy for that betrayal is to re-create the Sunday liturgy of the mid-1950s as it imagines that liturgy to have been celebrated in many Catholic parishes. The problem here is that that liturgy is largely a fantasy: anyone who imagines that the twenty-first century's solemn celebration of the Extraordinary Form of the Roman Rite according to the Missal of 1962 is a replication of what happened at 7 A.M., 8 A.M., 9 A.M., 10:30 A.M., and 12:15 P.M. in Catholic parishes across America every Sunday in, say, 1955, is imagining a dream world. More often than not, that liturgy was poorly celebrated, its Latin ill-pronounced, and its music more saccharine than Gregorian.

The same Catholic Antiquarianism can bedevil the twenty-first-century Church's intellectual life, as when one style of Thomism is thought to be the only possible way of doing Catholic theology. It can contribute to twenty-first-century forms of clericalism, when priests frightened by the cross-currents of contemporary culture and the pastoral problems they create retreat into the safeties and sureties of a clerical caste. And it can confuse the quest for an evangelically Catholic aesthetic in architecture, art, and music, imagining that "old" is always "beautiful," when "old" can in fact be ugly.

In pondering the theology, catechetics, liturgy, piety, and art of the Catholic past (including the theology, catechetics, liturgy, piety, and art of Counter-Reformation Catholicism), Evangelical Catholicism takes with great seriousness the Lord's injunction to "Gather up the fragments left over, that nothing may be lost" [John 6.12]. But because Evangelical Catholicism does not imagine that the catechetical-devotional Catholicism of the Counter-Reformation was the final and definitive historical expression of the Christ-bestowed form of the Catholic Church, and because Evangelical Catholicism recognizes the unique challenges to fulfilling the Great Commission posed by the postmodern world, it believes that the Church of the twenty-first century should "gather up the fragments" across the entire panorama of Catholic history, and then judge them according to the two criteria of authentic Catholic reform, truth and mission. Does a given fragment bespeak a core truth of "the faith which was once for all delivered to the saints" [Jude 1.3]? Will this fragment, once fitted into the Cosmatesque mosaic of Evangelical Catholicism, advance the mission of the Church under twenty-first-century circumstances?

IN THE FIRST FOUR DECADES AFTER THE SECOND VATICAN COUNCIL, however, Catholic Presentitis—a lust for "relevance" according to postmodern cultural and intellectual canons—was a far greater impediment to the maturation of Evangelical Catholicism and authentic Catholic reform than was Catholic Antiquarianism. Its originating image—some might say, its original sin—was to imagine Vatican II as the Council that "opened the Church's windows to the modern world" in order to initiate a "dialogue" with secular modernity—a dialogue it imagined secular modernity craved, and which it thought had been impeded by mid-twentieth-century Catholic intellectual intransigence (usually called "Neo-Scholasticism," often without any secure purchase on the actual meaning of that philosophical term of art). There were multiple difficulties here.

In the first instance, Catholic Presentitis misread the Second Vatican Council's evangelical intention. Even in that most optimistic of conciliar documents, the Pastoral Constitution on the Church in the Modern World, the Council's "opening the windows of the Church," was not intended to start a generic conversation about generic human goods. It was a dialogue that, from the Church's point of view, was intended to propose to the world two essential truths: that Jesus Christ reveals the full truth about the human person, and that human beings only come into the fullness of their humanity through a sincere gift of themselves.[8] In 1965, when the Pastoral Constitution was adopted by the Council, as in the first decades of the twenty-first century, these proposals were deeply countercultural. They were reference points for a dialogue with edge, not a dialogue of accommodation.

Catholic Presentitis has also misread the depth of the cultural crisis of the West since the mid-1960s. If the windows to be opened in the Church by Vatican II are imagined to be windows on a train, well, as philosopher Michael Novak once observed, the blinds were raised and the windows opened just as the train entered a dark tunnel full of toxic gases. (Pope Paul VI put it even more sharply, asking aloud in the post-conciliar years how the "smoke of Satan" had entered the Church.) In the revolutionary upheavals that are typically described there as, simply, "1968," Europe celebrated a deliberate cultural rupture with the past; that rupture did not welcome a dialogue with Catholicism, which the children of "1968" imagined to be an integral part of the history and culture they were determined to overthrow.[9] In the last decades of the twentieth century, the nineteenth-century "atheistic humanism" analyzed by the French Jesuit theologian Henri de Lubac became the "Christophobia" analyzed by Jewish constitutional scholar Joseph Weiler: that is, the idea that the God of the Bible was the enemy of human maturation and freedom became the idea that the Catholic Church is the last institutional obstacle to the revolution of debonair nihilism. That was not a Church with which post-1968 secular modernity was much interested in conversing; it was a Church that was to be driven to a privatized, marginalized place on the far outskirts of public life, by coercive state power if necessary.

This cultural crisis was most acute—and was most misread by the proponents of Catholic Presentitis—in the intellectual life. The enthusiasts of dialogue in the immediate aftermath of Vatican II did not imagine a

Western world that would, within a few decades, become nihilist in its overall philosophical position, radically skeptical about the human capacity to know the truth of anything, and thus wholly relativist in its theory of morals. The authors of the Pastoral Constitution on the Church in the Modern World may have imagined that they would be in dialogue with honest agnostics who thought like Albert Camus, or post-Stalinist reform Marxists like Ernst Bloch and Roger Garaudy; they simply could not imagine a world in which a Spaniard, Juan, could walk into a civil registry office and, by signing a form, declare himself to be, now, Juanita (and without any surgical alteration). Yet that is the world in which the Gospel must be proclaimed in the twenty-first century. And it was created in no small part by late-modern and postmodern intellectual life, which Catholic intellectuals, infected by Catholic Presentitis, imagined to be the essential reference point for their own work.[10]

John 6.12—the injunction to gather the fragments so that nothing of value may be lost—applies to those tempted to Catholic Presentitis just as much as it does to those tempted to Catholic Antiquarianism. The maturation of Evangelical Catholicism requires gathering up and incorporating into the Church's proclamation all of the bits and pieces of modernity and postmodernity that can aid the Church's mission: from the art of Georges Rouault and the music of Gabriel Fauré and Maurice Durufle to the researches of historical-critical students of the Bible and learned modern theologians. Indeed, the evolution of Evangelical Catholicism, as noted previously, was accelerated by the mid-twentieth-century Catholic intellectual renaissance that emerged from the Leonine reform of the late nineteenth century and paved the way to the Second Vatican Council. No serious proponent of the deep reform that is Evangelical Catholicism will imagine a twenty-first- or twenty-second-century Church that is not in debt to that renaissance and its key figures: men and women of genius, such as Karl Adam, Romano Guardini, Henri de Lubac, Jacques Maritain, Etienne Gilson, Marie-Joseph Lagrange, Augustin Bea, Edith Stein, Hans Urs von Balthasar, Yves Congar, and Joseph Ratzinger, whose work was foreshadowed in different respects by the greatest of nineteenth-century Catholic thinkers, John Henry Newman. What the Evangelical Catholicism of the future will remember is not just the intellectual accomplishments of these indisputably modern Catholics, however. It will also remember that their quest for a new Catholic self-understanding was informed by a thirst for holiness. For holiness is the essential (and most compelling) expression of the truth the Church bears and of the mission to which the Church is called.

Thus holiness is that quality that draws together the twin criteria of truth and mission in Evangelical Catholicism. Holiness is the frame that measures whether something old, or something new, gathered from the fragments of the ancient past, the recent past, or the present, can be aptly fit into the Cosmatesque mosaic of Evangelical Catholicism in the future.

Holiness is the ultimate antidote to infidelity, fear, and the evangelical paralysis that follows from infidelity and fear. Holiness is what binds together a Church in which centrifugal forces are always at work.

Holiness is what Christ, who instructed his Church to always pick up the fragments, that nothing might be lost, constantly and lavishly gives his friends as he gives himself, the Bread of Life [John 6.35].

Wheat and Weeds, Always

The fear that caused Peter to cry out in panic as he began to sink into the Sea of Galilee was born of a form of infidelity: trusting in himself rather than keeping his gaze fixed on Christ. Peter's infidelity in some respects mirrors the fall in the Garden, where Adam and Eve trusted in their own cleverness rather than obeying the command of God. In any case, the challenge to fidelity is a perennial feature of the Church's life, this side of the Wedding Feast of the Lamb. Guided by the twin criteria of truth and mission, and ordered to holiness of life, the authentic reform of the Church that will yield the maturation of Evangelical Catholicism will address infidelity in its sundry twenty-first century forms. At the same time, however, any authentically Catholic reform, leading to a robust

Evangelical Catholicism rather than to Catholic sectarianism, will attend to another gospel story, which occurs in Matthew just before the Lord comes walking across the water:

> Another parable he put before them saying, "The kingdom of heaven may be compared to a man who sowed good seed in his field; but while men were sleeping, his enemy came and sowed weeds among the wheat, and went away. So when the plants came up and bore grain, then the weeds appeared also. And the servants of the householder came and said to him, "Sir, did you not sow good seed in your field? How then has it weeds?" He said to them, "An enemy has done this." The servants said to him, "Then do you want us to go gather them?" But he said, "No; lest in gathering the weeds you root up the wheat along with them. Let both grow together until the harvest; and at harvest time I will tell the reapers, 'Gather the weeds first and bind them in bundles to be burned, but gather the wheat into my barn.'"[11]

Like the boat in the story of Jesus walking on the Sea of Galilee, the field of this parable is an image of the Church. The Catholic Church has contained wheat and weeds, saints and sinners (saints being sinners who know that they are sinners), for two millennia. The Church was wheat and weeds in the immediate, post-Pentecostal fervor of its first days: then, amid the conversion of thousands, thanks to compelling preaching and miraculous healing, Ananias and Sapphira tried to con Peter and were struck dead [see Acts 5.1–11]. The Church was wheat and weeds in the struggle to wrest the papacy back from the tenth-century Ottonian emperors; when Catherine of Siena besought a weak and vacillating pope to return to Rome from exile in Avignon; when Catholic reformers contested with corrupt churchmen for the soul of Catholicism in the Renaissance; when every English bishop but one bent to the will of Henry VIII and his fraudulent title, "Supreme Governor of the Church in England." The Catholic Church was wheat and weeds when the Church bowed to royal absolutism; when some churchmen dallied, at least briefly, with fascism; when priests betrayed their vocations by cooperating with communist secret police agencies; when postconciliar Catholic intellectuals took their cues from the cultured despisers of religion; when priests abused the young people entrusted to their care, and their bishops accepted the shibboleths of the therapeutic society in responding to such infidelity.

The Catholic Church will be wheat and weeds throughout the maturation of Evangelical Catholicism and beyond. The deep reform of the Church suggested in what follows—in which certain key issues of deep Catholic reform are discussed—is not a matter of preemptively burning out the weeds, although it will involve some radical clarification of what are in fact weeds. Still, if the Church's character is primarily evangelical, meaning ordered to conversion, then that applies inside the Church as well as to the Church's proposal to the world. Evangelical Catholicism is, first and foremost, a call to conversion.

Beyond Fear, Through the Cross

The final perfection of the Church will come at the end of history, when history itself is consummated in the Wedding Feast of the Lamb, in the New Jerusalem, which has no Temple because "its Temple is the Lord God Almighty and the Lamb," who are also the city's light and lamp [Revelation 21.22–23]. Between now and then, and whenever "then" may be, we have the revealed and trustworthy divine assurance that in "the holy city, new Jerusalem," the "dwelling of God is with men. He will dwell with them, and they shall be his people, and God himself will be with them; he will wipe away every tear from their eyes, and death shall be no more, neither shall there be crying nor pain any more, for the former things have passed away" [Revelation 21.2–4].

Between then, when the Lord will "make all things new" [Revelation 21.5], and now, there is the call to courage: "Be not afraid." That call is no psychological trick. For when it comes from the Risen Lord, it is a call that comes on the far side of the Cross. On the Cross, the Son of God who shared our nature took upon himself all the world's sin. And by burning that sin in the fire of obedience to the Father's will, the Son made it possible for all those who grasp the outstretched hand of the Risen Lord to live, not without fear but beyond fear; to live courageously in truth; and to live fearlessly for mission.

The Cross leads to the Wedding Feast of the Lamb. That is why "the sufferings of the present time are not worth comparing to the glory that is to be revealed to us" [Romans 8.18]. That is why our "momentary affliction is preparing us for an eternal weight of glory beyond all comparison" [2 Corinthians 4.17]. That is why twenty-first-century Catholics can cherish the Church, this "treasure in earthen vessels" [2 Corinthians 4.7], even as they strive to bring Evangelical Catholicism to maturity.

The Cross leads to the Wedding Feast of the Lamb.

PART TWO

The Reforms of Evangelical Catholicism

CHAPTER FIVE

The Evangelical Catholic
Reform of the Episcopate

THE FIRST VATICAN COUNCIL (1869–1870) INTENDED TO DISCUSS THE theology of the episcopate and the ministry of bishops in the Church after it had dealt with the question of the papacy and its prerogatives, which led to the Council's teaching on the pope's infallibility when teaching definitively on matters of faith and morals. But the Franco-Prussian War broke out; Vatican I was suspended; and for a variety of reasons it was never reconvened. Thus, for almost a century, between Vatican I and Vatican II, there was something of an imbalance in Catholicism's self-understanding about the order of bishops. There was considerable clarity about the nature and prerogatives of the Bishop of Rome, who, as Peter's successor, was chief among the bishops. But there was less clarity about the Church's other bishops (themselves the successors of the apostles), their relationship to each other, and their relationship to the Bishop of Rome.

The Second Vatican Council was determined to rectify this imbalance. Thus, in its Dogmatic Constitution on the Church and its Decree on the Pastoral Office of Bishops in the Church, the Council clarified several important points that had previously been contested.[1] First, the episcopate is an *order*: it is the highest order within the sacrament of Holy Orders and it confers a unique character upon the men who are ordained bishops, configuring them to Christ the Good Shepherd in a singular way. Second, the world episcopate forms a "college," with and under the Bishop of Rome, who is the head of the college; and this college, as successor to the Twelve upon whom the Holy Spirit descended at Pentecost [see Acts 2.1–5] has, with and under its head, supreme authority in the Church by the will of God. Third, ordination to the episcopate obligates every bishop to three missions—the mission of teaching [*munus docendi*], the mission of sanctifying [*munus sanctificandi*], and the mission of governing [*munus regendi*]; these three missions reflect the Church's understanding of Christ the Lord as prophet, priest, and king. The Council also emphasized that it was the prophetic mission, the ministry of preaching and teaching, that held pride of place in the work of a Catholic bishop (as indeed it had for the apostles whom the bishops succeeded).[2]

An Incomplete Renewal

In the decades after the Council, it was often said that these teachings made clear that the bishops were true vicars of Christ in their own dioceses; they were not branch managers of Catholic Church, Inc., in which real authority remained with world headquarters (i.e., the Bishop of Rome, understood as a kind of global CEO). Like all clichés, this postconciliar cliché was true as far as it went. But its emphasis on the mission of governance, as if the *munus regendi* constituted the irreducible essence of the episcopate, tended to obscure the Council's emphasis on the bishop as prophet: the bishop as preacher, teacher, and guarantor of the truth of Catholic faith for the sake of the Church's mission and the sake of the flock the bishop shepherded. Intersecting with the historical fact that, in the late twentieth and early twenty-first centuries, most diocesan bishops led considerable organizations, this emphasis on the *munus regendi* has led, in many instances, to an imbalance in the way the episcopal office has actually been lived out. Most bishops in the developed world spend most of their time on administrative matters. And although many of these administratively burdened bishops cherish the *munus docendi* and the *munus sanctificandi,* their lives, judged by imaginary time sheets, might bring to mind the complaint of the Church's first bishops, two millennia ago, about having to spend time "to serve tables"—a complaint that did not reflect the early emergence of a clerical caste system but rather the urgency the apostles felt about "preaching the word of God" [Acts 6.2].

The Council also taught that the collegial character of the episcopate should be given organized expression in the formation of national episcopal conferences, of which all the active bishops of a country would be members. It was thought that these conferences would build episcopal fraternity, give bishops an opportunity to discuss their problems and challenges with their peers, and provide for a unified and powerful Catholic voice in a nation's public affairs. The conferences were formed (or transformed from preexisting bodies). It being the late twentieth century, most conferences in the developed world were then rapidly and massively bureaucratized; and like all bureaucracies, the conference staff began to devise various ways to keep those for whom the staff worked—the bishops—in line (a process in which many bishops acquiesced, thinking their staffs more "expert" than themselves in matters ranging from liturgy to catechetics to the application of Catholic social doctrine to public life). Many bishops' conferences also took on the character of men's clubs, which was theoretically no bad thing (bishops needing club-like friendship as much as anyone else), but which in practice virtually eliminated the ability of bishops to criticize one another or to call one another to account for doctrinal errors and failures of governance, even behind closed doors. In an odd variant on George Orwell, episcopal conferences that were intended to give all bishops a voice within a collegial body also began to display the characteristics evident among the denizens of *Animal Farm* shortly after the revolution: which is to say, it quickly became clear that some bishops were more equal than others.[3]

Other difficulties in implementing the evangelical reform of the epis-copate mandated by Vatican II have been caused by the process by which the Church selects bishops—nominees are proposed by the Vatican rep-resentative in a given country and vetted by the Congregation for Bish-ops in Rome for presentation of a slate of three possible appointees (a *terna*) to the pope for his decision. That process tends to privilege po-tential candidates who are primarily known for administrative skills displayed in various diocesan, national, or global Catholic offices, a ten-dency further reinforced by the criteria the Holy See asks its represen-tatives to use in vetting candidates, which stress reliability, managerial acumen, and ability to get along with other clergy rather than other gifts and accomplishments.[4]

Yet another difficulty came into sharp and disturbing focus during the scandal-time of the clergy sex-abuse crisis, which was also a grave crisis of episcopal malfeasance and misgovernance: the Church had no established mechanism for dealing with failed bishops. For two cen-turies, the Holy See had slowly, tenaciously, and skillfully regained the capacity to order the Church's internal life by appointing bishops with-out the interference of governments. Thus as the Catholic Church en-tered the third millennium of its history, the pope had a free right of appointing bishops everywhere except China and Vietnam—a situation far different from that faced by Pius VII during the early nineteenth cen-tury, when the pope had a free right of episcopal appointment in only a small minority of cases. Yet having gained the right to appoint the men it judged best suited for the high demands of the episcopacy, the Church seems to have no method at hand for dealing with those cases (which were not limited to the abuse crisis) in which a mistake had manifestly been made and the local bishop is an impediment to the Church's mission.

Vatican II, the Council that aimed to revitalize the order of bishop and restore its biblical and patristic dignity, achieved at least some of that. Many Catholic bishops of the early twenty-first century are impres-sive men, full of zeal and skill, who generously give their lives to the truths they bear. One can readily imagine these exemplary bishops prepared to give their lives literally, as martyrs, if circumstances demanded the final measure of fidelity to Christ.

The postconciliar decades also witnessed a crisis in the Catholic episcopate, however. The centrality of the *munus docendi* in the bishop's witness has not been seriously implemented in much of the Church. The exercise of the *munus regendi* has come to mean bureaucratic management, rather than pastoral shepherding, in too many instances. And although the reform of the liturgy has given many bishops the chance to get to know those intent on becoming part of the Church—as the local bishop typically meets the adult catechumens of his diocese prior to their Baptism or reception into full communion at the Easter Vigil—the hard fact is that most Catholics in most dioceses have little sense of their bishop as their primary leader in prayer and worship, as they have little direct sense of their bishop as pastoral shepherd.

Moreover, some of the Church's most deeply committed and intelligent lay Catholics cannot understand why the Church seems to have no established and timely method of removing incompetent, malfeasant, or dubiously orthodox bishops—the bishops who fail to live out the task of watchman as described by the prophet Ezekiel [see Ezekiel 3.17–21]; the bishops whom St. Augustine called "wicked shepherds" in his sermon *On Pastors* (which the Church reads annually in the Liturgy of the Hours): in other words, the bishops who are failures and whose failures touch both criteria of authentic Catholic reform, in that they fail to lead by the criterion of truth or otherwise impede the mission of the Church. The people most dedicated to the evangelical renewal of the Catholic Church often look at Catholicism's inability to hold bishops accountable, compare it to the rigorous accountability required of similarly situated leaders with grave responsibilities for the lives of others in other environments, and ask whether the episcopate, rather than being renewed as an order, has become a self-protecting and self-perpetuating caste.

It hasn't. But the fact that such questions are raised—not by professional carpers but by devout Catholics of mature faith—suggests something of the depth of the crisis of the Catholic episcopate. It also suggests the imperative of a deep evangelical reform of the appointment of bishops and the exercise of the office of bishop in the Church—a reform that would benefit from good models.

Happily, such a model is available, and from the very recent past.

A Model for Episcopal Reform

Cardinal John J. O'Connor, the archbishop of New York who died in 2000, liked to tell the story of bantering with John Paul II, Bishop of Rome, after the serious business of one of their meetings had been finished. "You know," O'Connor said, "I'm never going to get anywhere in this Church. I wasn't a bishop's secretary." "Neither was I," said the 263rd successor of St. Peter.

Yet Karol Wojtyła became one of the most consequential popes in two millennia of Catholic history, and no small part of that accomplishment was due to the fact that he had been one of the greatest diocesan bishops of the post–Vatican II Church. The story of his episcopacy in Kraków is worth revisiting as a model for the authentically Catholic and evangelical reform of the Catholic episcopate.

From 1964 until 1978, under exceptionally difficult circumstances, Wojtyła was the archbishop of a city he knew and loved. He was under constant surveillance by the Polish communist secret police, who electronically bugged his living quarters and offices, tried to suborn his associates, and in some instances beat them senseless. Protecting his priests from secret-police harassment was a constant problem (as, occasionally, was getting them out of jail when they were arrested on trumped-up charges). The Church was forbidden to run normal chaplaincy programs in health-care institutions or with the young. Seminarians were pressured and needed steady encouragement to persevere under police scrutiny and social pressure. The archbishop had meager financial resources with which to work, for much of the Church's patrimony had been expropriated by the state.[5]

Yet in circumstances far more challenging than those faced by most Catholic bishops in the Western world, Wojtyła led one of the most extensive diocesan implementations of Vatican II in the world Church: he strengthened an already vibrant local piety while encouraging new currents in Catholic thought and spiritual practice; he became a dynamic public figure in defense of the human rights of all Poles; and he played a considerable role both in world Catholic intellectual circles and in the deliberations of the Vatican. No doubt some of this success reflected the exceptional gifts of mind and soul that had been bestowed on Karol Wojtyła, gifts he had nurtured through a lifetime of spiritual and intellectual discipline. And no doubt the communist authorities made a perfect foil for a man of Wojtyła's Christian convictions and deep knowledge of Polish literature and history: in communist Poland, it was not difficult to make clear who was the authentic custodian of the nation's deeply Catholic memory and culture and who were the usurpers and liars—to see who was the true leader, and who were the charlatans.

Yet even taking account of these special personal and historical circumstances, Karol Wojtyła's fourteen-year episcopate in Kraków (which was preceded by two years of service as administrator of the archdiocese and another four as one of its auxiliary bishops) was an enormous success. Its success was intimately tied to his idea of the office of bishop and his methods of living out what he believed about his episcopal vocation. And it is from that idea and those methods that lessons for the evangelical renewal of the Catholic episcopate in the twenty-first century can be drawn.

As John Paul II joked with Cardinal O'Connor, he hadn't come up the normal clerical career track. He had been a parish priest, a university chaplain, and a professor; his vacations were spent with the young laypeople who called him *Wujek* [Uncle] and who were among his closest friends; he wrote plays and poetry and works of philosophy and theology; he was a demanding preacher and challenging confessor who likely didn't know much about how the archdiocesan bureaucracy operated, having never worked there; he was a skilled outdoorsman and an authentic mystic who spent hours in contemplative prayer. In the summer of 1958, when he was called away from a kayaking trip with lay friends to receive the news of his nomination as auxiliary bishop of

Kraków from the formidable Polish primate, Cardinal Stefan Wyszyński, he tried to decline on the grounds that he was too young, being only thirty-eight. Wyszyński replied that this was a problem that would readily take care of itself, Wojtyła accepted the appointment as an act of obedience—and an epic episcopal vocation was launched.

Wojtyła's idea of being a bishop was certainly shaped by the debates at the Second Vatican Council, in which he was a significant participant. But even before the Council convened in October 1962, Wojtyła had already defined his episcopal vocation by giving absolute priority to the missions of teaching and sanctifying, while attending to the tasks of governance as required. This pattern continued when he was named archbishop of Kraków in December 1963 and enthroned in the *cathedra* of St. Stanisław on March 8, 1964.

Karol Wojtyła's evangelical approach to leading a complex and (in his case, persecuted) local church comes into clear focus when one learns that, in facing any new problem, challenge, or opportunity as archbishop, he asked two questions: "What is the truth of faith that sheds light on this (problem, challenge, or opportunity)?" and "Who can we get—or train—to help?"

The first question (which John Paul II did not hesitate to apply on a global scale as pope) was an expression of Wojtyła's secure conviction that the truths of the faith, as borne by the Church in Scripture and apostolic tradition, set the standard by which all decisions ought to be made, all programs planned, and all newly proposed projects accepted or declined. In solving problems or undertaking pastoral initiatives, Wojtyła did not, in other words, look first to books of management theory or to the archdiocesan balance sheet: he looked to the Gospel.

The second question reflected Wojtyła's generous nature, his eagerness to bring out the best in others, and his willingness to take risks on people. But it also reflected a Gospel conviction that the disciples are all "in the boat" together, as on the Sea of Galilee, and that the captain of this particular boat in the Catholic flotilla ought to look widely around the crew and passenger lists to find help in meeting his own responsibilities as teacher, sanctifier, and governor.

This distinctively episcopal approach to leadership and decision making was complemented by Karol Wojtyła's intense life of prayer. As archbishop, he spent the first two hours of every day in his residence chapel before the Blessed Sacrament, praying, thinking, and writing. In that sense, Wojtyła governed the archdiocese of Kraków not from his desk, but from his knees: he led the 1.5 million Catholics who were his people out of his ongoing conversation with the Lord Jesus.

When he wasn't praying, thinking, and writing his way into the future in his chapel, Wojtyła spent considerable time in conversation with others: with his priests; with lay friends; with academics and artists and Catholic journalists; with political activists across the spectrum of opinion in the anticommunist opposition (including agnostics and atheists). Thus his information about the situation he faced as a bishop and as a de facto opposition leader to the communist regime was drawn from a remarkable breadth of sources, not from an ecclesiastical (and clerical) bureaucracy.

He spent even more time, however, in parishes, living with his people as well as visiting them. A pastoral visit to a parish by Cardinal Karol Wojtyła, archbishop of Kraków, was a multiday affair. In Wojtyła's view, a parish was not an accidental congeries of Catholics who happened to live in the same neighborhood or village; a parish was a way of living out what Vatican II's Dogmatic Constitution on the Church had described as the universal call to holiness in a specific, local, and distinctive human situation.[6] Thus Wojtyła came to the parishes of his archdiocese as shepherd, as high priest, and as teacher: he visited the sick in their homes; he conferred the sacrament of Confirmation; he celebrated special Masses for married couples, giving each couple a personal blessing; he visited the parish cemetery, if there was one, and prayed the rosary there with the parishioners while blessing any new graves. He of course met with the parish priests, with whom he stayed on these visitations; he also met with lay leaders, leaders of renewal movements and charitable activities, the young, and the local nuns. It all had the atmosphere of a parish retreat or mission led by the local bishop: a time of renewal in which serious conversations about serious matters could unfold during special days of grace.

Karol Wojtyła did not define himself as archbishop of Kraków or live out his sense of episcopal vocation as a bureaucratic manager; for him, parish visitations, not administration, were a unique expression of the bishop's vocation. He needed assistants; so he appointed men in whom he reposed trust to run the various offices of the archdiocese, and let them get on with their business. Meanwhile, he invested a lot of his time in a remarkable ministry of "presence" to his people—and did so out of deep Catholic conviction. For as he told the retreat he preached before the Roman Curia and Pope Paul VI in Lent 1976, a parish visitation was a moment to unveil, in a variety of circumstances and locales, the seal of Christian dignity that Christ had bestowed on all the people of his archdiocese at Baptism.[7]

Various lessons for the evangelical reform of the Catholic episcopate can be drawn from this model. Perhaps the most important is that, under very challenging circumstances, and notwithstanding the bishop's unavoidable administrative responsibilities, it is quite possible to live the episcopal missions of teaching, preaching, and sanctifying in the post–Vatican II Church. Doing so is a matter of conviction, deputation, priority-setting, and, above all, prayer.

Making Bishops

It would be a serious mistake, bordering on heresy, to think that God is any less generous in the gifts of grace bestowed on the Church of the twenty-first century than was the case when the Church was blessed with such great bishops as Ambrose and Augustine, Athanasius and John Chrysostom, Charles Borromeo and John Fisher, Francis de Sales and Alphonsus Liguori, Ildefonso Schuster and Clemens von Galen, Stefan Wyszyński, Andrey Sheptytsky, and Karol Wojtyła. The question is how to identify such men—men of competence and energy whose deep Catholic faith is wedded to courage and lived in holiness. This theological conviction, drawn from the truth of Catholic faith that teaches the Church about the abiding presence of the Holy Spirit in its life, suggests that *the* key to the evangelical reform of the Catholic episcopate in the twenty-first century involves a change in the criteria by which candidates for bishop are identified.

Some would doubtless argue that the entire bishop-making process as it operates in the first decades of the twenty-first century should be revamped. But as this is most unlikely to happen, the focus of evangelical reform in the appointment of bishops should be on the criteria that nuncios and apostolic delegates are instructed to use in formulating the nominations they send to the Vatican's Congregation for Bishops, which ought to be the same criteria that the Congregation and its prefect use in formulating nomination lists for the pope.

The criteria appropriate for finding bishops for the Evangelical Catholicism of the twenty-first century must reflect the realities of the challenging circumstances twenty-first-century bishops in the developed world will face. Twenty-first-century Western culture is bedeviled by fears among the faithful of being thought "intolerant" or "insensitive"—charges readily laid by the mass media and others against anyone asserting certain moral truths, no matter how winsome or logically compelling the assertion. Twenty-first-century societies are also saturated with bureaucracy, from the local Girl Scout troop to the Pentagon and the Ford Foundation. Put those fears of appearing "intolerant" or "insensitive" together with the bureaucratic mind-set endemic to postmodern society, and bishops can begin to imagine themselves as mitered referees, discussion-group facilitators whose primary task is to keep the "dialogue" going while keeping everyone reasonably content (and the diocese solvent financially).

That is not a model of the Catholic episcopate that would have made sense to the great bishops mentioned a moment ago. Nor does it embody for the twenty-first century the Second Vatican Council's recovery of the prophetic and sanctifying missions of the local bishop. No one is going to be converted to friendship with the Lord Jesus and enflamed with a passion for mission by a discussion-group moderator: not priests, not lay adults, not the young.

New criteria

If the object of the process of making bishops is to find men who can be twenty-first-century apostles, leading the Catholic Church out of the shallows of institutional maintenance and into mission amid the cultural whitewater of postmodernity, then criteria for the reformed selection of bishops must reflect the characteristics of deep Catholic reform that is Evangelical Catholicism. Thus, in addition to the obvious questions about background, education, habits of life, and character that can be found in the current questionnaire used to assess a possible candidate for the episcopate, the following questions should be addressed—and should be determinative:

1. In his manner of life and his priestly ministry, does this man manifest a deep personal conversion to friendship with Jesus Christ? Has he made a deliberate, conscious, and irrevocable choice to follow Christ? Has he responded to Jesus's question to the disciples, who were shocked by his command to eat of him, the Bread of Life—"Do you also wish to go away?"— with Peter's answer: "Lord, to whom shall we go? You have the words of eternal life, and we have believed, and have come to know, that you are the Holy One of God" [John 6.67–69]?

2. Does this priest take preaching and teaching as among his primary responsibilities? Does he preach clearly, biblically, and with conviction? Can he make the Church's evangelical proposal to unbelievers? Can he, with charity and under-standing, teach, and if necessary correct, Catholics who have embraced notions contrary to Scripture and apostolic tradi-tion? How many converts has this man made? How many Christians of other communities has he brought into full communion with the Catholic Church? How many baptized pagans has he brought back into a fuller communion with the Church?

3. If this priest has been primarily engaged in parish work, have his parishes grown through his ministry? If his principal

work has been in a seminary, college, or university, have his students flourished under his guidance, spiritually as well as intellectually?

4. How does this priest celebrate Holy Mass, in specific and concrete terms? Does his liturgical ministry lead those in his pastoral charge into a deep experience of the Paschal Mystery of the Lord's death, resurrection, and ascension? Does his manner of leading the Church in liturgical prayer honor the baptismal dignity of his congregants? Is he regularly found with his people in Eucharistic adoration?

5. How many men have entered the seminary under this priest's guidance? How many women have entered consecrated religious life through his influence? Does he foster holy marriages and stable Catholic families that are themselves "little churches"? Does he encourage lay movements of Catholic renewal? Does he guide popular piety well? Does he promote frequent reception of the sacrament of Penance, and does he devote significant time to his ministry as a confessor? Does he encourage his people to read the Bible daily? Is he, in other words, a man who can facilitate the universal call to holiness because he is a man of holiness himself?

6. Does this man have the strength of conviction and character to make decisions that, though faithful to the Church's teaching and practice, may be unpopular with other clergy and with lay Catholics?

7. Does this priest regard the study of Scripture and theology as an essential part of his vocation? Is he able to convey the best of the Church's theological traditions, across the centuries, to those without specialist training in theology?

8. Has this man reached a level of spiritual maturity in which his competence as a pastor and his security as a man and a Christian disciple express themselves humbly? Does he see his ministry as one of empowering in others the gifts the Holy

Spirit has bestowed on those in his pastoral charge? Does he treat those who help him implement his pastoral ministry as collaborators in the work of the Gospel, or as indentured servants? Does he foster talent, not being threatened by it?

Broadening the consultation

In identifying possible nominees according to these criteria, the nuncio or apostolic delegate to a given country should be instructed by the pope and the Congregation for Bishops to consult more widely than is typically the case. The episcopate is not a club in which the current club members have a privileged say in the future membership; nor is it a caste in which those who have achieved higher caste status determine who is fit for similar elevation. The office of bishop is an *order* that is ordered to the leadership of all the people of the Church in their common evangelical task. Thus nuncios and apostolic delegates should be instructed to consult widely: among bishops, to be sure, but also among priests, religious, and laity, both in seeking candidates for the episcopate and in assessing possible candidates according to the criteria noted above.

The absence of any serious lay input in this process is a mistake. Laypeople who are committed Catholics often see things that clergy miss, and can identify real leaders whom clergy or bishops miss. Some will object that broadening the consultation in this way risks the confidentiality that is essential to the process. But if the Church has survived the indiscretions of the clerical grapevine (which in the Internet age have now become universally available), those who are charged with finding bishops according to this model ought not fret unduly about the capacity of knowledgeable, faithful, and mature Catholic men and women to respect confidences.

The question of age

The evangelical reform of the Catholic episcopate would also be accelerated by considering younger men for the office of bishop than is often the case in the twenty-first century. It is true that prudence requires the Church to observe a man's capacity for pastoral leadership over a substantial period of time. It is also true, however, that the priests most likely to be displaying the kind of pastoral leadership that embodies Evangelical Catholicism in the first decades of the twenty-first century are the priests of the John Paul II Generation of clergy. The deep reform of the Church that is Evangelical Catholicism coming to maturity in the early twenty-first century will thus be more likely to be led by men who are chosen bishops when they are in their forties and early fifties; artificial and arbitrary decisions by nuncios to consider only men older than fifty should be reversed.[8]

History is also a good teacher here. True, men live longer in the twenty-first century and mature later than in previous eras. But is there nothing to be learned from the fact that St. Ambrose was thirty-four when he was chosen bishop of Milan, or that St. Augustine was forty-one when he became bishop of Hippo? Two great reforming bishops of the Counter-Reformation were ordained to the episcopate in their mid-thirties: St. Charles Borromeo and St. Francis de Sales. Stefan Wyszyński became primate of Poland and the de facto opposition leader of a country under communist occupation when he was forty-seven; Karol Wojtyła, as noted previously, was ordained a bishop at thirty-eight and became archbishop of Kraków before his forty-fourth birthday. Are men of that caliber, and that age, unavailable today? It seems unlikely.

Previous experience

There is no one set of experiences that best prepares a man for the demands of the episcopate. Effective parish leadership is often a good indicator of a possible bishop, but experience has shown that a priest who has been a marvelous pastor in a large parish can be an indecisive bishop. Effective parish leadership is an important indicator according to the criteria above, and ought to be given greater emphasis in developing lists of candidates for bishop than is now the case. But it is not an infallible indicator, which is another reason why the consultation process ought to be broadened to include those who might be able to sense that a man, while a fine pastor, is ill equipped for a larger responsibility.

Effective leadership of a seminary has in some cases proven to be a good indicator of a potential bishop, but if Evangelical Catholicism is to get the bishops it needs to accelerate deep Catholic reform, this general category of possible candidates should be broadened to include priest-academics working in other venues. There are twenty-first-century theologians, philosophers, and historians working in Catholic institutions of higher learning who have proven themselves able teachers, good liturgists, compelling preachers, and helpful counselors; their advanced degrees and scholarly careers ought not be impediments to the possibility of their being chosen bishops.

Campus ministry, especially on secular campuses, is often at the cutting-edge of evangelical Catholic renewal. Priests who are proven campus ministers—men working where the intellectual life and a distinctive form of parish life intersect—are rarely considered for the office of bishop; they should be.

Then there is the question of previous experience in church administration. The evangelical Catholic reform of the Church will draw on the talents of some priests who, having spent the bulk of their ministerial lives at chancery desks, can also make good bishops. At the same time, those charged with finding and approving candidates for the episcopate of the twenty-first century must recognize (a century after Max Weber!) that the classic bureaucratic cast of mind—in which efficient management and rapid damage-control are prized, and amelioration and accommodation are typically preferred to confrontation—can be, and often is, in deep tension with a Catholic bishop's triple mission to teach, sanctify, and govern. That, at least, ought to have been learned from the first decade of the twenty-first century, when bureaucratically driven episcopal misgovernance turned clerical scandal into genuine ecclesial crisis time after time.

The Roman process

The evangelical reform of the process of appointing bishops will also involve accelerating the evangelical reform of the Congregation for

Bishops in the Roman Curia, a process that began under the pontificate of John Paul II. The appointment of the prefect of the Congregation for Bishops in Rome is one of the two or three most important choices a pope makes: future popes would be well advised to seek prefects who have extensive experience as diocesan bishops in circumstances that reflect the primary challenges facing the proclamation of the Gospel in postmodernity. Moreover, the cardinal-members of the Congregation for Bishops (who work with the prefect in formulating the *terna* of candidates for each position that the prefect brings to the pope) and the congregation's staff must be carefully chosen; priests and bishops who have demonstrated a commitment to Evangelical Catholicism and an ability to bring it to life in a parish, a seminary, or a diocese are the kind of men needed.

Bishops' Conferences

National conferences of bishops are a permanent feature of post–Vatican II Catholic life. As they have evolved since the Council, however, these conferences have typically had more to do with institutional maintenance than with evangelism. Thus the new question for the deep reform of the Church is how national episcopal conferences can be fitted into Evangelical Catholicism and its commitment to mission as the *raison d'être* of the Church.

Circumstances differ from country to country. As a general rule, however, national bishops' conferences will advance the deep reform of the Church that is Evangelical Catholicism when they are genuine instruments of affective collegiality—supportive and, if necessary, corrective fraternity—among their member-bishops. Conversely, national bishops' conferences will impede the deep reform of the Church if they remain, or become, staff-driven or staff-dominated bureaucracies that are largely cut off from the Church's primary mission of evangelization, and that substitute themselves for the rich diversity of associational life in the Catholic Church.[9] National conferences of bishops ought to support that associational life, not stifle it.

Perhaps most crucially, the deep reform of the Church that is Evangelical Catholicism requires that bishops' conferences become forums in which the bishops, in private, can engage in a classic, but largely forgotten, aspect of episcopal collegiality: fraternal challenge and correction. Fraternal correction is a mandate of the Lord Jesus: "If your brother sins against you, go and tell him his fault, between you and him alone. If he listens to you, you have gained your brother" [Matthew 18.15]. Viewed through this biblical lens, fraternal correction is an ecclesial exercise of supernatural charity: if one sees a brother or sister in Christ in trouble, one has an obligation to seek to bring that brother or sister back into the truth, and thus back into the Church's mission.

Christian spouses do this all the time. Catholic bishops do not have wives, however. A priest cannot easily challenge his bishop, given the paternal dimension of a bishop's relationship with his priests. Who, then, is to tell a bishop that he is wrong on a point of doctrine or its application, or that he is making a mess of this or that situation, or that he has appointed an untrustworthy person of dubious orthodoxy to a key diocesan position, or that he is celebrating the liturgy in an unbecoming manner, or that he is, in some other fashion, impeding the Church's overall mission, unless it be a brother bishop or bishops? This kind of fraternal challenge and correction took place among the great men of the early Church: as Paul explained to the Galatians, he once rebuked Peter "to his face," charging that he was "not straightforward about the truth of the Gospel" and saying, "If you, though a Jew, live like a Gentile and not like a Jew, how can you compel Gentiles to live like Jews?" [Galatians 2.11, 14]. Fraternal challenge and correction was a staple feature of the interaction of bishops in the patristic era, generally regarded as one of the moments in Catholic history when the episcopal bench was replete with figures of consequence. Yet fraternal correction among bishops is virtually unknown today. And unless bishops are willing to challenge and, if necessary, reprove their brother bishops, examples of episcopal failure will continue to fester.

The recovery of the habit of fraternal challenge and correction in the episcopate is not a matter for national bishops' conferences only, however. Bishops within a province ought to exercise this service of charity when required, as should metropolitan archbishops with the suffragan bishops of their province. Given all the other difficulties that bishops know their fellow bishops face, the temptation to be understanding and accommodating, and not to ruffle feathers within the fraternity, can be powerful indeed—and not simply as a matter of weakness, but as a judgment of prudence (however mistaken). In the storm-tossed waters of postmodernity, though, getting along and not rocking the boat is a sure prescription for the boat capsizing, with damage to all hands.

Fidelity to Vatican II?

The Second Vatican Council's teaching on the renewal of the Catholic episcopate was not only a matter of resolving certain disputed questions on the nature of episcopal ordination, episcopal collegiality, and the relationship of ordination to the exercise of episcopal jurisdiction. The Council aimed to resolve these questions in order to foster the deep reform of the episcopate as a sacramental "order" that is, by the will of Christ, "ordered" to the tasks of preaching and teaching, sanctifying, and governing. Certain postconciliar practices, however, seem inconsistent with this intention, and thus incompatible with Evangelical Catholicism.

One such practice involves granting ordination to the episcopate as a reward for services rendered. Perhaps the most striking case of this was the 1998 appointment as a bishop of Piero Marini, the papal master of ceremonies from 1987 to 2007. Marini's tenure of that position was controversial; even those who applauded his masterful redesign of the ritual for a papal wake and funeral, which helped to make the wake and funeral of John Paul II a global catechetical exercise of unprecedented reach and impact, were unhappy with some of his innovations in papal liturgies (of which the use of something resembling smudge pots at the 2003 beatification Mass for Mother Teresa of Calcutta was perhaps the *ne plus ultra*). Putting aside questions of liturgical propriety and taste, however, the basic question remained: Was it congruent with Vatican II's teaching on the nature of the episcopacy for a papal master of ceremonies—who, if the image be permitted, is an exceptionally skilled and glorified altar boy—to function in that role as a bishop? Throughout the last seven years of John Paul II's pontificate and the first two years of Benedict XVI's, there was something jarring about Marini's presence at papal liturgies, moving this and that and guiding the flow of the ceremony while vested in a bishop's robes with pectoral cross and ring. Was this what Vatican II had in mind in its reform of the episcopate?

Questions might also be raised about the proliferation of bishops who are not ordinaries of dioceses, but who are auxiliary bishops within dioceses or administrators of various offices. The notion of an auxiliary bishop as a man "in training" for the duties of a diocesan bishop would seem to be in some tension with the Council's reform of the Church's understanding of what episcopal ordination is and does. Similar questions could be asked about what, in the early twenty-first century, is the seemingly settled practice of naming the deputy heads of many departments of the Roman Curia as bishops (indeed archbishops), although the matter is somewhat more complicated by the fact that these men, like papal nuncios (who are also archbishops) must deal with bishops in the exercise of their duties, and the assumption seems to be that "rank" is necessary for those interactions. But again, does this reflect the mind of the Council about the nature of episcopacy in the Catholic Church?

Then there is the question of the transfer of bishops: the bishop of X becoming, in due course, the bishop or archbishop of Y. There ought to be no hard and fast rules here; it may well be that the requirements for (arch)bishop of Y are best met, in some instances, by a man who is already bishop or archbishop of X. But if the bishop's relationship to his diocese is analogous to the "profound . . . mystery" of Christ's spousal relationship to the Church [Ephesians 5.32], then what does a bishop's transfer to another diocese say about that spousal bond? (One nuncio dealt with such an objection by saying, "Please: same woman, different address," which is clever, but not quite right.) Further, the "career path" by which a man becomes, first, an auxiliary bishop, then a diocesan ordinary, then an archbishop somewhere else reinforces every untoward image of the Catholic episcopate as a group of bureaucratic branch managers who can be readily moved around the corporation as the global chief executive officer directs. It also reinforces the tendency, in selecting bishops, to ignore the possibility of appointing to a major see a skilled priest-pastor or priest-scholar who is not already a bishop.

Here, too, there is a tension between existing practice (however prudent in certain cases) and the theology of the reformed episcopate taught by Vatican II.

Confronting Failure

The bishop is the chief custodian of the truth of Catholic faith in his diocese. As Pope St. Gregory the Great put it in a sixth-century homily, those whom the Lord calls to the office of bishop are like the prophet Ezekiel, to whom God said, "Son of man, I have made you a watchman for the house of Israel" [Ezekiel 3.17]. A "watchman," Gregory continued, "always stands on a height so that he can see from afar what is coming. Anyone appointed to be a watchman for the people must stand on a height for all his life to help them by his foresight."[10] The "height" on which bishops stand is the truth of the Gospel as conveyed by Scripture and apostolic tradition, which a man solemnly affirms before his ordination to the episcopate. If a bishop does not stand on that height, if he imagines that "faithful dissent" is a problem to be managed rather than a breach in the communion of the Church that must be challenged and corrected in charity, he cannot be a watchman for the New Israel, the Church. And he must be replaced.

The bishops are "servants of Christ and stewards of the mysteries of God" who must be "found trustworthy" of their charge [1 Corinthians 4.1–2]. A steward of "the mysteries," the sacraments, is bound by his episcopal oath of fidelity to see that the celebration of the mysteries takes place in his diocese according to Catholic truth. That truth teaches us that "whoever . . . eats the bread or drinks the cup of the Lord in an unworthy manner will be guilty of profaning the body and blood of the Lord," and that whoever does so "eats and drinks judgment upon himself" [1 Corinthians 11.27, 29]. Bishops who do not attend to the fundamental duty to protect the integrity of the sacraments in their diocese ought to be replaced.[11]

The bishop is the chief shepherd of his people, on the model of the Good Shepherd of the Gospel, who stands guard against the one "who does not enter the sheepfold by the door but climbs in by another way [and] is a thief and a robber" [John 10.1]. If the bishop fails in this responsibility to protect the sheep from the thieves and robbers of his time, as so many Irish bishops failed to do in matters of clergy sexual abuse, then other leadership for that diocese must be found.

In recent decades, the Catholic Church has moved with something approaching alacrity to replace bishops who have caused a financial shambles in their dioceses. But what of doctrinal shambles? What of disciplinary shambles? In most instances, the approach taken has been to allow a man to retire gracefully, and then to try and repair the damage by appointing a strong successor. Even in extreme cases of doctrinal and disciplinary disarray, it can take years to effect a change of governance in the diocese. In the Diocese of Toowoomba in Australia, for example, it took more than a decade, and the action finally taken by the Holy See was resisted to the bitter end by some members of the Australian episcopate.[12]

This inability to deal in a just, decisive, and timely manner with failed bishops is a major problem impeding the deep reform of the Catholic Church that is the maturation of Evangelical Catholicism. Some have drawn the analogy between this situation and that of the U.S. military after Vietnam, which was in crisis because senior management (i.e., officers wearing stars) had failed both the service and the country; thus the U.S. military after Vietnam was a disciplinary wreck; standards of behavior had dropped precipitously; and mission effectiveness was severely compromised. The crisis was resolved, and the situation reversed, by junior officers, first blooded during the Vietnam period, who were determined not to lead men futilely into harm's way, who were committed to the honor of their profession and were willing to stake their careers on deep reform. After two decades of intense and often wrenching challenge and correction, the reformers won the day, and the result was one of the best-functioning institutions in twenty-first-century American society.[13]

The reformers' victory in the battle over the future of the American armed forces depended on a development of doctrine and a willingness to replace superiors who were incapable of leading according to that developed doctrine. The analogy to the situation of the Catholic Church in the twenty-first century is not perfect, but analogies never are. The analogy is, however, suggestive.

The deep reform of the Catholic Church that is Evangelical Catholicism is built on a development of doctrine, a development of Catholic self-understanding, that began with Leo XIII. In the middle decades of the twenty-first century, that deep reform will be carried forward, in the main, by those bishops, priests, consecrated religious, and lay Catholics who have received the vision of Evangelical Catholicism, have made it their own, and are living it out both in the Church and in the world. Their efforts ought not be impeded by failed bishops—the equivalent of those senior officers who were fighting World War II in Vietnam.

Developing means of dealing decisively and justly with failed bishops is not an easy business. The question is how such means can be developed without further damaging the Church's integrity and evangelical mission. Yet the effort must be made, both to complete the deep reform of the Church and to remain consistent with the Church's just claim to be the final arbiter of its own internal life. As noted previously, the Church of the nineteenth and twentieth centuries sought to regain control over its capacity to choose its bishops according to its own criteria—and it largely succeeded. Having successfully claimed the right to do so, the Church of the twenty-first century must own the responsibility to deal with episcopal failures. It must do so for the sake of its own integrity. And it must do so to forestall new forms of state interference with the Church's life (often threatened in the wake of the abuse scandals) that would impede the Church's evangelical freedom of action. At the same time, having disentangled itself from the embrace of state power in the choosing of its bishops, the Church cannot mortgage that hard-won authority to popular-opinion plebiscites shaped emotionally by the passions of the 24/7 news cycle and the blogosphere.

Advancing the evangelical mission of the Church and safeguarding the *libertas ecclesiae*, the freedom of the Church, are the reasons why criteria and processes must be developed for determining, in a timely and just fashion, when a local bishop has lost, existentially, the capacity to govern his diocese—when he can no longer function as the good shepherd he was ordained to be. The Church ought to replace malfeasant, incompetent, or unorthodox bishops for its own evangelical reasons.

The Congregation for Bishops has an immense task on its hands in attempting to identify the men who could become the bishops the Church needs in order to further the deep reform of the Catholic Church. If the maturation of Evangelical Catholicism is to be accelerated in the twenty-first century, however, the Congregation, drawing on the full range of expertise across the world Church, must also devise the standards and methods by which episcopal failure is recognized and addressed.

In the same way, it should be made easier for bishops who are manifestly exhausted by their efforts to lay down their responsibilities so that more vigorous leadership can be given to a local Catholic community. Serious damage is often done to a diocese when the bishop is allowed to "see it out" after it has become clear, both to his clergy and to the diocese's lay leadership, that he is incapable of further leadership, whether for reasons of age or illness or both. There is no dishonor in a man becoming an emeritus bishop, and thereafter leading a life of prayer and charity, before he turns seventy-five and is canonically required to submit his resignation to the pope. Were that to be clear to all concerned, dioceses would not be left adrift, as they sometimes are now, in the last years of a man's active episcopacy.

A Question of Sacramentality

According to the Church's settled conviction, Catholicism is episcopally constituted or structured by the will of Christ himself. Episcopacy in the

Church, in other words, is not a historical accident, a reflection of certain patterns of social organization in the Mediterranean world of the first and second centuries A.D. In fact, the truth of the Catholic conviction about bishops as central to the divinely mandated framework of the Church's essential structure is confirmed by the fact that there was nothing like the Christian "bishop" in the religious life of the classical world—that is, a single man who combined the offices of teacher, sanctifier, and governor.[14]

Throughout history, the Catholic Church has been blessed with great bishops. Many of those great bishops were martyrs, including men of the twentieth and twenty-first centuries, such as the martyr-bishops of Ukraine and the other bishops who gave their lives in fidelity to their vocation under communist persecution. And although it is also true that the Church has known episcopal apostates and scoundrels, their infidelities do not alter the fact that the office of bishop and its unique place in the Church's mission are of the will of Christ for the Church, his Body.

If the reforms of Vatican II, as expressions of the pattern of Catholic reform that began with Leo XIII, are to be realized in a deep reform of the Catholic episcopate in which the bishops embrace Evangelical Catholicism and lead the Church in putting out "into the deep" of twenty-first-century evangelization, then perhaps the basic issue is that of the bishop's sacramental identity. The episcopate is an office, but before it is an office it is an *order*: the highest expression of the sacrament of Holy Orders, the unique configuration of a man to Christ, the Good Shepherd and Spouse of the Church.

When the full and immense meaning of that identity is understood, both by those choosing bishops and those chosen as bishops, the reform of the episcopate will be secure, and the bishops will be the leaders of Evangelical Catholicism they are called to be.

CHAPTER SIX

The Evangelical Catholic
Reform of the Priesthood

T HERE ARE HUNDREDS OF THOUSANDS OF FAITHFUL CATHOLIC PRIESTS
throughout the world Church. Those among them who have taken
Blessed John Paul II as their role model live their priesthood as an evangelical adventure; inviting men and women into deep and personal
friendship with Jesus Christ, through Word and Sacrament, defines their
ministry—which they further understand to be an extension of the
priestly ministry of the Lord himself. As the evangelical Catholic reform
of the priesthood unfolds in the twenty-first century, it is these priests
who will be the role models for those entering seminaries and houses of
priestly formation.

Yet while that seed of priestly reform has been germinating throughout the Church, it is also true that the past half-century has been a very
difficult one for the priesthood—and for priests. More men left the active
ministry in the years immediately following the Second Vatican Council
than at any comparable period since the Reformation. And no sooner
had that hemorrhage been stanched than, throughout much of the Western world, revelations of the sexual abuse of the young by Catholic priests
began to fill the headlines. In some instances, notably Ireland and Canada,

these crimes and sins were institutionalized, in that religious congregations and dioceses covered up abuse, suborned false and exculpatory testimony from victims, and provided shelter to perpetrators. These patterns of corruption called to mind the dominical condemnation of those who corrupt the Master's lambs: "Whoever causes one of these little ones who believe in me to sin, it would be better for him to have a great millstone fastened around his neck and to be drowned in the depth of the sea" [Matthew 18.6].

There were other factors at work in the abuse crisis, of course. In some instances, men who should never have been ordained in the first place slipped through a seminary system that had, from the late 1960s through the late 1980s, looked more to psychology and psychiatry than to moral theology and sacramental theology in dealing with aberrant personalities and grave sins. This overconfidence in the ability of the therapeutic arts was often replicated by bishops facing abuse cases. In all cases, however, the fundamental reality of the sexually abusive Catholic priest remained: abusers were and are men who have betrayed the truth of their priestly vocation.

Infidelity and sin are at the root of sexual abuse by priests. Fidelity and deeper conversion to Christ the High Priest, who offers his own life in sacrifice for the flock, are thus the essential characteristics of any genuine reform of the Catholic priesthood—not "reforms" that would repattern the Catholic priesthood on the ministry of Protestant communities.[1]

The story of clerical sexual abuse is not, however, the whole story of the Catholic priesthood, media distortions and exaggerations notwithstanding. Evangelical Catholicism recognizes that the fidelity of the overwhelming majority of Catholic priests is itself a resource for future reform. In the first decades of the twenty-first century, many, perhaps most, Catholic priests in the developed world still live a Counter-Reformation model of Church and a Counter-Reformation model of priestly ministry in which the priesthood is a kind of religious trade union. They believe, with real conviction, in the truths of the Creed in which they lead their people in prayer on Sunday, but their lives are more consumed with management than with evangelism; they talk more easily of "the Church" than they do of "the Lord Jesus"; and for all their devotion—and it is genuine devotion—the career aspects of their lives fill the horizon of their imaginations (and dominate their conversations, especially among themselves) rather more than the vocational aspects of their ministry.

Still, the fidelity of these priests is, to repeat, a resource for authentic, evangelical Catholic reform. There are things these priests have learned—about patience; about ministering to parishes full of the incompletely converted; about the importance of routine and steadiness, as well as adventure and boldness, in the spiritual life—from which priests who are already living an evangelical Catholic model of priesthood can benefit. Thus there should be no disdain for—indeed, there should be appreciation for—those priests who will likely live out their lives within a Counter-Reformation model of the priesthood and the clerical life. But neither should there be any doubt that that model is dying—just as there should be no doubt that, in too many instances, the corruptions of that model had a lot to do with the Church's seeming inability to come to grips with sexual abuse by priests. Reform is essential, for the late Counter-Reformation model is inadequate to the tasks of the New Evangelization, which cannot be advanced by the concept of the Catholic priest as man-licensed-to-perform-certain-types-of-ecclesiastical-business.

According to the *Catechism of the Catholic Church*, the priest is not a religious functionary, but a man who has been ordained to a unique, priestly share in the eternal priesthood of Jesus Christ, the one true Mediator who shows us the face of the Father and the truth about our own humanity.[2] If that truth is to be lived out by the Church's priests in the Evangelical Catholicism of the twenty-first century, however, further reform of priestly formation, priestly self-understanding, and priestly life is essential.

Radical Discipleship

The settled conviction of the Catholic Church is that the Catholic priest, an earthen vessel to whom a great supernatural mystery has been entrusted, is an *alter Christus* [another Christ]. Ordination to the priest-hood changes a man not simply in what he can *do*, but in what he *is*. In-deed, what Catholic priests *do* is wholly dependent on what Catholic priests *are*. The Catholic priest brings Christ to the world, and brings the men and women of the world into friendship with the Lord Jesus, in a unique way: through his celebration of the sacraments; through his preaching and teaching; and through his exercise of pastoral charity and pastoral leadership. And Catholic priests can do those uniquely priestly things because ordination configures a man to Christ in a unique way. The fundamental reality of the priesthood, therefore, is sacramental, not clerical.

Parenthetically, this truth of Catholic faith helps to explain one root of the crime of abuse; it also sheds light on the problems of clericalism, in which ordination to the priesthood is understood as admission to a caste, and what ought to be a ministry of supernatural charity and service is lived as a ministry of domination. If a priest does *not* believe that his priesthood makes present in the world the eternal, mediating, and salvific priesthood of Jesus Christ, then, under certain cultural or institutional circumstances (or both), his desires may overwhelm his good intentions. And a life once intended to be a gift of self to Christ and the Church can become perverted into one in which the office and ministry of the priest becomes a tool of seduction or control.

Thus the fundamental requisite for a Catholic priest is that he be a radically converted disciple of the Lord Jesus Christ. Over the course of his life, his conversion must deepen; that is obvious. But what was not obvious in Counter-Reformation Catholicism is that a man must be thoroughly converted to Christ, must be living a life of friendship with the Lord Jesus, and must have shown at least some capacity to invite oth-ers to meet the Lord *before* he can be seriously considered as a candidate for the diocesan priesthood.[3] Even in the emerging Evangelical Catholi-cism of the twenty-first century, this is not always understood, as is clear from the fact that, even in the best twenty-first-century seminaries, a candidate for the priesthood hears far more about the Church, as a gen-eral rule, than he does about friendship with Jesus—just as, even in the best dioceses, the preadmission scrutiny of candidates focuses far more on psychological testing than on the exploration of a man's life as a missionary disciple. This is changing, but the change must be accelerated. For unless a man is a radically converted Christian disciple—one who, in gazing upon the Cross, knows himself to be looking at the great truth at the center of human history—he will not be able to bring to the world, through his ministry, the truth that "God so loved the world that he gave his Son, that whoever believes in him should not perish but have eternal life" [John 3.16].

This demonstrated ability of candidates for the priesthood to attract others to friendship with the Lord Jesus must be based on and spring from the power of their own conversion to Christ. "Missionary priests," in Counter-Reformation Catholicism, were those sent out to the ends of the earth to convert the heathen. In the Evangelical Catholicism of the developed world in the twenty-first century and beyond, *every* Catholic priest must be a missionary priest. For every territory is mission territory, and there are both the unbaptized and baptized pagans who must be called to radical conversion of life. If a man contemplating the priesthood does not understand this—if he thinks of the priesthood as a career option, albeit one with certain demanding requirements, such as celibacy—then he should be invited to think again, and be encouraged to live a more evangelical form of discipleship, before he applies again as a candidate for the diocesan priesthood.

Celibacy and Obedience

Radical conversion is also the prerequisite to priestly ministry in Evangelical Catholicism because radical conversion enables the Catholic priest to live his life, and his celibacy, as a sign of contradiction—to live as one set apart from the world for the world's sake. In this respect, Evangelical Catholic priests are indeed different from their fellow evangelical Catholics (not to mention different from their fellow denizens of postmodernity). But that difference is not an end in itself, a matter of personal idiosyncrasy or caste rules. It is difference for the sake of conversion, so that the world may learn the truth about itself and come to embrace the Gospel.

Thus the radical reform of the Catholic priesthood will include a deepening, not a weakening, of the link between priestly celibacy and the priestly ministry.

Calls for the abolition of celibacy as a requisite for priestly ordination in Latin-rite Catholicism have been a staple of the waning Counter-Reformation Catholicism in the post–Vatican II period. Evangelical Catholicism, by contrast, embraces priestly celibacy as an essential part of the Church's countercultural challenge to the postmodern world in which the Gospel must be preached in the twenty-first century.[4] The radical openness to complete dependence on God that is one hallmark of a celibate life; the radical self-giving in celibacy that testifies to the truth that self-gift, not self-assertion, is the path to goodness in the human condition—these are essential messages with which Evangelical Catholicism challenges the self-absorption of postmodernity. And while those challenges to the ambient public culture are also mounted by consecrated religious men and women, they will be most effectively and directly mounted for most Catholics—and for most of those whom all Catholics are called to evangelize—by celibate priests. Lived in integrity, and happily, priestly celibacy is a powerful sign to the culture of the imperial autonomous Self that there are things worth dying for—including things worth dying-to-self for.

A similar Gospel-centered dynamic ought to inform priestly obedience in the Evangelical Catholicism of the twenty-first century and beyond. As the clerical system of the Counter-Reformation tended to regard celibacy as a requirement for admission to a caste, so that same system saw a priest's obedience to both the truths of faith and to the will of his bishop as a part of the caste rules and ethos. In Evangelical Catholicism, by contrast, the first criterion of authentic Catholic reform is the criterion of truth. Thus, in a postmodern culture in which truth is a chimera and obedience is bondage, the obedience of the Catholic priest to the truths of the faith and to the discipline of the Church (manifest through the will of the local bishop) is a powerful witness to the Church's countercultural insistence that the truth binds and frees us at the same time. Liberated by obedience to the truth, the Catholic priest can invite others into the liberating power of truth in a unique way.

Seminary Formation, Theology, and Apologetics

In training priests to be leaders in the New Evangelization, seminary formation, and especially theological education, must emphasize that the story Christianity proposes to the world—the story of God's coming into history through Israel and the Church—is not one option in a supermarket of religious possibilities, but *the* truth of the human condition.[5] It is not a truth for Catholics only, or for Christians only, but a truth that demands of its very nature to be shared with everyone. That conviction, if properly developed and formed, does not shut the priest off from other truths, no matter what their sources in literature, the sciences, philosophy, music, art, or other religious traditions; it enables the priest, as a thoroughly converted Christian disciple, to understand and propose to the world that all truths, from whatever source, ultimately point toward the one Truth, who is God the Father of Jesus the Lord, who as Son of the Father, with whom he is "one," calls himself "the way, and the truth, and the life" [John 10.30, 14.6].

In the evangelical Catholic seminary of the twenty-first century, therefore, theological education will have a different intellectual texture than graduate theological studies in other institutions of higher learning. In the latter, a critical, sometimes deconstructive, approach to the Great Tradition of Christian faith is the norm. Evangelical Catholic priests must know the faith before they subject it to the tools of critical analysis. Thus many twenty-first-century seminary pre-theology programs emphasize, rightly, a thorough encounter with the *Catechism of the Catholic Church,* so that seminarians have a solid foundation in the symphony of Catholic truth before they begin to study its component instruments. Theological and biblical studies in the first years of seminary formation should build upon this solid foundation so that each candidate has a deep understanding of what the Church teaches—and why. Theological studies in the seminaries of twenty-first-century Evangelical Catholicism will thus be a discipline that leads seminarians to commit themselves to the practice of *sentire cum ecclesia*: to thinking deeply *with* the Church as the foundation from which to think critically about understanding the tradition, preaching it, and teaching it.

Intellectual formation in evangelical Catholic seminaries will also stress the importance of apologetics: the ability to make a compelling case for the truths of the Gospel when confronted by the counterclaims of the ambient culture. Evangelical Catholic apologetics is not so much a matter of winning arguments as it is of converting souls. Winning arguments can be an important part of converting souls and bringing men and women into deep friendship with the Lord Jesus, but it is the encounter with Christ that the twenty-first-century apologist will offer, and he will do this through a variety of tools. A fine model for this kind of "apology" can be found in the ten-part film series *Catholicism*, hosted by Father Robert Barron. Barron's apologetic skills are built upon a solid foundation of theological knowledge.[6] Thus the two—serious engagement with theology, and apologetics—ought to go together in the evangelical Catholic seminary formation of the twenty-first century and beyond.

A Catholic theology faculty will know that it has done its job well when the men it recommends for priestly ordination think of theology (including biblical studies) as their professional intellectual discipline and have developed the skills necessary to turn theology into apologetics, evangelism, and challenging preaching—all in service to the call to friendship with the Lord Jesus.

The Imperative of Preaching Well

In a moment of considerable candor, doubtless mixed with chagrin, Pope Benedict XVI once observed to colleagues that the divine origins of the Church were confirmed by the fact that the people of the Church remained in it despite being subjected to dreadful preaching, Sunday after Sunday. The concerns of this master-preacher over the state of preaching in the Catholic Church were shared by one of his most distinguished predecessors, Pope St. Gregory the Great, who in the sixth century had this to say in his *Pastoral Guide*: "Anyone ordained a priest undertakes the task of preaching, so that with a loud cry he may go ahead of the terrible judge who follows. If, then, a priest does not know how to preach, what kind of cry can such a dumb herald utter?" Nor are these simply the criticisms of the professionals; vast numbers of committed lay Catholics would readily agree. For these men and women, whose number is legion, the preaching they hear is a burden to be borne rather than an integral part of their deeper conversion to Christ and an invitation to live their own evangelical responsibilities more intensively.

As Counter-Reformation Catholicism slowly gave way to Evangelical Catholicism in the late twentieth and early twenty-first centuries, there seemed to be three reasons for this sad state of affairs, and a clear path to the evangelical reform of Catholic preaching beckoned.

The first reason for the failure of too much Catholic preaching is that too many seminary faculties teach a deconstructive approach to the Bible, laying heavy emphasis on the historical-critical method of biblical interpretation—a method that often leads to a grave fragmentation of the biblical texts. The net result is that bits and pieces of the Bible appear as the detritus of the dissecting room and the laboratory, not as the living Word of God. An approach to preaching that draws only on the historical-critical method will have one of two unhappy outcomes: the preacher will cease to preach the Bible (an artifact too complex for the vulgar minds of the uninitiated) and will substitute various therapeutic recommendations for happy living; or the preacher will preach historical criticism, thus making his people fellow pathologists of a dead text.

The answer to all this is not, of course, to revert to a kind of Catholic biblical fundamentalism. As Pope Benedict pointed out in the introduction to the second volume of his Christological triptych, *Jesus of Nazareth*, the twenty-first-century Catholic exegete, and preacher, will gratefully accept the real accomplishments of the past two centuries in the historical-critical study of the Bible, and then build out from there a method of biblical interpretation and a style of biblical preaching that rediscovers the Bible as an integrated whole: the book of the Church from which the Church is daily fed on the Word of God.[7] Thus the evangelical Catholic preacher will enrich his preaching with information, drawn from historical-critical studies of the Bible, about the times and places in which Jesus lived, the people with whom Jesus dealt, and the controversies and concerns that shaped each Gospel writer's unique presentation of the *kerygma*, the Good News of Jesus Christ. But he will do all that in service to homilies and sermons that proclaim the Bible as the Word of God, that invite the people of the Church to meet the Lord through his holy Word, and that empower Catholic men and women to take the Gospel into the world and draw people to Christ. Benedict XVI himself offers a superb model of critically—and theologically—informed preaching that unpacks the truths of the faith and makes them "live" in the context of the twenty-first century; his collected homilies are a good star for Catholic priests to steer by in their preaching.

The second problem in the formation of Catholic preachers for the Church of the twenty-first century is that, in the homiletic programs that do exist for both seminarians and priests, too much emphasis is placed on storytelling, references from pop culture, humor, and other preaching "tricks" thought to make sermons relevant and engaging. Most often, they do not. The evangelical Catholic priests of the future must relearn the importance of expository preaching, which requires careful study of the liturgy's biblical texts through the use of good biblical commentaries, many of which will have been written by Protestant scholars. (Indeed, the revival of the theological interpretation of the Bible is one of the great ecumenical undertakings of the twenty-first century.)[8] Evangelical Catholic preachers will also find a rich resource for expository preaching in the Liturgy of the Hours; the Office of Readings is replete with excerpts from the expository preaching of the Fathers of the

Church—which was itself modeled on the Lord's own explanation of biblical texts in his own preaching and teaching. Evangelical Catholic pastors who preach in this style report good results from their congregations, many members of which have long been quietly unhappy, even distressed, at the attempts of their priests to be "user-friendly," as postmodern culture understands the term.

And the third reason for bad preaching is that few Catholic seminaries (and few clergy education programs for those already ordained) lay as heavy an emphasis as they should on developing preaching skills. Pope Benedict and other great preachers throughout Christian history did not just happen. Preaching is a skill and an art. That skill must be developed and honed in seminary formation, and its artistry further refined in continuing priestly education, with more intensity than is often the case in the first decades of the twenty-first century. A man who cannot preach well will not be a priest capable of being an icon of the priesthood of Jesus Christ, the Word incarnate, in the Evangelical Catholicism of the future. Attention must therefore be paid to this often-minimized aspect of priestly formation and clergy education. Homiletics is not an optional part of evangelical Catholic seminaries; it is at the heart of priestly formation, one of the facets of priestly formation where theory (theology and biblical studies) meets practice (preaching). The same holds true for the continuing education of priests.

Liturgical Presence

Another facet of seminary formation where contemplation of theological truth intersects with priestly activity is the training of priests as celebrants of the sacred liturgy. Here, again, a clear idea of what the liturgy *is* will inform and shape what the priest-as-liturgical-celebrant *does*.

If the liturgy is understood as primarily the action of the Church, something we create, then the priest will act as the "presider" in an "assembly" in which his personality is perhaps the single most important part of the action. If, in evangelical Catholic terms, the liturgy is understood as primarily the action of Christ, whose eternal priesthood is iconographically present in the liturgical ministry of bishops and priests, then the priest will act as *celebrant* of the *sacred mysteries*, leading the *People of God* into an experience of the liturgy of angels and saints at the Throne of Grace. His personality will not therefore be an essential part of the act of worship, except in the homily, where his own rhetorical skills will still be subordinated to the proclamation and explication of the Word of God.

The new English translations of the third edition of the Roman Missal, introduced in 2011, will be one aid in the evangelical reform of the liturgical ministry of Catholic priests in the Anglosphere; the more complex structure of the prayers forces the celebrant to pay closer attention to the text, so that he can speak those prayers intelligibly and intelligently. But the deeper reform of the liturgical presence of Catholic priests must come from an interior conviction, first bred in seminaries and then nurtured by bishops, that the priest is the servant of the liturgy, not its master, and that he must never think of the sacred liturgy as an occasion for the expression of his charming (or winsome, or glowing) personality. The priest's mission in the sacred liturgy is to lead his people into a profound experience of the presence of Christ, and through Christ, into the mystery of the Holy Trinity. It is not to lead others to himself. The priest, through his own dignified conduct as celebrant, leads his people into a dignified celebration of the sacred mysteries, and thus empowers them in their own priestly privilege of offering right worship.

Priestly Fraternity and Clericalism

Catholic priests share a unique vocational bond that has led over time to a unique form of fraternity. That sense of fraternity, of belonging to an "order" within the sacrament of Holy Orders, is different from the friendships shared by those in other professional careers. If it has any parallel, it is most likely that of the fraternity of military officers. But even that analogy limps, given the fact that the priests of Latin-rite Catholicism are celibate.

That fraternity is corrupted when a priest becomes the object of a fellow priest's sexual desires, which is one of the reasons why a deep-seated homosexual "identity" is incompatible with the Catholic priesthood. That homosexual corruptions have taken a toll on priestly life in recent decades cannot be denied, both in the diocesan priesthood and among religious communities of men such as the Jesuits and the Carmelites. Addressing existing problems of sexual corruption, both homosexual and heterosexual, is thus essential to the deep reform of the Catholic priesthood in the Evangelical Catholicism of the future. The witness of celibacy chosen for the Kingdom is gravely compromised by these corruptions, be they matters of homosexuality or clerical concubinage (a major problem in the Church of the Third World).

Clericalism, however, is likely the more dominant challenge to the evangelical reform of the priesthood in the developed world: the understanding of the priesthood as a caste, or, more vulgarly, a religious trade union, to which one gains membership by participating in certain initiation rites that confer a new and higher status on the initiate. In this case, the initiates identify themselves with "the Church," rather than understanding themselves as servant-ministers in a community in which all are called to holiness and mission.

The classic expression of this kind of clericalism is the question posed by Bishop William Ullathorne to Blessed John Henry Newman in the nineteenth century: Who are the laity? Well, the great theologian answered, the Church would look rather foolish without them. Newman's interlocutor may have been an extreme case, but the problem of clericalism—in which one must include the problem of clerical ambition—is a long-standing one. Its resolution is essential if Evangelical Catholicism is to be the Church as proclaimed by the Second Vatican Council: the Church of the universal call to holiness.

There is, obviously, an issue of theology here. How a man understands his priesthood will have a lot to do with whether he succumbs to the worst aspects of clericalism: pretentiousness, ambition, jealousy of others who are advancing faster in their "careers," and an inability to relate as both leader and brother to the people who have been given into his pastoral care. Thus, the way the theology of the priesthood is taught in seminaries will be a crucial factor in building the right kind of priestly fraternity, in which the priests of a diocese think of themselves as fellow members of a presbyteral college, with and under the local bishop, for the service of all the People of God.

Clericalism, understood as the identification of a priestly caste with "the Church," is an impediment to the full flowering of Evangelical Catholicism, and an antidote may be found to it in the example of Blessed John Paul II. Karol Wojtyła, Pope John Paul II, was a priest's priest and an inspiration to countless numbers of priests and seminarians. He nevertheless found many of his friends among laypeople—men and women whom he had first known as a university chaplain, and who remained among his closest friends throughout his life. There was no confusion of identities or roles in this network of friends; he was a priest, and they were not. But even more fundamentally, all were disciples who understood that the gifts they had been freely given, be they gifts of intellect, athletic or artistic skill, or personality, were to be shared freely with others. And in that mutual exchange of gifts between a priest and his lay friends, there was a continual growth in discipleship.[9]

It is a pattern that might well be emulated throughout the world Church.

Handling Crises

Like every other Christian, the evangelical Catholic priest will find himself, from time to time, in spiritual distress, even crisis. The crisis can become so severe that it causes a man to ask whether he should remain in the priesthood. When that depth of crisis occurs, however, the first question a man should ask is not "Why did I become a priest?" Rather, the first question is, "Why am I a Christian, a disciple of the Lord Jesus? Why am I a Catholic?"

When counselors, fellow priests, and bishops put those questions to wavering priests—and do so simply, directly, and with love—the fog of confusion that can enter priestly souls often dissipates. Then the crisis can be seen and addressed for what it is: a crisis of faith. Though the immediate cause of a "vocation crisis" is often a moral failing, every crisis in a man's priesthood is, first and foremost, a crisis of discipleship and Christian identity. It is also, in many cases, a specific question of Catholic identity. Addressing those questions is the beginning of spiritual growth and healing at the level necessary for the restoration of fruitful discipleship and ministry.

Signs of Contradiction, Making Saints

Evangelical Catholic priests in the twenty-first-century developed world will necessarily be signs of contradiction. Priests are "set apart" from the world by the vow of celibacy, but they are "set apart" from the world for the sake of the world: they live, in a heightened way, the reality of the Gospel as a truth that is against the world for the world. This contradictory character of the priest's life is not crankiness or idiosyncrasy; it is built into the nature of the Catholic priesthood—and in a cultural moment that combines Christophobia with profound spiritual boredom, the contradictions and tensions posed by the priesthood will be sharpened. The postmodern world believes that the royal road to happiness lies through self-assertion; the Catholic priest embodies in a special way the Gospel truth that human flourishing comes through self-gift, not self-assertion. The postmodern world celebrates the imperial, autonomous Self; the evangelical Catholic priest lives the life of an obedient, deeply ecclesial man-for-others.

There is also paradox in this being a sign-of-contradiction, but it is paradox that is evangelical and salvific. By renouncing the goods of marital communion and physical paternity, the priest's life is a paradoxical reminder to a confused, unisex world that these things are in fact *good*, just as his spiritual paternity is a sign of contradiction to the materialism of the developed world.

Evangelical Catholic priests understand that, by teaching the truths of the faith, by reverently celebrating the sacraments, and by justly governing and leading that portion of God's people entrusted to their care, they are empowering the men and women of the Church to become saints—and thus to fulfill their human, as well as their Christian, destiny. Saints, as C. S. Lewis taught, are people who can live comfortably with God forever. That is what God intended for humanity from the beginning. That is why the Son of God entered history as the full self-revelation of the God who had spoken through the Law and the prophets, and that is why the Son died in obedience to the Father's will. That is why the Holy Spirit came upon the apostles, equipped them for mission, and accompanied them—and the Church throughout the ages—to the ends of the earth. It's all about sanctity; it's all about grace, and grace making saints.

Making saints is what Catholic priests are for, by being instruments of the grace of God, who is the true author of sanctity. To be a living icon of the eternal priesthood of Jesus Christ is to live out a special vocation within the communion of the Church. Priests who understand that vocation in explicitly evangelical and sanctifying terms will live out the awesome truth of what was conferred upon them in Holy Orders in ways that advance the deep reform of the Church in the Evangelical Catholicism of the future.

CHAPTER SEVEN

The Evangelical Catholic Reform of the Liturgy

T HE RENEWAL OF THE CHURCH'S LITURGY IS AT THE CENTER OF THE
historical arc of deep Catholic reform that begins with the election
of Pope Leo XIII and runs through the pontificate of Pope Benedict XVI.
That renewal is the keystone of the edifice, both chronologically and
theologically.

The Liturgical Movement was not simply one important part of the
mid-twentieth century Catholic renaissance, alongside the renewal of
Catholic biblical studies, Catholic theology and philosophy, and Catholic
action for social justice. The reform of the liturgy was the spiritual hub
from which these other spokes of Catholic reform extended out into the
life of the Church, and the vital, sacramental center to which the reform
of the Church was always intended to return.

The Liturgical Movement was closely tied to kerygmatic theology,
the forerunner of the New Evangelization, in part because of the work
of Father Joseph Jungmann, S.J., of the theological faculty at Innsbruck,
who played a significant role in both liturgical studies and the development of kerygmatic theology. On the other side of the Atlantic, the close
links between the Liturgical Movement and the emerging discipline of

Catholic social thought were embodied in Father Virgil Michel, O.S.B., of St. John's Abbey in Minnesota, a leader in both liturgical reform and Catholic action. As the reform and renewal of the Church's liturgical life were thought essential to the development of a Catholic theology suitable for the evangelization of the modern world, so the liturgy was also understood to be the spiritual source from which Catholic action for justice in the world would spring. The liturgy would thus inspire and nourish Catholic action.

The Evangelical Catholicism of the twenty-first century will rebuild these linkages, which have become frayed, if not completely broken, in the decades since the Second Vatican Council.

The Council intended to vindicate the Liturgical Movement (always capitalized in those days) by a reform that repositioned the liturgy at the center of Catholic life in all its dimensions; it did not intend to detach the liturgy from the proclamation of the Gospel, or the works of charity, or the Church's social doctrine and public witness. Yet that is largely what happened.

Why it happened can be argued elsewhere. What is important to stress here is that the "reform of the reform" of the liturgy—which is the bringing to full maturity of the mid-twentieth-century liturgical reform—is not a matter of taste but of theology. The Church is most herself when she celebrates the liturgy, and especially the Eucharist, for at Holy Mass, the Church in the world is in touch with the Church of the saints in a unique way. The Eucharistic liturgy makes present the eschatological Christ—the Christ who, coming in glory, will draw all peoples to himself [cf. John 12.32]. In that holy presence, the Church experiences herself as the bride of the eschatological Bridegroom, the Christ who is to come and establish the Kingdom of the Father: "Behold, the bridegroom! Come out to meet him" [Matthew 25.6].

Thus, in its worship, the Church receives a supernatural gift: a foretaste of what Joseph Ratzinger once called "divinization, a world of freedom and love."[1] In the liturgy, the world of history (in which we, the Church, "groan inwardly as we wait for adoption as sons, the redemption of our

bodies" [Romans 8.23]) touches the future that is a redeemed cosmos—
a cosmos in which the Bridegroom of the Church, Christ the Lord, "de-
livers the kingdom to God the Father after destroying every rule and
every authority and power," including "the last enemy . . . death" [1
Corinthians 15.24, 26].

This powerful vision of the Church's worship as an experience of
the coming Kingdom was at the heart of the Second Vatican Council's
teaching on what the Council Fathers styled the Constitution on the *Sacred* Liturgy:

> In the earthly liturgy we share in a foretaste of that heavenly liturgy
> which is celebrated in the Holy City of Jerusalem toward which we
> journey as pilgrims, where Christ is sitting at the right hand of God,
> Minister of the sanctuary and of the true tabernacle. With all the war-
> riors of the heavenly army we sing a hymn of glory to the Lord; ven-
> erating the memory of the saints, we hope for some part and fellowship
> with them; we eagerly await the Savior, our Lord Jesus Christ, until he,
> our life, shall appear and we too will appear with him in glory.[2]

Evangelical Catholic worship is thus precisely that, *worship*, or, in
the technical term, *latria*: the communal celebration of the adoration
that is to be given to God alone. In the deeply reformed Catholic liturgy
of the twenty-first century, everything that is done at Holy Mass and in
the celebration of the other sacraments is ordered to that end: the adoration of God "through our Lord Jesus Christ," the Holy One received
who is also the One coming in glory. The worshipping community is not
focused on itself; as one body with many parts and many Spirit-given
gifts, it is focused on, and ordered to, the One who is to come, and who
even now brings us to the Father through the power of their Holy Spirit.

That is the truth to which the evangelical reform of the liturgy always
returns, and which it seeks to express. That is the Eucharistic ordering
that rightly orders all our earthly loves and loyalties toward the Kingdom
to come and the Wedding Feast of the Lamb.

The Question of Orientation

And that is why Evangelical Catholicism takes seriously the possibility of returning to the ancient orientation of the Church's liturgical prayer during the Liturgy of the Eucharist at Mass. There, both priest-celebrant and congregation pray in the same direction: toward the Christ who will return in glory and draw his Body, the Church, into the heavenly Jerusalem.

The issue here is not so much one of the priest celebrating Mass "facing the people" or "facing the altar" as it is one of the biblically and theologically correct orientation of the Church's liturgical prayer *for everyone.* Thus attempts to derail this discussion by dismissing the orientation question as a project of anti–Vatican II reactionaries eager for the priest to "turn his back to the people" should be dismissed for the distraction they are. The crucial point, as Uwe Michael Lang has written, is that "the Mass is a common act of worship where priest and people together, representing the pilgrim Church, reach out for the transcendent God."

And as we have seen, this is in fact one of the primary aims of the Eucharistic liturgy: it is meant to point "Christian existence toward Christ coming in glory." Has that aim been frustrated in what sometimes seems the "closed circle" of an orientation in which priest and people face each other across a free-standing altar? Some would suggest that it has. That loss can lead, in turn, to what Father Lang calls an "eschatological deficit" in the liturgy—a deficient sense of liturgical prayer as our privileged participation in the heavenly liturgy, which anticipates Christ's coming in glory. The "eschatological deficit" in the celebration of the sacred liturgy leads in turn to a kerygmatic deficit (the liturgy is less the encounter with the *truth* of Christ the Lord than it ought to be), and that kerygmatic deficit leads to an evangelical deficit (the liturgy does not inspire the people of the Church to become the agents of the Church's *mission* they have been baptized to be). Thus this "eschatological deficit" suggests that the common orientation of the Liturgy of the Eucharist since Vatican II comes up short on the two criteria of authentic Catholic reform: the criterion of truth and the criterion of mission.

As Father Lang demonstrates, the common orientation of priest and people toward Christ, returning in glory, is deeply rooted in the origins of Christianity. Then, it was a "matter of course" for Christians to turn in prayer toward the rising sun—an orientation that directed the Church's attention to Christ, the light of the world; an orientation that embodied the Church's hope for the Lord's return and the inauguration of the Kingdom of God in its fullness.[3] In addition to this eschatological or Kingdom-meaning of priest-and-people looking together toward the returning Lord, the common orientation of the entire worshipping community during the Liturgy of the Eucharist also symbolized "the journey of the pilgrim people of God towards the future." Thus two further questions: Does the now conventional, but hardly traditional, priest-facing-people-over-the-altar orientation contribute, however unintentionally, to a loss of the congregation's self-awareness as God's people on pilgrimage through history toward the fulfillment of God's promises? Has the typical postconciliar orientation of the Liturgy of the Eucharist seriously attenuated the Church's sense of the priest-celebrant leading God's people "in a [common] 'movement toward the Lord,' who is 'the rising sun of history'"?[4]

Thus an evangelical Catholic reform of the liturgy will give serious consideration to a recovery of the classic orientation of Christian prayer during the Liturgy of the Eucharist. During the Liturgy of the Word, priest and people would still face each other—an orientation appropriate for listening and for preaching. Then, in the Liturgy of the Eucharist, the entire congregation, including the celebrant, would turn toward the Lord: both priest and people would, in other words, turn as one toward the altar as the celebrant prayed the Eucharistic Prayer, all facing together toward Christ, whose coming in glory is anticipated in his Eucharistic Presence, which the worshipping community receives in the consecrated bread and wine of holy communion.

The liturgy can be reverently celebrated with priest and people facing each other during the Liturgy of the Eucharist; that is not in question. The question Evangelical Catholicism is pressing is a deeper one: Would a recovery of the Church's ancient practice of a common orientation of priest and people during the Liturgy of the Eucharist make such reverent celebrations more likely, while helping the Church recover the Kingdom aspect of its Eucharistic life, thus reconnecting the Eucharist to Christian truth, proclamation, and witness?

A change in orientation cannot (and must not) be achieved by fiat, for most Catholics are wholly unaware of the reasons behind the ancient orientation of the Church's prayer during the Liturgy of the Eucharist, which has never been explained to them. Thus priests will need to prepare their congregations carefully for change through extensive liturgical catechesis, best undertaken at the homily during Sunday Mass for a considerable period of time. When a return to the ancient orientation during the Liturgy of the Eucharist is properly introduced, experience shows that it is almost invariably well received.

Sacred Space

Postconciliar Catholic architecture has badly attenuated the sense of sacred space that is required for the liturgy to be celebrated in both a theologically rich and aesthetically dignified manner. In many Catholic parishes of the twenty-first century there is little sense of sacred space. The reverent silence that used to prevail in Catholic churches is rarely encountered, even in churches that have an ample narthex where the gathering congregation can greet one another before entering the church proper. Yet if the church proper is the *Porta Coeli*, the door of heaven and the portal of the Kingdom, then surely one ought to act in that space somewhat differently than one acts at the local mall or supermarket.

Thus evangelical Catholic church design will make clear that there is a border between sacred and profane space, and evangelical Catholic pastors will recatechize their people in the truth that the body of the church is a sacred space in which a new way of behavior is appropriate. That task, of course, will be easier in churches that eschew architectural modernism and that embody, in their very fabric, the orientation of the worshipping community toward the New Jerusalem.[5]

The eschatological or Kingdom character of the liturgy also demands that the Church's most solemn acts of worship be celebrated in a church.

Thus the use of large secular facilities for major Church ceremonies will cease in the Evangelical Catholicism of the twenty-first century. The ordination or enthronement of a bishop in a hotel ballroom, in a resort facility that includes casinos, bars, and bowling alleys, is sacramentally valid. But it seems very difficult, if not impossible, for the liturgy of ordination and installation to embody the truth and majesty of the office of bishop in a ceremony in which the ordinand lies prostrate on an oriental rug in front of the kind of drapes typically found in a convention hall during a meeting of the Rotary Club. The cathedral is the mother church of the diocese; if the cathedral is inadequate to the needs of a growing local Church, then a new cathedral should be built.

Liturgical Time as Countercultural Time

Postmodernity flattens and profanes time: thus the Sabbath becomes the "weekend," Advent and Christmas become "the holidays," Easter is the "Spring Festival," and so forth. Evangelical Catholicism, by contrast, lives *in* time in order to prepare the people of the Church for the time *beyond* time that is the Wedding Feast of the Lamb in the Kingdom of God. Rather than accommodating the conventions of secular time by transferring some holy days to Sundays and canceling other holy days of obligation when they fall near Sundays, the liturgical calendar of twenty-first-century Evangelical Catholicism should be deliberately countercultural, embodying a distinct way of life that points beyond the flattened "now" of a world without transcendence to the eschatological horizon of a future in which "God [is] everything to everyone" [1 Corinthians 15.28].

Thus the reform of the reform of the liturgical calendar ought to begin with the restoration of Sundays after Epiphany and Sundays after Pentecost, and the suppression of Sundays of "Ordinary Time." There is nothing "ordinary" about Sunday, the weekly festival of the Resurrection, the eighth day of the New Creation and the Sabbath of the New Covenant. Nor is there anything "ordinary" about the Sundays after the Epiphany—the great solemnity of the Lord's manifestation to the world and to history—and Pentecost—the birthday of the Church and the beginning of the mission to the nations. Catholics who live in the "time of the Church" will live in the penumbra of those two great feasts and will know that they are not "ordinary" in so living.

The restoration of Sundays after Epiphany will also permit a return to biblical and liturgical clarity in the celebration of the Christmas season, which has been turned impossibly inside-out by the transfer of Epiphany to Sunday and the imperative of beginning "Ordinary Time" immediately after the Solemnity of the Baptism of the Lord. Consider, for example, the thoroughly confused sequence of Gospel readings in 2010, according to the liturgical calendar in force at the time:

On December 25, Jesus is born.

On December 26, the Holy Family flees to Egypt and the Magi leave for home.

On January 2, the Magi (who have just been described as leaving) arrive.

On January 3, Jesus hears that John the Baptist has been arrested; Jesus leaves Nazareth and goes through Galilee.

On January 4, Jesus feeds the 5,000.

On January 5, Jesus walks on water.

On January 6, Jesus goes back to Galilee (when did he leave?) and reads in the synagogue of Nazareth.

On January 7, Jesus cures a leper.

On January 8, Jesus goes to Judea, where John the Baptist, who was arrested on Monday, has not been arrested yet.

On January 9, Jesus is baptized by John.

This is biblical insanity. And it is caused by the transfer of Epiphany to Sunday, the placement of the Feast of the Holy Family on the Sunday after Christmas, and a three-year reading cycle instead of a fixed cycle during the Christmas season. All of this can, and must, be reformed so that the liturgical calendar will reflect biblical truth, not the recreational and seasonal conventions of postmodernity.

In addition to restoring Epiphany to its traditional home on January 6 and making that solemnity a holy day of obligation on which all are called to the Eucharist, the Evangelical Catholicism of the twenty-first century should feature more, not fewer, obligatory days of Mass attendance during the week—thus demonstrating in the living practice of the Church that participation in the Eucharist is not another weekend recreational option. The Solemnity of the Ascension must be restored to its classic home on the fortieth day after Easter, a Thursday, rather than being transferred to a Sunday. Corpus Christi, the Solemnity of the Body and Blood of Christ, should be restored to its traditional home on the Thursday after Trinity Sunday and made a universal holy day of obligation. The celebration of these solemn feasts during the week once gave a distinctive character to the Counter-Reformation Church's temporal life; it can do so again in the Evangelical Catholicism of the twenty-first century and beyond.

That evangelical Catholics live in a different time zone, so to speak, can also be underscored by increasing, not minimizing, holy days of obligation, always with the pastoral understanding that if participation at Mass on these days works a real and true hardship, then the obligation ceases. Given the variety of historical and spiritual experiences in the world Church, local Catholic churches could adopt distinctive sets of holy days of obligation to meet their particular needs while observing such universal holy days as the Solemnity of Mary, Mother of God (January 1); the Solemnity of the Epiphany (January 6); and the Solemnities of the Ascension and Corpus Christi (the dates of which are governed by the date of Easter). In the United States, for example, an evangelical Catholic perspective on culture would suggest that the Solemnity of the Annunciation (March 25), the memorial of the Incarnation, be celebrated as a holy day of obligation and a special day of prayer for the development of a culture of life.[6] John Paul II described Our Lady of Guadalupe as a special Marian gift to the Americas; her liturgical feast on December 12 could be a holy day of obligation dedicated to reflection on Mary as the Star of the New Evangelization. And as twenty-first-century Catholicism lives the truth that the blood of martyrs is the seed of the Church, the liturgical memorial of the North American martyrs on October 19 might well become a new holy day of obligation. These holy days would, of course, be marked in addition to the Solemnity of the Assumption (August 15), which Evangelical Catholicism celebrates as the foretaste, in Mary, of the glory that awaits all the saints when the Lord comes in glory, and the Solemnity of the Immaculate Conception (December 8), the patronal feast of the United States.

The sanctification of time is an ancient challenge for the Church; one of the first communities of Christian converts had to be admonished by St. Paul for its quick return to the observation of secular "days, and months, and seasons, and years" [Galatians 4.10], all of which harkened back to the slavish worship of false gods. In every age, therefore, the rhythms of the Church's life should reflect the difference that the fullness of Catholic faith makes in the ways we perceive time—and the "goal" of time. A Church that accommodates its liturgical calendar to the imperialism of secular postmodernity (often from a misguided sense of pastoral sensitivity) is a Church prepared to make other concessions to the demands of the ambient culture. A Church that lives counterculturally within its own temporal rhythms is a Church that can say to that culture, with the Apostle to the gentiles, "And now I will show you a still more excellent way" [1 Corinthians 12.31b].

The Self-Discipline of the Celebrant

In the liturgy as celebrated by evangelical Catholic priests and bishops, the personality of the celebrant is not a crucial, much less *the* crucial, element of worship. Indeed, outside the homily or sermon, an evangelical Catholic celebrant will take care to keep his own personality out of the way of the liturgy by, among other things, avoiding various greetings or comments that are not found in the Church's official liturgical books and that, however well-intended, turn the liturgy into yet another form of communal self-celebration, fueled by sacerdotal self-expression.

As noted previously, Vatican II called its document on liturgical reform the Constitution on the *Sacred* Liturgy. Celebrants should understand that their task is to lead a community into true worship of the living God, not into an appreciation of the celebrant's personal charm. Psalm 96.9, as translated by King James's commission, calls us "to worship the Lord in the beauty of holiness." That is the task in which the celebrant of the sacred liturgy must lead his people, who are being called in liturgical worship to the threshold of heaven and the Wedding Feast of the Lamb.

Psychologist Paul Vitz has analyzed some of the worst abuses of liturgical propriety by celebrants as instances of "clerical narcissism." The deeper problem, as always, is theological. For as Vitz noted in a sharp critique of priests and bishops determined to impose their personality on the liturgy, such behavior (often driven by concerns for "relevance") intensifies the "now" aspect of the liturgical rite while minimizing, if not completely obscuring, the liturgy's orientation toward the future—its anticipation of the coming of the Lord, who will come in both glory and judgment.[7]

The culture of the postmodern West is obsessed with immediacy; the Church's liturgy is intended to lift us up from the present so that we might orient our lives against a more ample horizon of aspiration. Postmodernity celebrates the arrogance of the imperial autonomous Self; the liturgy teaches us humility before "so great a gift" as the Eucharistic Body and Blood of the Risen Lord. Priest-celebrants and bishops who make themselves and their personalities the focal point of the Church's worship should reflect upon St. Paul's admonition to the self-absorbed and rowdy Christians of Corinth: "Now we have not received the spirit of the world, but the Spirit which is from God, that we might understand the gifts bestowed on us by God. And we impart this in words not taught by human wisdom but taught by the Spirit, interpreting spiritual truths to those who possess the Spirit" [1 Corinthians 2.12–13].

Praying Twice, with Love

St. Augustine did not, as it happens, say that "he who sings well prays twice" [*Qui bene cantat bis orat*]. What he did say, in a commentary on Psalm 72, was that those who sing, sing praise; they do so joyfully, and thereby love him about whom they are singing. The Christian's song, in other words, is to be a love song. And love, as St. Paul taught, is the still more excellent way.

Thus music in the sacred liturgy can never be considered as mere filler: something to do while something else of relative unimportance is afoot; something, in other words, that is peripheral. Rightly understood, prepared, and executed, liturgical music is an integral, not accidental, facet of divine worship. Unfortunately, the stress that postconciliar Catholic liturgy tended to place on what some wags call the "hymn sandwich," the processional and recessional hymns, reinforces this sense of music as an "extra."

Throughout the world Church, the evangelical Catholic reform of liturgical music will begin by affirming the Second Vatican Council's teaching that Gregorian chant is "specially suited to the Roman liturgy" and "should be given pride of place in liturgical services."[8] Other musical forms will then be used in the sacred liturgy as local custom and prudent liturgical planning dictate. In the Anglosphere, the pride of place given to Gregorian chant will be complemented in evangelical Catholic liturgy by recognition of the uniquely beautiful patrimony of hymnody possessed by the English-speaking peoples. The art involved in good liturgy in the United States, for example, involves bringing these two truths together.

This is by no means as difficult or cumbersome as it may appear to those for whom the "hymn sandwich" is the only imaginable musical paradigm. At any Mass where there is to be singing, the procession can enter the body of the church while a hymn is sung, the hymn being completed as the celebrant venerates the altar; then, as the celebrant incenses the altar (or, in less "high" forms of celebration, moves from the veneration of the altar to the celebrant's chair), the choir sings the entrance antiphon in chant. At Masses when the choir processes into the church at the beginning of the celebration, the entrance antiphon and versicle are chanted at the back of the church as a call to worship at which the congregation rises; the processional hymn is then sung by all as the celebrant, his ministers, and the choir enter the church, venerate the altar, and take their places in the sanctuary.

A similar "both-and" approach to song during the communion rite honors the Council's injunction about chant while recognizing that almost fifty years of futile efforts to get congregations to sing during the communion procession are telling us something. Thus, during the distribution of holy communion to the congregation, the choir chants the communion antiphon with an appropriate psalm or canticle. Then, after holy communion has been distributed and the sacred vessels are being cleansed, the entire congregation sings a communion hymn of thanksgiving.

Congregations, it might be added, take easily to simple chant, either classic Gregorian or various modern adaptations of it. Chant in various forms, and often using Latin, has become a staple of international Catholic gatherings like World Youth Days and the annual meetings of various renewal movements. In chant, the Church is rediscovering its common tongue as well as its common musical grammar (albeit often in contemporary forms, such as the simple chants of Taizé).

Hymnody also has its rightful place in the liturgy of Evangelical Catholicism in the Anglosphere (and certainly elsewhere). The next question is, Which hymns?

An extraordinary number of trashy liturgical hymns have been written in the years since the Second Vatican Council: hymns whose texts reflect a treacly pseudo-theology of self-affirmation (often frankly Pelagian in character); hymns whose music is more redolent of Andrew Lloyd Webber musicals than it is of the hymn-tunes of Isaac Watts,

Thomas Tallis, or Ralph Vaughan Williams, much less the hymnody found in such classic collections as the 1623 *Geistliche Kirchengesange*, the 1828 *Katholisches Gesangbuch*, or the 1940 *Hymnal* of the Episcopal Church in the United States. The evangelical Catholic reform of the sacred liturgy is one in which hymns are chosen very carefully, both as to textual integrity (according to the criterion of truth) and musical dignity (which includes singability by untrained voices).

Hymns that teach heresy—hymns that make assertions contrary to Christian truth—have no place in the liturgy. The prime example here is "Ashes," frequently heard on Ash Wednesday throughout North America: "We rise again from ashes to create ourselves anew." No, we do not, and we are condemned if we imagine that we do. Christ creates us anew, for Christ alone has the power to forgive the sins that Lenten ashes call us to repent. It is unconscionable that such Pelagian drivel, which would have sent St. Augustine's head spinning, should be a part of Catholic liturgy; it is even more unconscionable that "Ashes" appears in hymnals and missalettes that carry the episcopal *imprimatur*, the official warrant that a text is free of doctrinal error.

Another contemporary hymn, "For the Healing of the Nations," deplores "dogmas that obscure your plan" as the congregation addresses God. But what can this possibly mean, except to reflect some kind of down-market, anti-intellectual, do-it-yourself Christianity for dolts? Dogmas illuminate God's plan and liberate us into the freedom of the truth in doing so. That is what the Catholic Church teaches, and that is why hymns like "For the Healing of the Nations" have no business being sung in Catholic worship.

Less dangerous, but still theologically troublesome, are those hymns in which the congregation speaks as if it were Christ himself. A prime example is "Love One Another": "Love one another as I have loved you / Care for each other as I have cared for you / Bear each other's burdens, bind each other's wounds / And so you will know my return." The confusions here are striking. Who is praying to whom? Is the Lord's return confined to our doing his will? Or do we somehow facilitate his return by doing his will? It all seems rather distant from the testimony of Scripture: "But of that day and hour no one knows, not even the angels of heaven, not the Son, but the Father only" [Matthew 24.36]. "Be Not Afraid," "You Are Mine," and "I Am the Bread of Life" are three other frequently encountered contemporary hymns that fit snugly within this "We Are Jesus" paradigm, which reinforces every bad cultural temptation to celebrate the self-worshipping community, the closed circle of witness to our own rectitude and niceness. Sung on Corpus Christi, as it not infrequently is, "I Am the Bread of Life" contradicts every lesson the liturgy of the day teaches: for we are not a self-feeding community giving each other the "bread of life," but a Eucharistic community nourished by the Lord's free gift of himself. "I Am the Bread of Life" inverts, even falsifies, the truths that Corpus Christi teaches. So why do parishes sing it?

Because, most probably, they haven't thought this through, and in any case they think of music as filler, not as an integral part of the kerygmatic dimension of the liturgy.

A great cleansing of hymnals and missalettes will therefore be an important part of the evangelical Catholic reform of the liturgy; at the same time, the Church in the Anglosphere will rediscover the glories of Anglophone hymnody and fit those glories into the celebration of the Eucharist and the other sacraments, along with the great Latin-rite tradition of chant.[9]

Liturgy, Kerygma, Justice

The celebration of the sacred mysteries of the liturgy is not a means to an end; we worship God because God is to be worshipped. Nevertheless, the reform of the reform of the liturgy in the Evangelical Catholicism of the twenty-first century and beyond will once again unite the liturgy to the Church's kerygmatic and charitable work. Thus the Church's *munus sanctificandi* [mission of sanctification] will be integrally related to the *munus docendi* [the mission of teaching] and the external or public aspects of the *munus regendi* [the Church's service to the world by its leadership in the works of justice and charity], as envisioned by the Liturgical Movement of the mid-twentieth century.

The three-year Sunday reading cycle and the two-year cycle of biblical readings during daily Mass are among the finer accomplishments of the post–Vatican II liturgical reform (the confusions of the Christmas season notwithstanding). They offer the people of the Church, and the Church's preachers, a rich feast of biblical texts that, over time, should steep the people of the Church in the depths of biblical wisdom.[10] Those depths are plumbed during the liturgy by kerygmatic and expository preaching that links the witness of the Bible to the teachings of the Church. Thus evangelical Catholic preachers will prepare their homilies and sermons with both a good biblical commentary and the extensive Scripture index to the *Catechism of the Catholic Church* ready at hand. In that way, biblical preaching will be linked to catechetical preaching for the deepening of Catholic faith, which is the essential prerequisite to effective Catholic witness in the world and service to those in need.

In the liturgy, the Church steps outside the ambient culture and its rhythms and passions to enter what is really the "real world": life within the light and love of the Holy Trinity. In this anticipatory participation in the Trinitarian life that the liturgy makes possible, the Church learns the meaning of Christ's promise that "I came that they may have life, and have it abundantly" [John 10.10]. Thus, in the unique microculture of dignified liturgical worship celebrated according to the mind of the Church, evangelical Catholics of the twenty-first century will learn an understanding of the dignity of the human person, who is capable of worshipping the one true God in spirit and in truth; they will learn the inalienable worth of every human life from conception until natural death; they will learn that religious freedom is the first of human rights; and they will learn the supernatural charity that completes, even as it transcends, the essential works of justice in and for the world. This is not didactic learning so much as it is a matter of absorption: the liturgy invites us to a richer, nobler apprehension of the human condition than the world offers. Formed by that liturgical experience, which transmits a special kind of knowledge, evangelical Catholics come to be the servants of justice and the agents of healing in a broken and fragmented world.

Reform, Not Nostalgia

The reform of the Church's liturgy in Evangelical Catholicism is emphatically not an exercise in nostalgia; nor does it begin from the premise that the *Novus Ordo* of Pope Paul VI—the form of the Roman Rite developed by the Concilium for the implementation of Vatican II's Constitution on the Sacred Liturgy—was a serious mistake. There were certainly grave mistakes in the implementation of the *Novus Ordo* liturgy. Thus Evangelical Catholicism welcomes the revival of the Missal of 1962 (the Extraordinary Form of the Roman Rite) for its capacity to inspire a more dignified celebration of the *Novus Ordo*. But the evangelical Catholic liturgical renewal of the twenty-first century will be built from the *Novus Ordo*, particularly as embodied in the Third Edition of the Roman Missal, not from a return to the preconciliar liturgy.

For a small minority of Catholics, the Missal of 1962 offers a way of prayer most conducive to the worship they seek to offer. For the overwhelming majority of Catholics, however, the reform of the reform will be an ongoing reform of the *Novus Ordo* as outlined above. That reform will be retarded, not advanced, by exercises in liturgical nostalgia that, by seeking to re-create an imagined past (which is, in truth, barely recognizable as the "past" that Catholics who lived in the 1950s would recognize), fail to set an appropriate course for the future. This kind of ill-informed nostalgia cannot contribute to the development of Evangelical Catholicism in the twenty-first century; the reform of the reform of the liturgy will not be advanced by a return to the use of the maniple, or by the widespread revival of fiddleback chasubles, or by a proliferation of lace surplices and albs, or by other exercises in retro-liturgy.[11]

By conventional postconciliar standards, evangelical Catholic liturgy is certainly "high." But it is not precious, and it is most certainly not prissy.

Beyond the Sacramental Service Station

Despite the decline of Catholic practice in the decades since Vatican II, it is also true that many Catholic parishes take their sacramental life—and the liturgical life that is related to it—with great seriousness. The deep reform that proceeds from Evangelical Catholicism will take this seriousness even further through a serious commitment to sacramental preparation.

In one (booming) American parish where the vision of Evangelical Catholicism is being lived in a radical way, members of the parish, or those who wish to be members of the parish, are required to demonstrate the seriousness of their commitments to living a life ordered by the Church's sacraments to the Sacrament who is Jesus Christ. Thus parents seeking Baptism for their children, if they are not members of the parish or are only occasional Mass attenders, are required to attend Sunday Mass on a weekly basis for six months prior to their child receiving Baptism—and during those six months, the parents are catechized (or, in many cases, recatechized, this time seriously) by the parish's deacons and catechists.

Couples seeking to be married in this parish are asked to demonstrate a similar sacramental seriousness: not simply by coming to the parish to fill out various forms and to plan their wedding, but to attend Sunday Mass together during a six-month period of marriage preparation. Cohabiting couples are similarly required to live the six months before their wedding according to the Church's understanding of the ethics of love—precisely so that the sacrament of Holy Matrimony can be celebrated and experienced in its fullness at their wedding, and thus set the platform on which a truly Christian marriage can be built.

Carrying out this kind of serious sacramental preparation as a means of embodying in local parishes the vision of Evangelical Catholicism can be advanced through cooperation among the priests of a deanery, vicariate, or diocese. It can also be impeded by those pastors who continue to run something like sacramental service stations, requiring little or nothing of those who come except their interest in being married in church or having their children baptized. If one parish requires a serious program of sacramental preparation, *not* to lay down the law but to deepen the encounter with Christ, and the neighboring parish is less than vigorous in inviting people to take Baptism and Matrimony seriously, the evangelical Catholic possibility of deep reform is undercut.

That is why the deep reform of the Church requires that the Church's bishops—who are the only ones who can bring evangelical and sacramental order into a diocese—not think of themselves as moderators of discussion groups, either of clergy or laity. The bishop's first task is to be the local Church's chief custodian of the truth of the Gospel, which includes custody of the integrity of both Word and Sacrament.

The Custody of the Sacred Mysteries

The evangelical Catholic reform of the liturgy depends, in the main, on the Church's priests and on trained lay experts in music, the decorative arts, and architecture. Their work will be supported by a revival of the understanding of the local bishop as the chief guarantor of the liturgical integrity of his diocese; their work will be impeded if bishops default on their responsibilities as the shepherds of the Church's worship. Bishops who, on one hand, allow liturgical aberrations to go uncorrected are damaging the worship of the Church, the kerygmatic mission of the Church, and the Church's ministry of service. Bishops who, on the other hand, guide their priests and people into the dignified celebration of the sacred mysteries are energizing and empowering every other facet of Catholic life in their dioceses. That is why cathedral liturgy is so important: as the mother church of a diocese, the cathedral church ought to set an example of dignified, beautiful worship, amplified by challenging and compelling preaching, which is emulated by every parish.

And that is why bishops must take far more seriously their responsibility to ensure that the people of the Church receive the sacraments worthily. When priests establish standards for the administration of Baptism or the celebration of weddings that are intended to guarantee the integrity of the sacraments—by, for example, insisting on regular Mass attendance by parents for several months before a child is baptized, or by teaching that cohabitation is not a proper preparation for marriage—they must be supported by their bishops. When a bishop determines, after consultation and conversation, that a public official is acting in a way that is gravely contrary to the moral law and the requisites of justice in carrying out his or her legislative or executive responsibilities, and should therefore not present himself or herself for holy communion, that bishop must have the support of his priests.

The celebration of the sacred liturgy is not a recreational activity in which anyone may legitimately engage as he or she determines. The Eucharistic liturgy is an act of worship in which all are called to participate, but in which only those in a state of grace may participate fully. A clear understanding of this, coupled with the appropriate disciplinary measures, is essential to the integrity of the sacramental life of Evangelical Catholicism, from which all else proceeds.

CHAPTER EIGHT

The Evangelical Catholic Reform of Consecrated Life

CATHOLICS IN CONSECRATED RELIGIOUS LIFE—MEN AND WOMEN WHO take public vows of perpetual poverty, chastity, and obedience— constitute about 1 percent of the world Church in the twenty-first century. Yet throughout history, what has always been a small minority has also been an essential part of the Church and a key to its renewal. That will be the case in the Evangelical Catholicism of the future, as men and women living the consecrated life of the vows will be the vital center of the Church's growth—a kind of spiritual reactor core from which new energies of grace will flow to all the members of the Body. Far from being peripheral to the evangelical mission of the Church of the twenty-first century, the consecrated life is essential. Its deep reform is an integral part of the deep reform of the entire Church.

The charter for this twenty-first-century reform will be *Vita Consecrata*, a 1996 apostolic exhortation on "The Consecrated Life" written by Pope John Paul II to complete the work of the 1994 Synod of Bishops. The Synod met to consider the state of consecrated religious life in the Church after Vatican II and immediately found itself in difficulties, given the wide variety of experiences that congregations of religious men and women (often called "religious orders") had undergone since the Council. In Africa and Asia, religious communities were growing rapidly, particularly women's orders. The exact opposite situation prevailed in Western Europe and North America, where religious vocations had plummeted since the mid-1960s and a large-scale exodus from religious life had taken place. That exodus had a profound effect on Catholic educational, charitable, and health-care institutions, many of which had formerly counted on abundant numbers of religious men and women for staff.

At the same time, both men's and women's religious communities in the West began to develop vocational theories that bore little resemblance to the ways the Church had always understood the "evangelical counsels" of poverty, chastity, and obedience. Those theories both reflected and accelerated a dramatic change in the mode of life lived by these religious communities. The reasonable modernization of religious habits mandated by Vatican II became the wholesale abandonment of a distinctive garb among many religious women. The Council's call to religious superiors to exercise authority through consultation aimed at a conscientious discernment of religious obligations became a virtual abandonment of authority (including the authority of the Holy See) in the name of "maturity" and "empowerment." The renewal of chastity proved exceptionally difficult amid the sexual revolution of the late twentieth century; religious communities of men that once prided themselves on a robust, soldierly masculinity were beset by homosexual practice, among both candidates for religious life and those who had already professed their vows.

There was great irony in all of this. Throughout history, authoritarian systems had marked out religious communities for especially stringent persecution; twentieth-century communism, the greatest persecutor of the Church in two millennia, was no exception. Then, just as communism began to wane as a force in Western history, religious communities themselves began a process of auto-deconstruction that weakened them beyond the imagining of the most ardent commissar for religious affairs or communist secret police agent. What persecution had failed to do in revolutionary France, anticlerical Mexico and Portugal, republican Spain, Nazi Germany, and the communist countries of Central and Eastern Europe, bad theology succeeded in doing in much of the post-Christian West: it reduced too much of consecrated religious life in the Catholic heartland to a bizarre, and sometimes sinister, simulacrum of itself.

Transformation through Transfiguration

John Paul II, determined to address these problems, invited the 1994 Synod of Bishops to look into the situation and propose remedies. The Pope was likely disappointed with the quality of discussion at the 1994 Synod on religious life, however. An inordinate amount of time was spent debating whether religious life was in crisis, which it clearly was; almost three decades into renewal-as-deconstruction, the leaders of many religious orders of men and women (and the bishops who spoke for them, out of conviction or weakness) refused to concede that the approach they had taken since Vatican II had failed. Rather than debating the obvious further, John Paul focused his attention, in the lengthy postsynodal apostolic exhortation *Vita Consecrata*, on the evangelical renewal of religious life. It was a project in which he saw boundless opportunities—if the project were well-grounded, biblically and theologically.

The primary biblical iconography that disclosed the truths of an authentic and deep reform of consecrated life was the Gospel story of the Transfiguration, the Pope proposed. Like Peter, James, and John, awestruck at the beauty and majesty of the Lord, whose "face shone like the sun" and whose "garments became white as light" [Matthew 17.2], men and women living religious life ought to be dedicated to contemplating, loving, and proclaiming the glory of the Lord, whether in active service ministries or in cloistered lives of contemplative and intercessory prayer.[1] Thus the consecrated men and women of the twenty-first century would learn to walk the spiritual path that the ancient Greek Fathers of the Church called *philokalia*, the "love of the divine beauty," which the

Pope then linked to both the continued outpouring of the Holy Spirit on the Church and the mission of all the Church's people:

> Like the whole of Christian life, the call to the consecrated life is closely linked to the working of the Holy Spirit. In every age, the Spirit enables new men and women to recognize the appeal of such a demanding choice. Through his power, they relive, in a way, the experience of the Prophet Jeremiah: "You have seduced me, Lord, and I have let myself be seduced" [Jeremiah 20:7]. It is the Spirit who awakens the desire to respond fully; it is he who guides the growth of this desire, helping it to mature into a positive response and sustaining it as it is faithfully translated into action; it is he who shapes and molds the hearts of those who are called, configuring them to Christ, the chaste, poor and obedient One, and prompting them to make his mission their own. By allowing themselves to be guided by the Spirit on an endless journey of purification, they become, day after day, *conformed to Christ*, the prolongation in history of a special presence of the Risen Lord. . . .
>
> The same Spirit, far from removing from the life of humanity those whom the Father has called, puts them at the service of their brothers and sisters in accordance with their particular state of life, and inspires them to undertake special tasks in response to the needs of the Church and the world, by means of the charisms proper to the various Institutes. Hence many different forms of the consecrated life have arisen, whereby the Church is "adorned by the various gifts of her children . . . like a bride made beautiful for her spouse" [cf. Revelation 21:2] and is enriched by the means necessary for carrying out her mission in the world.[2]

The Pope used other biblical vignettes to illustrate crucial aspects of the consecrated life as a life transformed, in the power of the Spirit, by an ongoing encounter with the Transfigured Lord and his glory. Mary's anointing of Jesus at the home she shared with Martha and Lazarus in Bethany speaks of the "unbounded generosity" that the consecrated life demands of those who would practice it. And as Mary's anointing in

John 12.1–7 anticipated Jesus's death and burial, the radical openness to others lived by those in consecrated life would be a sign, to the Church and the world, of the fullness of life in the Kingdom.[3] The vigil of the Virgin Mary and the apostle John at the foot of the Cross is a biblical icon of the discipleship that is the foundation of the consecrated life. The vigil of Mary and the apostles in the Upper Room, waiting for the gift of the Spirit after the Resurrection, is a perennial reminder that "spousal receptivity" to God's grace—the receptivity born of a deep and committed love—must constantly and prayerfully await further outpourings of the Holy Spirit.[4]

All these biblical images, John Paul II wrote, illustrated *the* crucial point in the reform of consecrated life in the twenty-first century: the life of the vows is not a life of self-assertion but of radical self-gift. The sanctity that had been experienced in consecrated life over the millennia, from the eremites of the Egyptian desert and the first Benedictine monks and nuns down to the wholly unexpected flowering of religious life in the nineteenth and twentieth centuries, demonstrated the truth that there is a Law of the Gift, a moral law of self-giving, built into the human condition. And according to that deep truth, men and women come to the fullness of life through the gift of self to others, not the assertion of self against others.[5] This Law of the Gift, in turn, is lived in a unique way through the vows of poverty, chastity, and obedience, in a witness the Pope believed was badly needed by both Church and world as history turned into the third Christian millennium.

Thus, the vow of obedience in consecrated life challenges the world's assumption that obedience to any "external" authority is demeaning, while demonstrating that obedience to the truth makes a genuine human freedom possible.[6] The vow of poverty challenges the world's materialism and the ethics of conspicuous consumption, while affirming the goodness of Creation and illustrating how simplicity of life can be liberating.[7] As for what seemed to many late moderns and postmoderns the most implausible of the vows, that of chastity, John Paul wrote that consecrated chastity should not be viewed only in negative terms, as a reproach to hedonism, but positively. For chastity, lived in integrity amid struggle, is "a witness to the power of God's love manifested in the weakness of the human condition. The consecrated person attests that what many have believed impossible becomes, with the Lord's grace, possible and truly liberating."[8]

In all of this, John Paul wrote, the consecrated religious man or woman is practicing, in contemporary form, what Christians had long called the "imitation of Christ":

> By professing the evangelical counsels, consecrated persons . . . strive to reproduce in themselves . . . that form of life which he, as the Son of God, accepted in entering this world. By embracing chastity, they make their own the pure love of Christ and proclaim to the world that he is the Only-Begotten Son who is one with the Father. By imitating Christ's poverty, they profess that he is the Son who receives everything from the Father and gives everything back to the Father. By accepting Christ's filial obedience, they profess that he is infinitely beloved and loving, as the one who delights only in the will of the Father, to whom he is perfectly united and on whom he depends for everything.[9]

These themes in John Paul's Transfiguration-driven proposal for the deep reform of consecrated life were taken seriously by a team of American religious women in a 2009 study, *The Foundations of Religious Life: Revisiting the Vision*, sponsored by the Council of Major Superiors of Women Religious (CMSWR)—a new body formed by consecrated women religious who judged that the Leadership Conference of Women Religious (LCWR), a kind of trade association of the religious orders whose members comprised the majority of American sisters, had fallen into the deepest of theological confusions.[10] In *Foundations*, theologically competent women religious, scholars who had taken *Vita Consecrata* seriously, affirmed that lives of evangelical poverty, chastity, and obedience were in fact the baptismal call and responsibility of all Christians; thus, consecrated life is a unique working-out of the implications of the grace of God poured forth into Christians at the very beginning of their Christian life. Some, however, are called to a more radical living-out of this baptismal call, and in responding generously to the vocational call to consecrated life, in either active or contemplative life, the vowed religious open channels of grace that support the entire Church in its striving for holiness and in its work of mission.

The life of the vows, the CMSWR team insisted, is a life *in* and *for* the Church in which personal responsibility is deepened by being conformed to the Church and its Bridegroom in a more radical way. The consecrated religious man or woman is thus not just joined to his or her religious community (order) by the profession of the vows; through that consecration, he or she is also joined to the entire Church, its life and its mission, in a distinctive vocation.

The authors of *Foundations* thus challenged those (whose voices were dominant, for example, in the LCWR) who had reinterpreted the vows, especially the vow of obedience, in a manner that seemed to reflect the solipsism of the imperial autonomous Self more than the obedience of the Son of God:

> In recent years, some have questioned whether superiors in fact "hold God's place" . . . [and] call for a "theology of discernment" and a "theology of mediation," stating that each religious can best mediate and determine her own life, for "a person chooses to shape his or her Christian discipleship within the framework of a particular state of life." St. Basil the Great's blunt observation from the fourth century comes to mind: "If [the monk] . . . wishes to do his own will, why has he placed himself under the obedience of a superior?" In reality, the vow of obedience is rooted in the willed choice of an individual, that is, in her intellect and will. Obedience is not conformity. Its exercise is voluntary and responsible. Acting in true obedience, the religious, far from being repressed and dehumanized, is exercising the most mature act that the will can make. . . . Thus the [Second Vatican Council] includes among the benefits of the religious state "liberty strengthened by obedience"

and stresses that such obedience "does not diminish the dignity of the human person but rather leads it to maturity through that enlarged freedom that belongs to the sons of God."[11]

All of this, the *Foundations* team stressed, returned, ultimately, to the central truths of Catholic faith: for the Council's effort aimed to "plant religious obedience even more deeply in the Paschal Mystery[,] wherein, 'taking the form of a servant,' Christ learned obedience through what he suffered. The obedient religious imitates Christ's obedience."[12]

Decidedly Mixed Results

John Paul II's vision of the deeply reformed religious life in the Evangelical Catholicism of the future, which deepened and broadened the vision of consecrated life proposed by Vatican II, was taken seriously by some provinces of some religious congregations of men throughout the world, but was largely ignored by others.

Among religious congregations of the early twenty-first century, the vision of *Vita Consecrata* was lived by the fast-growing religious communities of women in Africa and parts of Asia (including the sometimes hard-pressed Church in Vietnam) and in North America by the communities that formed the Council of Major Superiors of Women Religious—which also happened to be the religious congregations of women that were growing in the United States and Canada. One such community, the Dominicans of St. Cecilia, based in Nashville, Tennessee, attracted so many young women that a new novitiate had to be built; bishops and pastors throughout the United States vied to get Nashville Dominicans to work in their parishes as they built the Evangelical Catholicism of the future. The CMSWR's constituent congregations also set up a graduate residence in Rome, the Domus Guadalupe, for sisters who wished to take advanced degrees at pontifical universities before returning to their various apostolates. Among the congregations represented in this venture was the Religious Sisters of Mercy of Alma, Michigan, a community that blended a classical approach to the vows with a commitment to graduate education, encouraging its members to pursue terminal degrees in fields ranging from philosophy and theology to canon law and medicine. Still another group living the life of the vows according to the vision of *Vita Consecrata* was the New York–based Sisters of Life, founded by Cardinal John O'Connor and Mother Agnes Mary Donovan (a former professor of psychology and clinical practitioner at Columbia University) to build the culture of life in an abortion-riddled America while providing pregnancy and maternity services to women in crisis.

For their part, the religious communities of women that had formed and dominated the Leadership Conference of Women Religious continued along a different path—the path for which the 1994 Synod and *Vita Consecrata* were intended to provide a major course correction. Their attitude was aptly captured by one of the chief theological proponents of the postconciliar revolution in religious life, Sister Sandra Schneiders, I.H.M., a longtime professor at the Jesuit School of Theology in Berkeley, California. Schneiders was nothing if not honest about the gulf that existed between the vision of religious life she espoused and that of those officially charged with the implementation of Vatican II, a gulf she attributed to "conflicting ecclesiologies":

> The leaders of women's religious life in [the United States] have come to explicit awareness . . . that the underlying conflict between, on the one hand, Vatican officialdom in its attempt to dictate the parameters and control the practice of religious life and, on the other, women religious in their claim to self-determination and adult responsibility, is not only a clash between medieval patriarchs and modern democrats, but, more deeply, a clash between two incompatible ecclesiologies.[13]

That was true. The question that remained, of course, was whether the ecclesiology, the idea of the Church, promoted by Dr. Schneiders and her colleagues of the LCWR was not in serious, and perhaps terminal, tension with Catholic orthodoxy. The further question was whether that disconnect between the LCWR's idea and manner of living the life of the vows, on the one hand, and the doctrine of the Church, on the other, was a principal reason why the religious communities that had deconstructed themselves since Vatican II were dying, while those that had embraced the Council's teaching and that of *Vita Consecrata* were growing. Yet when this question was raised, LCWR leaders refused to engage it, suggesting that their goal was not to grow, but to be. How one could "be" without "growth" was not addressed.[14]

The Difficulties of Reform

The difficulties in effecting a deep reform of consecrated life that were evident in the decades after Vatican II reflected various factors in the life of the Church and illustrated several of the institutional tensions involved in the transition from Counter-Reformation Catholicism to Evangelical Catholicism. Those problems included the relative autonomy of religious communities within the Church (a good thing, until autonomy became virtual disengagement); the unwillingness of the Holy See to risk schisms (an exercise of pastoral prudence that could blur into irresponsibility in the exercise of Church governance); and the reluctance of many post–Vatican II bishops to be the guarantors of Catholic identity in their dioceses (a reflection of the false idea of the bishop as a discussion-group moderator). All of these problems must be overcome if the evangelical reform of consecrated life is to make its appropriate contribution to the deep reform of the entire Church. Three failed attempts to address the severe problems that had beset certain communities of men and women religious since the Council illustrate how things ought not be done in the future.

John Paul II's Jesuit intervention

At a September 1979 meeting with international Jesuit leaders in Rome, John Paul II bluntly told the members of a religious community explicitly pledged to the service of the papacy that "you were a matter of concern to my predecessors and you are to the pope who is talking to you." The concerns of the moment included the involvement of numerous Jesuits in revolutionary politics in the Third World, but could well have included novel interpretations of the vows of poverty, chastity, and obedience that were rife throughout this elite corps of religious men, the largest in the Church.[15] The Society of Jesus, long known for its formidable intellectuals, had also developed a well-deserved reputation for theological dissent since Vatican II—a reputation in starkest contrast to the image of Jesuits in the preconciliar years.

Two years later, in October 1981, John Paul took the Society into a form of papal receivership, placing his own delegate, Father Paolo Dezza, S.J., and a coadjutor (or deputy), Father Giuseppe Pittau, S.J., at the head of the Society's governance. It was a form of shock therapy, intended to convey the deep concern of the Holy See for the theological and pastoral direction taken by Jesuits since the Council.

That concern was not shared by a critical mass of Jesuits. Thus this dramatic papal intervention must be reckoned one of the failures of John Paul's pontificate, in that it did not lead to substantial theological reform, or to a reform in the way in which the vows of consecrated life were lived, within the Society of Jesus.[16] The degree of failure may be measured by citations from prominent Jesuits themselves in a 2002 book whose very title spoke volumes: *Passionate Uncertainty: Inside the American Jesuits.* As reviewer Paul Shaughnessy, himself a Jesuit, pointed out, the one thing postconciliar Jesuits were not uncertain about was their own rectitude:

> One of the signal services of *Passionate Uncertainty* is that it lets us hear influential Jesuits—those who shape policy—speak their minds frankly, in words unsoftened by the public relations personnel in their fund-raising offices. "I am appalled by the direction of the present papacy [i.e., John Paul II's]," says a university administrator. "I am scandalized by Rome's intransigent refusal to re-examine its doctrines regarding gender and sex. . . . Frankly, I think the Church is being governed by thugs." "The Church as we have known it is dying," a retreat master insists. "I hope and pray that the Society of Jesus will help facilitate the death and resurrection." An academic gloats, "The Society

has not sold its soul to the 'Restoration' of John Paul II." Another Jesuit scholar, a Church historian, ranks John Paul II as "probably the worst pope of all times"—adding, "He's not one of the worst popes; he's the worst. Don't misquote me." The respondents made it clear that their contempt for the Pope is based almost entirely on his . . . unwillingness to imitate their own adaptability in the matter of doctrine.[17]

These attitudes, which were widespread throughout the Society (if rarely expressed so bluntly in public), involved no small degree of cognitive dissonance.[18] For as Father Shaughnessy went on to remark, "As do all priests, the speakers above took a solemn oath swearing that they 'firmly embrace and accept everything concerning the doctrine of faith and morals' proposed by the Church." Yet as Shaughnessy concluded, one cannot assume that these men do not perceive the discrepancy between what they have promised and what they believe and live. "Their willed imbecility derives not from a lack of brainpower or ingenuity but from a deliberate decision to ignore the clash of commitments and to suppress insurgent attempts to throw light on what, for tactical reasons, is better left in the darkness."[19]

The Jesuit situation was discussed at the conclave of 2005. One proposal floated at the time called for an even more dramatic papal intervention, in which a future pope would release all Jesuits from the distinctive fourth vow that all fully professed members of the Society take—an act that would, in effect, dissolve the Society of Jesus. A papal commission (including now-former Jesuits with a reputation for sanctity and orthodoxy) would then review applications for membership in a refounded religious community whose members would explicitly commit themselves to live the consecrated life according to the vision of St. Ignatius Loyola, in full fidelity to the teaching authority of the Church.

Perhaps a future pope, determined to revitalize within the Church an elite corps of highly educated religious men for the sake of the New Evangelization, will do something like that. Until then, and despite the younger Jesuits who have entered the Society in recent decades and who fully embrace John Paul II's vision of the Church of the future, it is not easy to see how the Society of Jesus, once the glory of Catholic religious life, will make any corporate contribution of note to building the Evangelical Catholicism of the future.

The visitations of American religious women's communities

In the decades after Vatican II, the Holy See made several attempts to initiate a truly evangelical reform of women's religious communities in the United States; all were failures, if for different reasons. A 1983 commission of U.S. bishops led by Archbishop John R. Quinn of San Francisco produced a bland document on essential elements of the religious life; even that was too much for many members of the Leadership Conference of Women Religious, who repudiated a document produced by a commission largely sympathetic to their point of view. The Congregation for the Doctrine of the Faith issued a warning to the LCWR in 2001, cautioning against its members' dissent on a variety of theological matters the Church considered settled; LCWR's leadership continued to insist on its understanding of religious life as one of "loyal dissent." Then, at the 2007 assembly of the LCWR, Sister Laurie Brink, O.P., noted with evident approval that some religious communities of women had, in the course of their "sojourning . . . grown beyond the bounds of institutional religion. . . . Religious titles, institutional limitations, ecclesiastical authorities no longer fit [such a] congregation, which in most respects is post-Christian. . . . [And] who's to say that the movement beyond Christ is not, in reality, a movement into the very heart of God?"[20]

In response to this and other expressions of deep (even bizarre) incongruity in religious life, yet another Vatican visitation of American women's religious communities was mounted—and yet again, the response from most LCWR congregations was noncooperation. The LCWR itself took a measured (if disingenuous) line, expressing surprise when the visitation was announced in January 2009. It was the redoubtable Sister Sandra Schneiders, I.H.M., who, once again, offered an honest, if wholly defiant, response:

I am not inclined to get into too much of a panic about this investigation—which is what it is. We just went through a similar investigation of seminaries, equally aggressive and dishonest. I do not put any credence at all in the claim that this is friendly, transparent, aimed to be helpful, etc. It is a hostile move and the conclusions are already in. It is meant to be intimidating. But I think if we believe in what we are doing (and I definitely do), we just have to go peacefully about our business. . . .

We cannot, of course, keep them from investigating. But we can receive them, politely and kindly, for what they are, uninvited guests who should be received in the parlor, not given the run of the house. When people ask questions they shouldn't ask, the questions should be answered accordingly. I just hope we will not . . . think that by total "openness" and efforts to "dialogue" we are going to bring about mutual understanding and acceptance. This is not mutual and it is not a dialogue. The investigators are not coming to understand—believe me, we found that out in the seminary investigation. So let's be honest but reserved, supply no ammunition that can be aimed at us, be non-violent even in the face of violence, but not be naïve. Non-violent resistance is what finally works as we've found out in so many areas.[21]

Sandra Schneiders need not have worried about mounting a non-violent resistance campaign of Gandhian proportions, for before the visitation was even completed, the Vatican went into full retreat. In 2010, the new secretary of the Holy See's Congregation for Religious, Archbishop Joseph Tobin, an American Redemptorist, essentially eviscerated the entire process. Tobin, speaking with the *National Catholic Reporter*, said that the Holy See had to acknowledge the "depth of hurt and anger" among the LCWR religious and promised a "strategy of reconciliation" that would avoid "punitive or overly prescriptive norms."[22] Eight months later, Tobin said that the Congregation for Religious had to "rebuild a relationship of trust" with the LCWR congregations: "I'm an optimist, but also trying to be realistic: The trust that should characterize the daughters and sons of God and disciples of Jesus isn't recovered overnight. I think women religious have a right to say, 'Well, let's see.'"[23]

It would, in other words, be business as usual in the LCWR congregations of women religious. The Holy See had surrendered; the serious questions of orthodoxy and orthopraxis that obviously beset the LCWR congregations would be ignored again. And deep Catholic reform was off the agenda, as far as the Congregation for Religious was concerned.[24]

Thus for what seemed the foreseeable future in 2011, any serious reform of women's religious communities along the lines proposed by the Second Vatican Council and *Vita Consecrata* would have to be carried out within individual congregations. Happily for those committed to deep reform, those were the communities likely to have members in the mid-twenty-first century, after the LCWR congregations disappeared as a result of their own inherent implausibility. What would happen to the billions of dollars of property held by those dying congregations was another question; but the debacle of the most recent visitation did not augur well for retaining those resources within the Catholic family to which they had originally been given.

The Legionaries of Christ

In 2006, it became unmistakably clear that Father Marcial Maciel, founder of the Legionaries of Christ, a relatively new and growing religious congregation of men, had been a pathological personality, serially abusing seminarians, fathering children out of wedlock, and using funds donated to the Legionaries to maintain his dissolute life. The Legionaries were taken into a yet another kind of Vatican receivership, with Cardinal Velasio de Paolis, C.S., a distinguished canonist with expertise in the law governing religious life, appointed as pontifical delegate to oversee reform. De Paolis, many hoped, would lead a reform process that asked the hard questions about the Legion's history, governance, and internal formation practices so as to create conditions for the possibility of a new path forward.

Yet Cardinal de Paolis refused to engage the most urgent question that Maciel's sins and crimes raised: Was the Legion of Christ a work of God? No one doubted that individual Legionary vocations were works of God, for there were many good Legionary priests. The question that demanded an answer, and that de Paolis refused to entertain, was whether and how a religious congregation founded by a sociopath, who framed its internal practices and culture to support his wickedness, could be the work of God. Cardinal de Paolis suggested that the answer to the question of "whether" had been given when the Holy See approved the Legion's constitutions. But that was to confuse a question of legality with the deeper theological question, which could only receive a theological answer.[25] By declining to face the harder, theological issue, de Paolis effectively took off the table a resolution of the Legion crisis similar to that proposed to deal with the Jesuits: dissolution followed by refounding. Yet it was difficult to see how the Legion of Christ could maintain any public credibility, in the Church or the world, absent the definitive break with Maciel that a dissolution-plus-refoundation would represent.

This failure had important parallels to the Church's failure to come to grips with the crisis of the LCWR congregations. In both instances, high officials shied away from the obvious, urgent, and hard question: Irrespective of their canonical status, were these communities Catholic in any meaningful theological sense? No doubt some of their members were in full communion with the Church, often in difficult institutional circumstances. But what about the institutions, the congregations, themselves? In what sense, if any, were they in full communion with the Catholic Church?

Truth and Mission, Again

Crisis in consecrated religious life is nothing new in the history of the Church; the corruptions of some religious congregations were one cause of the Reformation. The very demands of the consecrated life tend to dramatize the problems of religious communities when they fall into theological incoherence: here are communities, founded to embody the noblest and most difficult path of discipleship, unraveling and sowing discord and confusion as they decompose. The entire Body of the Church is wounded as a result.

The reform of these communities in the post–Vatican II period posed unique problems for Church leadership. In the past, individual religious had fallen into heresy and left the Church. In the post–Vatican II turmoil, however, entire communities became dubiously orthodox while insisting that *they* were in fact the Church of the future, and subsequently fell into what might be called psychological schism: they did not leave the Church in a legal or canonical sense, but they had no affective connection to the institutional Church and its supreme authority, and they regarded similarly situated men and women religious who had not followed their path with barely disguised contempt. That much, at least, was clear from books like *Passionate Uncertainty* and the works of Sandra Schneiders.[26]

In the Evangelical Catholicism of the future, the deep reform of consecrated life will, like every other facet of authentic Catholic reform, be measured by the twin criteria of truth and mission. Religious congregations that deny the constituent elements of the Catholic symphony of truth will not contribute to the sanctification of the Church or the conversion of the world. In the fifth decade after Vatican II, the strategy taken by the highest authorities of the Church in the face of these de facto schismatics seemed to be one of letting them die a natural death— a strategy that, admittedly, had the advantage of keeping a peace of sorts.

Yet how such a default in the exercise of pastoral authority contributed to the deep reform of the Church, the "endless journey of purification" of which John Paul II wrote in *Vita Consecrata*, and the progress of the New Evangelization was another hard question that remained unanswered.

CHAPTER NINE

The Evangelical Catholic Reform of the Lay Vocation

A T THE VERY BEGINNING OF ITS DECREE ON THE APOSTOLATE OF THE Laity, the Fathers of the Second Vatican Council described the lay mission in the Church and the world as an "apostolic" calling "indispensable" in the Church's work of evangelization, sanctification, and charity.

The lay mission derives, the Council Fathers wrote, "from the layman's very vocation as a Christian." And although the lay mission was evident from the very beginnings of the Church [see Acts 11.19–21, 18.26; Romans 16.1–16; Philippians 4.3], the circumstances of modernity "demand" from lay Catholics "infinitely broader" fields of mission and a "more intense" commitment to those multiple spheres of apostolic action. For all the members of the Body of Christ share in the Church's evangelical mission: "to spread the kingdom of Christ over all the earth for the glory of God the Father, to make all men partakers in redemption and salvation, and through them to establish the right relationship of the entire world to Christ."[1]

It was a grand vision. Some of it was realized in the decades after the Council, particularly in the rise of new lay renewal movements, and in the expansion of such expressions of the lay mission as Opus Dei, throughout the world Church. But in the main, this conciliar prescription for the reformed Evangelical Catholicism of the third millennium has not been filled. Rather than empowering the laity to enter the mission fields of the family, culture, politics, business, and media as agents of conversion, postconciliar Catholicism in the developed world often displayed a tendency to clericalize the laity—in tandem with the tendency in some quarters to laicize the clergy. Thus "lay mission" often came to be understood as ecclesiastical work that laypeople, both men and women, did *in* the Church, not apostolic work that they did *from* the Church *in the world*.

Some of this broadening of lay roles within the Church was entirely welcome. Enhanced lay participation in the liturgy has been a source of spiritual growth and evangelical fervor for many lay Catholics. In the postconciliar period, circumstances also dictated that lay Catholics fill important roles in Catholic institutions that were previously the preserve of priests and religious men and women. As the numbers of men and women in consecrated religious life plummeted in the West, lay Catholics assumed responsibilities previously held by religious priests, brothers, and sisters in Catholic education, Catholic health care, and Catholic social service—and in some notable instances took the Catholic identity of these enterprises more seriously than the remaining religious were inclined to do. Lay Catholics have also been at the forefront of the New Evangelization in the twenty-first-century Church through renewal movements that seek to reconvert baptized pagans and invite new Christians into the Church; through new initiatives in campus ministry and other forms of evangelism; and through the pro-life movement in its activism and its service to women in crisis pregnancies.

Yet in the early twenty-first century it seems obvious that many other fields of what the Council called the "lay apostolate" have not been well tilled; in some cases, there is less Catholic "density," although there is more numerical Catholic presence, in these fields of Catholic action than there was when the Council concluded in 1965. To take the United States as an example: while there are far more Catholics in public life in America than there were at the time of the Council, one would be hard put to say that the moral reasoning embedded in the social doctrine of the Church has been effectively seeded into the Congress or the state legislatures over the past four decades.[2] The same holds true for the media, where Catholics are well represented numerically, but where there is little serious and sustained Catholic impact. And although there are many new lay-evangelism initiatives aimed specifically at the business community, they have yet to have a major influence on the way the American economy functions.

Meanwhile, confusion over what constitutes "lay mission" continues. Some insist that only when laypeople are fully engaged in the governance of the Church at all levels will their dignity and equality as baptized Christians be recognized—a claim that is the mirror image of the very clericalism it typically condemns, but which is nonetheless tenaciously clung to in some circles. But the challenge is even greater than that posed by this curious progressive Catholic clericalism. At every Easter Vigil, the Church welcomes hundreds of thousands of adults into its ranks, adults who have been catechized for months through the Rite of Christian Initiation of Adults; yet how many of those new Catholics think of themselves as missionaries with a distinct evangelical vocation?

The deep reform of the Church in the Evangelical Catholicism of the twenty-first century demands that laypeople take possession of their unique responsibilities as *lay* agents of the Church's mission to the world. Certain laypeople will find their vocational responsibilities lived within the walls of the Church, so to speak; some of them will bring badly needed managerial, intellectual, financial, and communications skills to their work with the Church's pastors; others will take administrative responsibility for Catholic educational and health-care institutions and social service agencies. Yet for the great majority of Catholics, the Council's lay apostolate will consist of "extramural" apostolic activity: work for the evangelization of the world outside the walls of the Church, amid the cultural confusions of postmodernity. It is their work—which is the "lay mission" rightly understood—that is the focus of the balance of this chapter.

The Radical Proposal of John Paul II

Although the Second Vatican Council's Decree on the Apostolate of the Laity remains an important reference point for Evangelical Catholicism in the twenty-first century, the Magna Carta of the deep reform of the lay mission will be found in the 1988 postsynodal apostolic exhortation *Christifideles Laici*, a bold exploration of the various evangelical roles of "Christ's Faithful Laity," written by a pope, John Paul II, who until his young-adult years intended to live out his Christian life as a layman, and who as a priest and bishop had a broader pastoral experience of the lay apostolate than any pope since the early Christian centuries. John Paul II signaled his determination to implement the Council's vision of an engaged laity in his very first homily as Bishop of Rome, delivered on October 22, 1978:

> Our time calls us, obliges us, to gaze on the Lord and to immerse ourselves in humble and devout meditation on the mystery of the supreme power of Christ himself.
>
> He who was born of the Virgin Mary, the carpenter's Son (as he was thought to be), the Son of the living God (as confessed by Peter), came to make us all a "kingdom of priests."
>
> The Second Vatican Council has reminded us of the mystery of this power and of the fact that Christ's mission as Priest, Prophet-Teacher, and King continues in the Church. Everyone, the whole People of God, shares in this threefold mission. Perhaps in the past the tiara, that triple crown, was placed on the pope's head in order to signify by that symbol the Lord's plan for his Church, namely, that all the hierarchical order of Christ's Church, all "sacred power" exercised in the Church, is nothing other than service, service with a single purpose: to ensure that the whole People of God shares in this threefold mission of Christ and always remains under the power of the Lord; a power that has its source not in the powers of the world, but instead in the mystery of the Cross and the Resurrection.[3]

Ten years later, in *Christifideles Laici*, John Paul, who had worked among laypeople as a manual laborer, and who had taken his vacations with lay friends until his election to the Chair of Peter, laid out a radical vision of a fully catechized and sacramentally prepared laity at work throughout society and culture, kneading the leaven of the Gospel into fields of human endeavor and situations that only laypeople could reach.

The basic challenge was put forcefully, even bluntly: "It is not permissible for anyone to remain idle."[4] For lay Christians, the universal call to holiness of which Vatican II spoke was "intimately connected to mission," for to the lay faithful is given the responsibility to continue Christ's salvific mission in "the world"; for "the world," the Pope wrote, "is the place and means for the lay faithful to fulfill their Christian vocation." And what is that distinctive lay (or, if you will, "secular") vocation? It is nothing less than the sanctification of "the world"—society, culture, politics, economy—through lay witness, lay evangelism, and the lay modeling of a more humane, nobler way of life.[5] The ordained ministers of the Church can play useful, supplementary roles in these fields of mission in the Evangelical Catholicism of the future. But the lead must be taken by lay Catholics who are empowered by Word and Sacrament to be the true evangelists they were baptized to be.

Being a Christian—being an evangelical Catholic—is a full-time occupation, according to John Paul II. The Church cannot evangelize or sanctify the world if the Church is imagined to be a kind of clerical game preserve into which the laity are occasionally permitted entry in order to observe what's going on. No, *the Church* is every baptized Christian, and every one of those baptized Christians is called to both holiness and mission. To foster that holiness among laypeople, and to serve and empower that lay mission, is the task of those in Holy Orders. The mission, however, is for everyone.

The Evangelical Power of Lay Example

Those hundreds of thousands of adult men and women who are baptized or received into the full communion of the Catholic Church at the Easter Vigil every year "convert" for many reasons. For some, like John Henry Newman in the nineteenth century and Evelyn Waugh in the twentieth, conversion is an intellectual matter: this is the truth; one should adhere to it. Others find their way to Catholicism out of the doctrinal and moral confusions of liberal Protestantism, where the tether to Great Tradition Christianity has become severely attenuated and political correctness often trumps theological conviction. Some evangelical Protestants yearn for a richer liturgical life and chart a path into Catholicism by following that desire of the heart and soul. Others, both baptized and unbaptized, find their way into Catholicism through the lives of the saints and martyrs, ancient and modern. All these reasons are good reasons; lay Catholics attentive to their evangelical responsibilities will be aware of the many paths to full communion with the Catholic Church, and from that understanding will invite others into fellowship, and later into mission.

As Evangelical Catholicism considers the distinct lay vocation at the beginning of the third millennium, it is worth pondering just why Christianity "won" in the first centuries of the first millennium. In the vast supermarket of spiritualities that was the Mediterranean world of the first centuries A.D., what was it about *this* proposal, this Way [Acts 22.4], that carried the day? Hard as it may be for theologians and other Christian intellectuals to admit it, argument was not the crucial factor. Example was.

As Rodney Stark has demonstrated in several books that examine the question of "why Christianity won" from a sociological point of view, the Christian "Way" triumphed because it modeled a more humane mode of life in a brutal world. Supernatural charity and sacramental fellowship, extended to women, slaves, foreigners, and the sick, proved an attractive incentive to join what had begun as a tiny messianic sect on the outer edge of the Roman *imperium*. Christian respect for women was particularly important, Stark argued, for it led to large numbers of conversions among women: women who then married pagans, whom the wives in turn converted while giving birth to large families. Christian selflessness in the face of plagues and the other vicissitudes of life-before-modern-medicine was another compelling feature of life according to "the Way," as was Christian indifference to ethnicity, race, or civil status.

Of course, Christian doctrine made far more sense than the Mithras cult or the fast-fading cults of the Roman gods.[6] But it was Christian example, including but not limited to the example of the martyrs, that in Stark's judgment brought Christianity to a point of cultural critical mass, from the periphery of Roman society and culture to the center—and thus to the Church's recognition by Constantine.[7]

What does this have to do with the lay vocation "in the world" in twenty-first-century Evangelical Catholicism? Everything. For the greatest tool of evangelism at the disposal of evangelical Catholics, be they single or married, is the humaneness and nobility they embody in the way they conduct their own lives. This mode of life is, of course, necessarily counter-cultural in the twenty-first century. Evangelical Catholics do not live according to the dictates of the imperial autonomous Self: they live in and for the One who calls them to a radical gift of self, not an obsessive asser-tion of Self. Those interested might even find, in the second-century *Letter to Diognetus*, a job description of the lay Catholic of the twenty-first cen-tury, whose basic work of evangelism is one of countercultural example:

> Christians are not distinguished from the rest of humanity by country, language, or custom. For nowhere do they live in cities of their own, nor do they speak some unusual dialect, nor do they practice an ec-centric life-style. . . . But while they live in both Greek and barbarian cities, as each one's lot was cast, and follow the local customs in dress and food and other aspects of life, at the same time they demonstrate the remarkable and admittedly unusual character of their own citizen-ship. They live in their own countries, but only as aliens; they partici-pate in everything as citizens, and endure everything as foreigners. Every foreign country is their fatherland, and every fatherland is for-eign. They marry like everyone else, and have children, but they do not expose their offspring. They share their food but not their wives. They are "in the flesh" but they do not live "according to the flesh." They live on earth but their citizenship is in heaven. They obey the established laws; indeed in their private lives they transcend the laws. . . .

. . . They are poor, yet they make many rich; they are in need of everything, yet they abound in everything. They are dishonored, yet they are glorified in their dishonor; they are slandered, yet they are vindicated. They are cursed, yet they bless; they are insulted, yet they offer respect[;] . . . when they are punished, they rejoice as though brought to life. . . . Those who hate them are unable to give a reason for their hostility.[8]

In the lay vocation as lived by twenty-first-century evangelical Catholics, holiness not only impels to mission; holiness converts. Thus the first missionary responsibility of the lay evangelical Catholic is to be an evangelical Catholic in every facet of life, beginning with the family. At a historical moment of severe family fragmentation throughout the Western world, the example of evangelical Catholic families that share joys and burdens, and do so with wit and grace, is one of the most powerful conversion tools available to the Catholic Church.

So, of course, is the local parish when it lives its evangelical Catholic witness in full: in its worship, in its catechetical programs for the young and for adults, and in its service to the local community. Thus the renewal of parish life is an integral part of the deep reform that is Evangelical Catholicism. The evangelical task is not for renewal movements and new Christian communities only. Every parish in the postmodern Western world lives in mission territory, and every parish sends its people into mission territory from the Sunday or daily Eucharist. Thus every parish is a missionary enterprise.

That is why the liveliest, most prayerful, and most generous Catholic parishes tend to be parishes that take their evangelical responsibilities seriously: parishes that offer thoughtful (not silly) Christian Initiation programs for adults and that bring large numbers of new adult converts into the Church at the Easter Vigil. Dozens of receptions and adult baptisms in a parish do not simply happen; they happen because a critical mass of the parish thinks that its Catholic responsibilities include extending an offer of fellowship to those outside the family of the Church.

Pastors and deacons will of course play a crucial role in the catechesis and spiritual formation of those seeking to enter the Church. But in many, if not most, cases, the original "offer" comes from a lay Catholic, either explicitly or by the example of personal or family life.

The Reform of Catholic Marriage

Marriage is the basis of the family, which is both the fundamental unit of society and, from a Catholic perspective, the *Ecclesia domestica*, the "domestic Church."[9] As the Catholic Church understands it, marriage between two baptized persons is a sacramental reality, a covenant relationship that transcends, even as it includes, the legal-contractual relationship of civil marriage law. Whether viewed sacramentally or legally, however, marriage is under assault throughout the Western world in the first decades of the twenty-first century.

The assault began in the twentieth century with the easing of the cultural, social, and legal barriers to divorce. The net result of that misguided effort was to make a strange new form of polygamy—marriage with multiple partners, although one by one—something approaching a norm in the developed democracies. Intended to ease the burdens of couples caught in failing marriages and to make life less difficult for their children, divorce-virtually-on-demand created disincentives for repairing damaged relationships and made children the hostages of their parents' difficulties even more than before.[10]

The assault on marriage is continuing with the movement to redefine marriage as the union of any two adults, of whatever gender. The damage that this effort has done to the basic self-understanding of the world's democracies will be considered in another chapter. For now, let it be noted that this movement has further reduced marriage to a matter of civil contract, thus continuing to empty the marital bond of its covenantal richness.

In these circumstances, one tremendous challenge to the lay vocation and the lay mission in the twenty-first century will be the redemption of marriage: the reestablishment of the covenant character of this first of human bonds, which was intended to be a source of fruitful love "in the beginning" [Genesis 1.1, 27–28], a beginning that established a pattern for every "present" and for any possible human future.

Meeting this challenge will require a deep reform of the Church's pastoral approach to the sacrament of Matrimony. The issues in this reform are not so much legal as they are theological, evangelical, and pastoral. The practice of Catholic marriage, and of pastoral preparation for marriage, must be deeply reformed so that this great gift of love, which the world treats increasingly as a mere contractual arrangement for mutual convenience, effectively makes present the spousal or nuptial relationship of Christ the Lord to his bride, the Church, in the Evangelical Catholicism of the twenty-first century and beyond. The *Catechism of the Catholic Church* aptly sums up this dimension of Christian marriage in these terms:

> The entire Christian life bears the mark of the spousal love of Christ and the Church. Already Baptism, the entry into the People of God, is a nuptial mystery; it is so to speak the nuptial bath [see Ephesians 5.26–27] which precedes the wedding feast, the Eucharist. Christian marriage in its turn becomes an efficacious sign, the sacrament of the covenant of Christ and the Church. Since it signifies and communicates grace, marriage between baptized persons is a true sacrament of the New Covenant.[11]

The burden of reforming Catholic marriage so that it becomes an integral part of the Evangelical Catholicism of the twenty-first century falls on pastors and married couples alike.

Pastors must recognize that, in many instances, couples come to the local parish to "arrange our wedding" with little or no understanding of what the Church means by "marriage," and how this sacramental concept of a covenant of love differs from what the state means by "marriage." Thus the first step toward the evangelical Catholic reform of marriage practice in the Church will be for pastors and parishes to think of the time-before-the-wedding, the months of marriage preparation, as a crucial catechetical moment. Marriage catechesis must begin with a fundamental catechesis (or recatechesis) of the Creed, focused on the Christian life as friendship with the Lord Jesus through his Church. The Bible is replete with spousal imagery in both the Old Testament, with its witness to God's nuptial relationship to the People of Israel, and the New Testament, which testifies to Christ's nuptial relationship to the Church. These biblical themes and images offer a unique opportunity to reopen the entire Christian kerygma for barely catechized (or even well-catechized) couples in a fresh and compelling way at a crucial moment in their lives. Such marriage-preparation programs, which are best led by teams of priests and married couples, will spend far more time on the Bible and the *Catechism* than they do on the Myers-Briggs Personality Inventory and other diagnostic toys used by many post–Vatican II marriage-preparation programs. Catechesis, not pop psychology, ought to be the paradigm for marriage preparation in the Church.

Bishops' conferences could be helpful in the work of recatechizing the Church on this "most ancient sacrament," as John Paul II called it.[17] To provide a needed resource for an entire local church, the local bishops' conference would mandate a complete course on marriage from an evangelical Catholic perspective and make such a course available on the Internet and in book form. The conference would then strongly suggest, and perhaps even require, that the course, adapted appropriately for each circumstance, be taught in all Catholic high schools, in campus ministries, and in diocesan-sponsored marriage-preparation programs.

The pastor's work in the redemption of marriage amid a toxic cultural environment will necessarily involve a certain exercise of pastoral discipline. If couples who are living together before marriage, or men and women who are not regularly attending Sunday Mass (whatever their domestic arrangements), are married in the parish church in a public liturgy, the Church undercuts its own teaching on the sacramental covenant of marriage and its relationship to the symphony of Catholic truth. Chaste living and a regular participation in the sacramental life of the Church in the months before marriage must therefore be required of any couple seeking to celebrate their wedding in the parish church, in order to safeguard the integrity of the sacrament and to invite couples—who are more likely confused than malicious—into a deeper relationship with Christ the Lord.

Couples who come to the local parish but who do not yet understand what it means to be a disciple and friend of the Lord Jesus cannot grasp what the Church means by "marriage," as distinguished from what the state means by "marriage."[13] That is why Evangelical Catholicism regards the vast confusions over marriage, in both twenty-first-century Western culture and in the minds of many ill-formed Catholics, as a great field of mission: the mission to convert poorly catechized Catholics to a deeper understanding of their discipleship; the mission to redeem marriage in a secular society that is so focused on the contractual relationship that it finds it difficult to imagine the covenantal one and the nobler human lives that living in covenant-relationship makes possible. Meeting the challenge of that vast field of mission requires leadership from bishops and pastors. It also requires the deep commitment of Catholic married couples who live one part of their lay vocation as evangelists of marriage with young people.

Lay Leadership in Business, Politics, and Culture

The teaching of the Second Vatican Council on the "lay apostolate" reflected one of the facets of the renaissance of Catholic life in the mid-twentieth century that preceded and made Vatican II possible: in this instance, the great flowering of Catholic associational life in groups as varied as Young Catholic Workers, the St. Vincent de Paul Society, the Holy Name Society, the Catholic Family Movement, the Catholic Youth Organization, the Association of Catholic Trade Unionists, the Catholic Rural Life Movement, the Legion of Decency, various Catholic student and professional associations, and a variety of Catholic fraternal associations, of which the Knights of Columbus was the largest and most prominent. One of the tragedies of the immediate postconciliar period was that this rich associational matrix quickly withered, and then died, as virtually all Catholic organizational energies were absorbed into newly created or rapidly expanded bishops' conferences, with their various offices aimed at "coordinating" (but in fact taking over) virtually every aspect of Catholic life.

Catholic renewal movements and new Catholic communities filled some of this associational void, and they will continue to do so in the Evangelical Catholicism of the twenty-first century and beyond. The challenge to these movements and communities will be to integrate themselves into the normal pastoral life of the Church without losing their own special charism, yet also without becoming sects within the Church.[14]

Other parts of the associational void were filled by new Catholic organizations, many of them formed as conscious responses to John Paul II's call to the New Evangelization. Legatus, an association of Catholic executives, entrepreneurs, and professionals, is one example of this dynamic in late twentieth- and early twenty-first-century Catholic life. So is the Fellowship of Catholic University Students (FOCUS), which trains and deploys recent Catholic college and university graduates to become missionaries on campuses throughout the United States for several years. St. Thomas More Societies in various dioceses have become venues in which Catholic lawyers and public officials can meet to deepen their understanding of the faith and to consider the evangelization of their own professional fields.

And then there is the Knights of Columbus, which in the twenty-first century has become an international network of Catholic laymen who are robustly and dynamically orthodox and who undertake various charitable and educational activities. The Knights are also a major factor in Catholic philanthropy throughout the world Church.

The Evangelical Catholicism of the twenty-first century will encourage and nurture these organizations, associations, renewal movements, and new Catholic communities. At the same time, Evangelical Catholicism will seek to empower individual Catholic laymen and laywomen to bring the social doctrine of the Church into business, politics, and culture by giving them the intellectual tools necessary to be agents of evangelical reform in those spheres of society.

Catholic social doctrine has been largely a clerical preserve since the time of Pope Leo XIII: the social teaching of the Church has been developed by Catholic professors (some of whom were priests and bishops) and formulated as magisterial teaching by the popes. Yet the social doctrine is clearly intended to inform and embolden lay Catholics, who, unlike the clergy, can actually bring the social doctrine to bear in the political world of legislation and executive decision, in the courts, in business and professional practice, and in the arts and the media. Thus Evangelical Catholicism, in fostering the lay vocation in the world, will nurture and develop cadres of Catholic laymen and laywomen who realize that discipleship is a full-time occupation and who know the social teaching of the Church: well-formed Christians—successful politicians, corporate and small-business executives, jurists and attorneys, entrepreneurs, medical professionals, authors, composers and sculptors, and major media figures—who will not leave their Christianity in the sanctuary (or the Church's social doctrine on a library shelf) but will live the multifaceted truth of Catholic faith in a compelling way as they go into the world.

Evangelical Catholicism will, in that sense, declericalize the social doctrine and its interface with society—even as Evangelical Catholicism redeploys the energies of its episcopal leaders and their coworkers in the public policy arena, as discussed in Chapter Eleven.

The Marian Symphony of Evangelical Mission

If, as John Paul II taught in introducing the *Catechism of the Catholic Church*, there is a "symphony of truth" in which various instruments form a harmonious doctrinal and catechetical whole, then there ought to be a "symphony of mission" in the Church as well: a harmonious blending of gifts and talents in a concerted, mutually supporting, dynamic response to the Great Commission.

Lay Catholics do not need anyone's permission to be the evangelical witnesses they were called to be: to be an evangelist is a baptismal obligation, not a privilege conceded by ecclesiastical authority. Still, the evangelical Catholic laity will welcome the sacramental, homiletic, and catechetical support of their pastors, and will undertake their unique forms of mission in obedience to appropriate guidance from those to whom the Lord has given the role of shepherds. Those in Holy Orders, in turn, ought not regard lay activism in the vast and varied fields of the apostolate as either a threat to their authority or an encroachment on their prerogatives.

In the early Church, "mission" and "missionary" typically connoted the Twelve as well as those other first disciples who went from Galilee *ad gentes*, "to the nations." Yet there is a sense in which Mary, Mother of God and Mother of the Church, is the first Christian "in mission." Mary's articulated *fiat* ("Let it be to me according to your word" [Luke 1.38]) was the essential human response in faith to the divine initiative in the Incarnation—and through that *fiat*, Mary became the first of disciples. The deepest contours of her discipleship became evident in the silent *fiat* at the foot of the Cross, captured by Michelangelo in the *Pietà*: discipleship is always a matter of submission to the divine will, however incomprehensible it may be at the moment.

In her articulated *fiat* and constant pointing beyond herself to her Son ("Do whatever he tells you" [John 2.5]), as well as in her silent *fiat*, Mary sets the pattern for all subsequent Christian discipleship: discipleship begins in acts of obedience to God's will that always lead to God's Son—and through him, into the very Trinity itself. Evangelical Catholicism understands that this basic pattern of discipleship is common to lay Christians and those in Holy Orders. Indeed, as John Paul II pointed out to the Roman Curia in his 1987 Christmas address to his clerical collaborators, the powers of office and jurisdiction in the Church exist solely to foster the discipleship of all the members of the Body of Christ: the powers conferred by Holy Orders have no other purpose "except to form the Church in line with the ideal of sanctity already programmed and prefigured in Mary," the first of disciples, and thus the first Christian "in mission."[15]

In this Marian symphony of evangelical mission, there is more than enough work to do for everyone. All who recognize that will welcome the gifts of others and see those gifts as complements to their own.

CHAPTER TEN

The Evangelical Catholic
Reform of the Church's
Intellectual Life

IN THE POST-CHRISTIAN WEST OF THE THIRD MILLENNIUM, THE CHURCH of the New Evangelization must proclaim the Gospel to educated men and women trapped in the slough of spiritual boredom, frightened by Christophobia, or both. And although the humaneness, dignity, and compassion displayed by evangelical Catholic communities will likely be the strongest magnet in attracting the curious, the interested, and the despairing to consider the possibility of faith in God and friendship with the Lord Jesus, Evangelical Catholicism must be prepared to engage minds as well as hearts. That is why the reform of theology—the intellectual science of the faith—must be an integral part of the deep reform of the Church. Good theology is essential to effective evangelization and solid catechetics, whether those to be catechized are children, adolescents, or adults.

Theology is composed of many subdisciplines. Fundamental theology explores the conditions for the possibility of belief; systematic theology explicates the teachings of the Creed and pushes out the frontiers of Catholic self-understanding; moral theology explains the Church's answer to the question of how we may live virtuously and happily. A special division of moral theology, Catholic social doctrine, explores the ways in which a Catholic view of the human person and human communities can inform the quest to build free societies on solid cultural foundations. All these theological disciplines are shaped by the Church's study of the Bible and by theology's dialogue with philosophy.

The Church's intellectual and cultural life involves more than theology, of course. But the best of Christian art, architecture, sculpture, literature, and music has always been theologically informed: think of Dante, Michelangelo, and Palestrina, among the giants of any age, or the theologically acute novels of Evelyn Waugh or Graham Greene, in modern English literature. This kind of culture-shaping theology has always had the Church as its principal referent: it is theology done from the Church and for the Church—and sometimes in challenge to the Church. Theology, then, is not another academic discipline; it is not "religious studies"; and it is certainly not a matter of games-intellectuals-play. Theology is an ecclesial activity, and in the Evangelical Catholicism of the future, theologians will understand their vocations in explicitly ecclesial, and explicitly evangelical, terms. As Father Thomas Weinandy has put it, the theologians' vocation "compels them to evangelize in every situation and to every audience. To evangelize is not beneath the dignity of theologians; it is to their honor that they are divinely called to do so."[1]

When that ecclesial and evangelical mission is embraced and lived by Catholic theologians, the Evangelical Catholicism of the future will know that another step has been taken toward the deep reform of the Church. Unfortunately, the tether between theologians and the Church, between Catholic intellectual life and Catholic mission, became seriously strained, sometimes to the point of rupture, in the decades after Vatican II. The strains were typically described as issues of an "authoritarian" Church uncomfortable with "academic freedom." In fact, the strains arose because of serious intellectual difficulties within theology itself.

Theology in Distress

In his 2009 presidential address to the Catholic Theological Society of America (CTSA), Dr. Terrence Tilley, a layman and chair of the theology department at New York's Fordham University, questioned whether the Christology of the Council of Chalcedon, which had been regarded as the baseline of orthodoxy since A.D. 451, had in fact set the normative framework for understanding the relationship of divinity and humanity in the one person of Christ—a proposal that would have been regarded as simply bizarre at the founding of the CTSA in 1946.[2] Over the course of six decades, something had clearly happened at the higher altitudes of Catholic intellectual life, in the United States and elsewhere.

What happened poses serious obstacles to the deep reform of the Church.

The problem is not theological controversy, per se. Theological controversy has been a part of Christian life since the earliest days of the Church, when Paul rebuked Peter "to his face" [Galatians 2.11]. Theological controversy and debate among knowledgeable theologians can be a source of real insight into the symphony of Catholic truth; theological debate is an essential part of what the Church calls the "development of doctrine." Serious problems do occur, however, when theological controversy is conducted without stable reference points in Scripture and apostolic tradition—and when new reference points are found in the conventions of the postmodern academy. When that happens, as it did in the decades since Vatican II, theology gets unmoored from the doctrinal foundations of the Church; speculation becomes dissent and filters throughout the Catholic community (ideas always having consequences); and the evangelical witness of the Church is weakened: for who can preach and bear witness to a series of question marks?

Thus one of the striking features of Catholic life in the first four decades after the Second Vatican Council was the transformation of post-conciliar Catholic theology from a discipline that understood itself to be at the service of the Church and its mission, to a discipline that sought, above all, the approbation of the university-based academic guilds of late modernity and postmodernity. This was a dramatic shift and it took place with striking rapidity. The immediate preconciliar renewal of Catholic theology that made Vatican II possible was self-consciously at the service of the Church and its mission: thus the linkages already noted, in discussing the sacred liturgy, between the kerygmatic theology of the 1930s and 1940s and the Liturgical Movement, on the one hand, and the Catholic social justice movement, on the other. Yet within a decade and a half after the Council concluded, Father David Tracy, a brilliant American theologian highly attuned to the guild atmospherics at the University of Chicago, where he taught, was arguing that theology had three "publics"—society, the academy, and the Church.[3] Soon enough, the generation of theologians that followed Tracy came to think and act as if it were the second public, the academy, that really counted, and that the Church, and especially its teaching authority, had no role in theology.

The proponents of this change sometimes compared the postconciliar transformation of Catholic theology, through its embrace of many of the shibboleths of late modern and postmodern intellectual life, to Thomas Aquinas's embrace of the philosophy of Aristotle in the thirteenth century, which had been controversial at the time. What Aquinas had done with Aristotle, it was claimed, Catholic theologians of the late twentieth and early twenty-first centuries would do with Karl Marx, or with the postmodern philosophers and literary critics. The difficulty with this suggestion is not hard to grasp: put most simply, Aristotle was right about many things, and Marx and the postmoderns were wrong. As Marxist and postmodernist thought shaped the reflection of theologians, they did not provide new materials from which a nobler and more evangelically compelling theological edifice could be constructed; they became solvents eating away at the substance of Catholic faith.

Thus the notion of a Catholic symphony of truth (or indeed any "symphonic" or coherent understanding of truth) got lost in the postconciliar Catholic academy in the Western world. Deconstruction, not harmonization, was the new methodological passion, and deconstruction inevitably led to a flagging of evangelical energies. For if there is no such thing as "the truth," but only "your truth," and "my truth," why evangelize? Why witness? Didn't such evangelizing suggest an imposition of sectarian views, even a manipulation of psyches and consciences?

The inherent implausibility of a Catholic theology that had lost its tether to truth and mission (and indeed regarded both "truth" and "mission" as impossibly old-fashioned notions) led, within two generations, to a revolt—or at least to the beginnings of a course correction. The pontificates of John Paul II and Benedict XVI, which developed the Church's teaching by putting Scripture and tradition into conversation with the best of modern thought, attracted younger scholars. And this third postconciliar generation, having discovered that there was something compelling about the idea of a symphony of truth, found the deconstructive and dissenting tendencies of their elders uninteresting, even boring. Engaging the thought of some of the great figures of the mid-twentieth-century Catholic intellectual renaissance, such as Henri de Lubac, S. J., and Hans Urs von Balthasar, while reengaging the patristic and medieval classics of Catholic thought, they began to craft a fresh approach to doing theology in a post–Vatican II Church. The distinctiveness of that approach was neatly summarized in the name of one of this generation's principal international theological journals: *Nova et Vetera* [New and Old].[4]

Although the third generation of post–Vatican II Catholic theologians was moving in a markedly different direction, eagerly exploring the fullness of Catholic faith and seeking ways to put those explorations at the service of the Church's evangelical mission, the damage that had been done to the Church's intellectual and cultural life by the first two generations remained. Deconstructive theology may have lost its intellectual momentum, but through that reactionary institution known as the academic tenure system, it continued to shape (and misshape) the life of many Catholic institutions of higher learning throughout the world, even as it weakened catechetics, disempowered evangelism, distorted interreligious dialogue, and reduced ecumenical theological conversation to a zero-sum game analogous to labor negotiations.

Gnosticism and Sacramentality, Again

Catholics concerned about the ongoing and sometimes scandalous effects of theological deconstruction and dissent on the intellectual life of their colleges and universities could point to any number of problems that occurred within months of each other in 2011.

In May, Georgetown University, the first Catholic institution of higher education in America, held a "Lavender Graduation" that was attended by the university's president and chaplain; the speaker at this "commencement" was U.S. Representative David Cicilline, a promoter of "gay marriage" and "full reproductive freedom," including abortion on demand.[5] That same month, Seattle University's director of campus ministry, Father Mike Bayard, S.J., defended an on-campus drag show: "My understanding of a drag show is that it's men dressing up as women; now what is wrong with that? . . . To be Catholic at Seattle University means to be totally inclusive."[6] In June, the Catholic Theological Society of America voted 147–1 to reject the cautions raised by the U.S. Bishops Committee on Doctrine about the theology of God proposed by Fordham University's Elizabeth Johnson, C.S.J., in her book *The Quest for the Living God.*[7] In September, Fordham hosted a "Sexual Diversity" conference that was noteworthy for the lack of any serious attention to, much less explication of, Catholic sexual ethics; during the conference, a New York priest advised a young gay man to lie to the archdiocesan vocation director about his sexual desires, because the "system" of the Catholic Church was broken.[8] In October, Loyola University of Chicago's office of Student Diversity and Multicultural Affairs posted on its Web site an invitation to the school's "Advocate Annual Drag Show," which had begun three years earlier, in 2008, under the sponsorship of the university's "Official GLBTQ Organization."[9] And throughout the year, the University of Notre Dame's board chairman, Richard Notebaert, refused to concede that support of proabortion organizations was incompatible with service on the governing body of that institution.[10]

These examples could be multiplied dozens of times over. What is striking about them, from a historical point of view, is that many such aberrations in Catholic intellectual life—and especially those that reject the Church's sexual ethic—reflect the contemporary revival of the oldest of Christianity's intellectual opponents: the protean heresy of Gnosticism, whose role in shaping the culture with which Evangelical Catholicism must contend has already been noted.

Gnosticism has come in many guises, from the Manichaeism that once seduced the great Augustine of Hippo to the medieval weirdness of the Albigensians and the Cathari. Its twenty-first-century forms share key characteristics with these ancient models: a radical denial of the *givenness* of things, including the physical givenness of the human condition; a deprecation of the material world; and an exaltation of esoteric knowledge that lifts the initiate out of the grittiness of the world. In the twentieth and twenty-first centuries, the Gnostic heresy has become exceedingly clever, cloaking its deprecation of the material world in what appears, on the surface, to be a deep-seated materialism. The most prominent example of this expression of the New Gnosticism is, of course, the sexual revolution, which sexualizes everything while concurrently insisting that maleness and femaleness are social constructs—not givens that reveal deep truths about the human condition, both in themselves and in their complementarity. What it claims to exalt, the Gnostic sexual revolution in fact demeans.

From the point of view of Christian orthodoxy, the chief theological problems with Gnosticism are that it denies the goodness of Creation and empties the Incarnation of its transformative power. Gnosticism is resolutely anti-incarnational; Evangelical Catholicism, like all Christian orthodoxy, is determinedly, even doggedly, incarnational. For, as the Creed affirms, God fully entered history in the person of his Son, the second person of the Holy Trinity, so that we might be redeemed and sanctified *in* our humanity, not fetched out of it by some sort of Gnostic insight. And God does that because, in the beginning, God found the world he created to be good, even very good [Genesis 1.31]. Thus what is effected in the redemption, St. Paul taught, is the restoration of the entire cosmos to the path on which God had originally set it—the path toward the light and love of the Trinity itself [cf. Colossians 1.13–29; Ephesians 1.3–10; Philippians 2.9–11].

The Catholic sacramental system, as noted previously, is a sevenfold rejection of Gnosticism. Water and oil are the tangibles by which the saving grace of the sacrament of Baptism is conferred. Bread and wine are the materials through which the Lord Jesus gives himself, body and blood, to his people in the sacrament of the Holy Eucharist. In the sacrament of Matrimony, the consummation of marital love completes and ratifies the vows made at a couple's wedding. In the sacrament of the Anointing of the Sick, holy oils confer spiritual, and sometimes physical, healing, and oil is an integral material in the sacrament of Holy Orders. The words of absolution and acts of contrition and penance are the materials by which the forgiveness of sins takes place in the sacrament of Penance. None of this is magic; none of it is witchcraft. Because the world was sacramentally configured "in the beginning" [Genesis 1.1]—because the materials of Creation are the materials through which we perceive the extraordinary that lies just beyond the ordinary—what the world calls the "real world" is in fact a window into the world of Trinitarian love, which infuses it. God uses the ordinary material of the world to bring us into communion with the extraordinary: with God himself, in the Trinitarian life of superabundant grace.

Too much of Catholic intellectual life has lost its grounding in the sacramental imagination since Vatican II and is thus ill-equipped to challenge (much less convert) the ambient public culture, saturated as it is with Gnosticism. This sacramental imagination is one of the tethers to the Church that the theologians of the Church must recover if their work is to support the Catholic mission to evangelize (or re-evangelize) the Western world of the twenty-first century.

Interestingly enough, some of the materials for such a "resacramentalizing" of Catholic intellectual life are ready to hand in John Paul II's Theology of the Body, written in response to the Gnosticism of the late twentieth-century sexual revolution and what was supposed to be the Catholic Church's inability to mount any sort of effective response to it.

This striking reimagining of the Catholic sexual ethic through a deep reading of Scripture and a profound meditation on the fact that "male and female he created them" [Genesis 1.27] is more than that, however. By taking Creation and Incarnation with utmost seriousness, John Paul II laid down a challenge to the entire world of Catholic theology: to look afresh at God, Christ, the Holy Trinity, grace, the Church, prayer, the sacraments, and the Church's worship through the prism of the rich personalism that undergirds and informs the Theology of the Body.

If they accept that challenge, the theologians of Evangelical Catholicism will rediscover the truth that Christ the Lord—in his Incarnation and in the redemption he wrought by his passion, death, and resurrection—is the final measure of all our knowledge: "For in him the whole fullness of deity dwells bodily, and you have come to fullness of life in him, who is the head of all rule and authority" [Colossians 2.9–10].

The Evangelical Catholic University

The evangelical Catholic college or university of the twenty-first century will measure itself and its aspiration by criteria other than those typically found in Western institutions of higher learning. This emphatically does not mean a slackening of commitment to intellectual excellence. But it does mean locating intellectual excellence within the mission of the Church, which is the sanctification of the People of God and the conversion of the world. For as Pope Benedict XVI said to the leaders of Catholic higher education in the United States in April 2008, "fostering personal intimacy with Jesus Christ and communal witness to his loving truth is indispensable to Catholic institutions of learning." It might seem an obvious thing to say, even a truism. But that has not been the self-understanding of many Catholic colleges and universities since Vatican II, and it must become so again if these institutions are to participate in the deep reform of the Church that is measured by the twin criteria of truth and mission.

Or, to put the matter bluntly: Catholic universities that sponsor productions of the *Vagina Monologues* and whose student-life offices encourage LGBTQ clubs, but which do not require their students to take courses in Augustine and Aquinas, or to read and absorb such key documents of Vatican II as its Dogmatic Constitutions on the Church (*Lumen Gentium*) and on Divine Revelation (*Dei Verbum*), have not begun to grasp the unique nature and mission of a Catholic institution of higher education.

In that same 2008 address at the Catholic University of America, Benedict XVI located the Catholic college or university firmly within the evangelical mission of the Church:

> All the Church's activities stem from her awareness that she is the bearer of a message that has its origin in God himself; in his goodness and wisdom, God chose to reveal himself and to make known the hidden purpose of his will. God's desire to make himself known, and the intimate desire of all human beings to know the truth, provide the context for human inquiry into the meaning of life. This unique encounter is sustained within our Christian community: the one who seeks the truth becomes the one who lives by faith. It can be described as a move from "I" to "we," leading the individual to be numbered among God's people.[11]

Catholic higher education, in other words, must reject the postmodern subjectivism that speaks only of "your truth" and "my truth," confident in the conviction that every genuine search for truth eventually leads to *the* Truth who is God the Holy Trinity. Human inquiry is thus not drudgery; it is an exercise of love, for the deeper penetration of the truth leads us deeper into the divine mystery of love. The evangelical Catholic searches for truth in Catholic institutions of higher learning knowing that the Truth has been given to us, in Christ, even before we begin our inquiry into the many truths of the world. In this way, Catholic higher education can help lead postmodern culture out of the sandbox of subjectivism and into the adult world of genuine inquiry and learning.

Evangelical Catholic higher education in the twenty-first century can also help the Western world retain its cultural memory, which is in danger of being lost under the pressures of "relevance" and an overwrought worry about developing marketable skills. Those skills are important; but what is even more important (as the economic disasters of the early twenty-first century should have reminded the world) is the character of the people who deploy those skills in the world of work. And the West has devised no better way of forming the character of the young than by immersing young men and women in the classics of Western civilization, so that their lives become a practice of the ecumenism of time—and their journey through life is enriched by having, as partners along the way, Homer and Plato and Aristotle and Virgil; Augustine and Aquinas; Dante, Milton, Shakespeare, and Cervantes; and those moderns who were themselves steeped in the classic liberal learning of the West. The curriculum of evangelical Catholic colleges and universities will thus lay heavy (and required) stress on an encounter with the classics, including that classic of biblical religion, the Bible.

Curriculum, though, will not be the only distinctive marker of an evangelical Catholic college or university in the twenty-first century and beyond. Mode of life on campus; regular availability of the sacraments; an active, catechetically engaged campus ministry; and ample opportunities to serve society will distinguish the Catholic institution of higher learning from the debaucheries limned (and not exaggerated) by novelist Tom Wolfe in *I Am Charlotte Simmons*.[12] Evangelical Catholic colleges and universities will sponsor study-abroad programs specifically aimed at deepening their students' appreciation of Catholic culture, especially the Christian culture of Europe, site of the Gospel's first inculturation. Similarly, the evangelical Catholic campus will itself bear witness, especially in its chapel, to the truth stressed by Hans Urs von Balthasar and Benedict XVI: that beauty is a privileged path to faith in the postmodern world and a means of opening up deeper reflections on the true and the good—and, ultimately, on the glory of the Lord.

Making Distinctions

In the United States, the evangelical Catholic reform of Catholic higher education has been making considerable progress in the first decades of the twenty-first century through a variety of models: the Great Books approach of Thomas Aquinas College in Santa Paula, California, and the Great Books Plus approach of the University of Dallas are two principal examples. Variations on those models could be found in schools as diversely located as Christendom College in Front Royal, Virginia, and Benedictine College in Atchison, Kansas. An alternative approach to the evangelical revitalization of Catholic higher learning could be found in the development of Catholic Studies programs on large Catholic campuses, of which the pacesetter was the Catholic Studies Program at the University of St. Thomas in St. Paul, Minnesota. All these institutions and programs self-consciously sought to "think with the Church," even as several of them made academic demands on their students as rigorous as any to be found in American higher education.

Some Catholic universities that had effectively divorced themselves from the Church in the aftermath of Vatican II have struggled, with some success, to recover a more robust Catholic identity. Thus ongoing battles over what "Catholic identity" required, and what it would lead a school to reject, were regularly visible at what was, emotionally at least, the flagship Catholic institution of higher learning in America, the University of Notre Dame. These battles have not infrequently involved defining a university's relationship to the local bishop; as one prominent bishop put it to a Catholic university in the last years of the twentieth century, "You say you're a part of the local Church; I'm the bishop of this local Church; where do *I* fit into *you*?" Wise bishops have no interest in micromanaging the affairs of complex educational institutions with their own unique histories and missions. At the same time, responsible bishops know that the exercise of their ministry of vigilance over the symphony of Catholic truth in their dioceses sometimes requires truth-telling with university presidents and boards of directors—publicly, if necessary.

In the Evangelical Catholicism of the twenty-first century and beyond, however, the full exercise of the bishop's stewardship of the truths
of the faith and the identity of the Catholic institutions in his diocese will
likely require something more: at times, the determination by the bishop
that an institution has forfeited any meaningful claim to the name
"Catholic," and a public statement of that sad fact. For if it was true, in
the early decades of the twenty-first century, that there had been some
recovery of Catholic identity on some campuses, and a welcome number
of new initiatives in Catholic higher education in response to the meltdown of the postconciliar period, it was also true that some institutions
seemed irretrievably lost, and had in fact become obstacles to the New
Evangelization in the dioceses where they were located.

Seattle University, a Jesuit institution, provided one sharp example.
In a 1999 meeting with the editorial board of the *Seattle Times*, the university's president, Father Stephen Sundborg, S.J., noted that his student
body was only 40 percent Catholic. When asked how he intended to
market the university to new students, Sundborg replied that, as some
radio stations advertised themselves as "Country Lite," his school was
taking an approach to Catholic higher education that might be called
"Catholic Lite."[13]

Sundborg's Jesuit colleague, Father Ryan Maher, S.J., associate dean
and director of Catholic Studies at Georgetown, went even further some
years later, while discussing his university's mission: "Our job as educators and as priests is not to bring God to people, or even to bring people
to God. God's already there and the people are already there. Our job,
our way of living out our educational vocation, is to ask the right questions, and to help young people ask those questions."

It may be safely assumed that this kind of vacuity is not what John
Paul II had in mind in his apostolic letter *Ex Corde Ecclesiae* [From the
Heart of the Church], when he penned this summary description of
the unique mission of a Catholic institution of higher learning: "By
means of a kind of universal humanism, a Catholic university is completely dedicated to the research of all aspects of truth in their essential

connection with the supreme Truth, who is God."[14] And it is certainly not what Archbishop John Carroll, founder of Georgetown, and the Jesuit founders of Seattle University had in mind. It might even be suggested that this is not what alumni, alumnae, and major donors have in mind when they support Catholic higher education, or what serious Catholic parents have in mind when they entrust their children to Catholic colleges and universities.

What, then, is the local bishop to do when it becomes clear that a Catholic college or university has lost its Catholic identity and that that institution's structures of governance make it virtually impossible to recover that identity in faculty-hiring practices, curriculum, and manner of life on campus? If the determination is made that this is in fact the sad state of affairs, then a bishop who takes seriously his responsibilities as the guardian of Catholic identity in his diocese will state publicly that the institution in question can no longer be considered a Catholic institution, and ought not to market itself as such to prospective students, prospective faculty, or prospective donors. This is not, it must be stressed, a matter of retribution; it is a matter of honesty and a matter of self-respect.[15] Evangelical Catholicism will not be the vibrant missionary movement it must be if its self-understanding is so weak, and its hold on the truth of its own identity so attenuated, that it cannot, in a calm and reasonable way, determine that an institution has so thoroughly lost its Catholic identity that it is unlikely to be recovered.

Both criteria of deep Catholic reform, the criterion of truth and the criterion of mission, demand that these distinctions be made when necessary.

CHAPTER ELEVEN

The Evangelical Catholic Reform of the Church's Public Policy Advocacy

T HE WITNESS OF EVANGELICAL CATHOLICISM IN PUBLIC LIFE IS DISTINCTIVE, both conceptually and operationally. It flows from discipleship as well as citizenship. It reflects the social doctrine of the Catholic Church, a rich tradition of thinking about public affairs that, in its papal form, traces its lineage to Pope Leo XIII. Like every other aspect of Catholic life, public policy advocacy in the Evangelical Catholicism of the future must be a deeply reformed witness issuing from a deeply reformed Church. Elements of this facet of deep Catholic reform were evident in the pontificates of both John Paul II and Benedict XVI.

John Paul II embodied Catholic social doctrine's capacity to bend history in a more humane direction through his pivotal role in the collapse of European communism. John Paul also pointed the Church's social doctrine firmly into the twenty-first century with his great 1991 social encyclical, *Centesimus Annus*. There, in an encyclical inspired by and named for the centenary of Leo's XIII's *Rerum Novarum*. he brilliantly analyzed the dynamics of the threefold free and virtuous society, which is composed of a democratic political community, a free economy, and a vibrant public moral culture, while teaching that the moral health of a culture is the key to living freedom nobly.[1]

Benedict XVI's contributions to the Church's public witness received less public notice, but were substantial, nonetheless. The discussion of "human ecology" in his third encyclical, *Caritas in Veritate*, brought the line of development that runs from Vatican II through the social magisterium of John Paul II to a sharp point of refinement. Thus Benedict XVI firmly cemented the life issues into the thinking of the Catholic Church as social justice issues, making clear that there are not, and cannot be, "social justice Catholics" *here* and "life issues Catholics" *there*.[2] Moreover, the discussion of "human ecology" in *Caritas in Veritate* underscored, even as it developed, John Paul II's teaching in *Centesimus Annus* on the moral truths that must be embedded in individuals, business enterprises, and law if the free economy is to function properly: hence the encyclical's title, which translates as "Charity in Truth." Further, Benedict XVI repeatedly pointed out the threats to religious freedom that are painfully apparent in twenty-first-century democratic societies, reminding the world that efforts to restrict religious freedom to the private practice of religion are a threat to the entire structure of human rights.[3] During his apostolic pilgrimages in the Western world, Benedict XVI also taught, with patience but also urgency, that nihilism, skepticism, and moral relativism erode the very foundations of the democratic project.[4]

Despite these achievements, however, much of the public policy advocacy of the Catholic Church—from the Holy See's commentary on world politics through the activities of the continental and national bishops' conferences to the work of many state Catholic conferences in the United States—is stuck in an older paradigm drawn from the days when the Church was a political actor in the old-fashioned sense: a player-among-players in a political power game. That older paradigm harkens back to the days when the Supreme Pontiff of the Universal Church was also the head of state of a minor European power, the Papal States. This way of thinking about the Church's public witness continued long after the demise of the Papal States in 1870; and traces of it can be found in the public policy advocacy of transnational, national, and local bishops' conferences in the early twenty-first century, as well as in the

Vatican's public policy commentary and diplomacy. In the Evangelical Catholicism of the future, a new paradigm of the Church's public policy engagement—more expressive of the post–Vatican II development of Catholic social doctrine, more congruent with the basic evangelical mission of the Church, more in harmony with the Second Vatican Council's teaching on the vocation of the laity in the world, and more attuned to the twenty-first-century realities of public life in the democracies—must take root.

In what follows, the shift that was underway in the second decade of the new century in the public policy advocacy of the United States Conference of Catholic Bishops—itself often a model for other bishops' conferences throughout the world—serves as an illustration of the kind of deep reform required throughout the world Church.

The Fundamental Life Issues

In *Evangelium Vitae*, his 1995 encyclical on "The Gospel of Life," and the life issues then pressing hard on all postmodern societies, Blessed John Paul II analyzed the effects of legalized abortion and euthanasia on democracies, teaching in perhaps the strongest language of his papal magisterium that democracies that erect clear moral wrongs into "rights" risk becoming "tyrant states."[5] In the 2009 encyclical *Caritas in Veritate*, Benedict XVI extended this analysis by teaching that the "human ecology" necessary to sustain decent, self-governing societies under the rule of law was being deeply damaged by an attitude toward life that measured human persons by their utility rather than their dignity. Embodied in law, that attitude risked destroying the human ecosystem by shredding the moral fabric of society, Benedict taught.[6] Thus, at this point in the history of the Catholic Church's engagement with public policy, there should be no question that the life issues are not only genuine social justice issues; the life issues are *priority* social justice issues. They touch the moral bedrock of the Church's social doctrine as an expression of the Gospel. And they engage the most fundamental issue being contested in the Western world of the early twenty-first century—the defense of the dignity of the human person, which is under assault from various utilitarian notions of human worth.

The bishops of the United States recognized this in their 1998 national pastoral letter, *Living the Gospel of Life*, which replaced the metaphor of the "consistent ethic of life" with the image of "the foundations of the house of freedom" as the U.S. Catholic paradigm for thinking about the life issues in relation to the many other questions of public policy. Every house needs a firm foundation, the Lord Jesus teaches in the Gospel [cf. Matthew 7.24]. The U.S. bishops taught in 1998, and have been teaching ever since, that the house of freedom that is the United States of America, and every other free society, must be built on the firm foundation of a respect for life that is embodied in both culture and law. The life issues are thus priority social justice issues theologically and in terms of both moral reason and democratic political theory.

Evangelical Catholic public policy advocacy must recognize that the life issues are *the* civil rights issues of the early twenty-first century. In defending the right to life from conception until natural death, in building a culture of life, and in helping design a legal architecture by which human life is legally protected at all stages and in all conditions, Evangelical Catholicism is heir to the U.S. civil rights movement in its classic phase, to the campaign against apartheid in South Africa, and to the witness of those human rights advocates who cracked the seemingly impermeable walls by which communism controlled entire societies. A deeply reformed Catholic public policy advocacy will put the life issues in precisely those terms: the defense of the right to life is a matter of the first principles of justice that can be known by reason. Anyone who claims that this is an example of Catholic sectarianism being "imposed" on a pluralistic society—and especially Catholic politicians and public officials who make that spurious claim—should be told politely, firmly, publicly, and relentlessly that they are wrong, and that their errors reflect ignorance, malice, or both. This is not partisanship. It is charitable correction, spoken in truth, for the sake of the common good.

Challenging the Totalitarian Temptation

Late twentieth-century political theorists across the ideological spectrum, including such major figures as Hannah Arendt and Leszek Kołakowski, were agreed on one crucial point: the essence of the two totalitarian systems that made a slaughterhouse of the mid-twentieth century was their attempt to remake human nature and accelerate humanity's march toward an ultramundane and hypersecular utopia through the ruthless deployment of coercive state power.[7] German National Socialism defended its brutalities and its utopian vision by crackpot racial theories; Marxism-Leninism did so by crackpot economic and historical theories. The totalitarian link between these two wicked systems is that both were determined to create worldly utopias by remaking human nature as theory required and to use the coercive power of the state to effect that remanufacture.

This temptation seems to be built into modern politics. The temptation, and the results of succumbing to it, were initially displayed in the first of the modern utopian political revolutions, the French Revolution. Various political monsters have followed in the wake of Robespierre: Lenin, Dzerzhinsky, and Stalin; Hitler, Himmler, and Heydrich; Mao Zedong, Ho Chi Minh, and Pol Pot. Contemplating that parade of ghouls, Americans and others who never experienced a totalitarian regime recoil in horror, all the while taking comfort from the conviction that "it couldn't happen here."

It is illusory, however, to imagine that the democracies of the West are immune to the totalitarian temptation to remake human nature by coercive state power. That dynamic is evident throughout the Western civilizational orbit in the first decades of the twenty-first century. It is evident in the attacks on biblical morality and moral reason that are a regular feature of the European Parliament and other bodies of the European Union. It is evident when the Star Chambers known in Canada as "human rights commissions" or "human rights tribunals" lay severe monetary penalties on evangelical Protestant pastors who dare to teach the biblical understanding of marriage. And it has become unmistakably evident in the debate over the state and marriage, for the "gay marriage" insurgency is nothing less than an effort to redefine human nature through the use of state power, coercively if necessary.

What is at stake in this and related arguments is nothing less than democracy itself, meaning limited constitutional governance based on the truth that the state is at the service of civil society. The current effort to define marriage as something it manifestly is not, and cannot be, is an attempt to remake human nature by means of law and to enforce that remanufacture by coercive state power. In adopting "gay marriage" statutes, the state is attempting something beyond its competence and is thereby doing grave damage to the civil society that the state is intended to serve. For if the state can redefine marriage and enforce that redefinition, it can do so with the doctor-patient relationship, the lawyer-client relationship, the parent-child relationship, the confessor-penitent relationship, and virtually every other relationship that is woven into the texture of civil society.[8] Any state that attempts to redefine these basic civil-society relationships, such that they become mere extensions of the state rather than forms of association that a just state must acknowledge and protect, undermines the social and cultural foundations of democracy, harms individuals (often the most vulnerable), and, in the case of redefining marriage, reduces to farce what it attempts to substitute for reality.[9] In doing so, the state also indulges and enforces what Pope Benedict XVI has aptly termed the "dictatorship of relativism."

Evangelical Catholic public policy advocacy must name this soft totalitarianism for what it is.

Catholic public officials who cannot be persuaded to recognize this form of the totalitarian temptation for what it is—and, even worse, Catholic public officials who seek to promote soft totalitarianism's coercive reach—should be informed by their bishops that they are in a defective state of communion with the Catholic Church, and further instructed in what an honest recognition of that fact requires from them. Bishops who do their evangelical duty in this respect must be given the full and unstinting support of those who work in their name in the fields of public policy.

That support is deficient when Catholic public policy advocates, licking their wounds after defeat on a basic question like the definition of marriage, assert that there are nevertheless other issues on which the Church can work happily with public authorities who have just indulged the totalitarian temptation. When politicians turn their backs on the first principles of justice, they must be made to understand that there are costs involved. When Catholic public witness fails to persuade on these fundamental questions, evangelical Catholics must understand that those failures are not compensated for by modest victories on other fronts.

A Necessary, Self-Denying Ordinance

In *Centesimus Annus*, Blessed John Paul II taught that the Church's "contribution to the political order is . . . her vision of the dignity of the person, revealed in all its fullness in the mystery of the Incarnate Word." Because of the distinctive nature of what the Church brings to the public square, the Church has no economic or political "models to present"; rather, the Church offers her social doctrine as "an indispensable and ideal orientation."[10] In two earlier encyclicals—one on "The Church's Social Concern" (*Sollicitudo Rei Socialis,* published in 1987), and the other on the evangelical imperative as an extension of "The Mission of the Redeemer" (*Redemptoris Missio,* signed in 1990)—John Paul similarly taught that the Church has no "technical solutions" to offer in the field of public policy.[11]

This modesty about the public policy competence of the Church *as Church* reflects basic doctrinal convictions about the nature of the Church. It also flows from an appreciation of what the Church uniquely knows about public life and what the Church uniquely brings to the public policy process.

As for what the Church knows, by virtue of her work among the poor and vulnerable and her intimate knowledge of the social realities of contemporary life (a knowledge that is arguably deeper and more extensive than that of many other civil society institutions), the Catholic Church knows, in a distinctive way, what is working, and what isn't, in cultures, economies, societies, and polities. Because of this grassroots-based knowledge, the Church is well qualified to ring the alarm bell, to identify what is wrong and what must be fixed, and to challenge the consciences of both citizens and political leaders to address real problems. That, for example, is how the Church helped shape the American civil rights revolution in its classic period.

What the Church brings to the public policy process is a clear understanding of the "first things" of public life in a free and virtuous society—"first things" that are mediated into the public policy process through the four core principles of Catholic social doctrine: personalism, the common good, subsidiarity, and solidarity.[12] This is what Vatican II, John Paul II, and Benedict XVI meant when they taught that the Church's social doctrine offers a principled framework for thinking through the requisites of the free and virtuous society, and that the Church does not have the competence *as Church* to offer "technical solutions" to those who have responsibility for the common good.

This sense of the limits of the Church's competence in advocating specific policies, solutions, and programs in the public square has not, to put it gently, been fully embraced by continental, national, or state episcopal conferences and their public policy agencies.[13] As these bodies have evolved since the Second Vatican Council, they have tended to take on the coloration of the surrounding political foliage: that is, they have often functioned on the model of other all-purpose public policy lobbies.

The self-imposed discipline evident in the magisterium's teaching that it is simply not within the Church's competence *as Church* to get down into the weeds of technical public policy questions does not reflect reticence, or a lack of passion about issues. Rather, it embodies a clear understanding of what the Church is, of what the limits of the social doctrine of the Church are, of how the social doctrine is an expression of the New Evangelization, and of the Second Vatican Council's teaching on the vocation of the laity in the world.

To begin with the last: The Second Vatican Council, John Paul II's encyclical *Redemptoris Missio,* and the late Pope's apostolic exhortation *Christifideles Laici* all teach unambiguously that it is primarily the responsibility of the laity to bring the Gospel and the social doctrine of the Church into the culture, the economy, and the political community.[14] The bishops, and, by extension, those who work in the name of the bishops, are to speak on issues of first principles, and their address to the public square should shape the contours of the public policy debate by bringing the leaven of moral reason into what might otherwise be merely utilitarian analyses. But the legislative process itself, save on questions of first principles, is not the primary field of activity for the Church's pastors and those who work directly for them.

Properly catechized, formed, and informed laypeople—both men and women who are serious Catholics and serious citizens—are the Church's principal agents in the legislative process. Those lay Catholics who work in state or national Catholic conferences, while members of the laity, are not "the laity" at work in "the world" as envisioned by Vatican II and the authentic papal interpretation of the Council. They are the agents of the Church's chief pastors, and the restraints the social doctrine imposes on the pastors apply to their public policy agencies as well. Catholic public policy agencies are not acting according to the settled self-understanding of the Church when they assume the role the Council envisioned for the laity and become simulacra or imitations of other all-purpose political lobbies.

This tendency is also problematic in its sense of the "reach" of the social doctrine. It is a distortion of the social doctrine of the Church, as well as a distortion of the right role of the lay faithful, to suggest, through a Catholic public policy agency's work in a transnational, national, or state legislature, that the Catholic Church has a settled position, based on its specific competence, on a vast array of questions that come before those political bodies. The Church does not.

The Church has no competence to state that the American presidential-congressional system is preferable to the Westminster parliamentary system. The Church has no competence to state that a bicameral legislature is superior to a unicameral legislature. The Church has no competence to state that legislative action should be subject to judicial review, or that there are "implied powers" in any executive office.

On many issues, including taxation and welfare policy, a boundary defining the limits of the Church's competence is not hard to determine. The Church has the competence to teach that taxation is just, for to pay taxes is a matter of exercising one's responsibility for the common good. The Church has no competence, however, to suggest that its social doctrine contains clear instructions on what constitute just rates of taxation, and it demeans its social witness (and misapplies its own social doctrine) when it does so through the public policy agencies of its pastors. The Church has the right and duty to teach that a just society makes provision for the elderly, the sick, and the severely handicapped, who, for reasons beyond their control, cannot care for themselves; the Church also has the right and duty to teach that a just society makes provision for the empowerment of the poor, the education of the young, and medical care for all. The Church, however, has no competence to pronounce on whether those societal obligations are best met by state-mandated and tax-funded programs, by private and independent-sector programs, or by some mix of the two.[15] Tax rates and social welfare policies are matters of prudential judgment, which is primarily exercised in the public sphere by the laity, not the pastors.

Then there is the question of priorities. When the Church's chief pastors or their public policy agencies intervene in the public policy process on a host of matters that do not, except in the remotest sense, touch on questions of first principles or on areas of the Church's special competence, they inevitably suggest that all issues are equal in the eyes of the Catholic Church. That is not the case, because of the nature of the issues themselves and the limits of the social doctrine. This lack of discipline in identifying and relentlessly pursuing those issues on which the Church has competence to speak, because those issues touch the first principles of justice, dissipates energies that could be better applied in a more focused way.

It also misconceives the Church's political effectiveness in the public policy arena. The Catholic Church simply does not deploy the same political weight across the spectrum of public policy questions, and it is both self-deluding and politically counterproductive for Catholic bishops and their public policy agencies to think that it does and act as if it does. The Church most effectively speaks truth to power in the public policy arena when it defends and promotes the dignity of the human person, religious freedom, and the integrity of civil society. It dissipates that effectiveness when it loses a sense of public policy priorities based on those bedrock concerns, which are the bottom of the bottom line both theologically and politically.

The deep reform of the Church's public policy advocacy will thus embody the self-discipline taught by the Council and the popes about the limits of the social doctrine's "reach." It will do this because it is the right thing to do from the perspective of the New Evangelization, which is harmed when the Church presents itself as a lobby-among-lobbies. And it will do so because it makes political sense. In the cacophony that is twenty-first-century democratic politics, less can be more, as any number of effective efforts to change hearts, minds, and laws demonstrate. Less-is-more will strengthen the pastors' credibility as teachers, and it will give the moral framework proposed by Catholic social doctrine a chance to be heard and received by the people of the Church, by the general public, and by public officials.

Education and Organizing

Even on questions of first principles, the Church's advocacy in the public policy arena has been weakened by the secularist tide throughout Western society; by two generations of ineffective catechesis, which have produced many Catholic politicians who are baptized pagans; and by the

Catholic scandals of the first decades of the twenty-first century. It is thus self-deluding to imagine that the Church's pastors have, in real political terms, the authority they enjoyed in the past (however well or poorly they deployed that authority). The same holds true, by extension, for those who represent the bishops in national and state legislatures. The question—to borrow a phrase from a most unlikely source, namely, Lenin—is, "What is to be done?"

What is to be done is to effect a paradigm shift: a shift in perspective and in action that is demanded by political reality and mandated by the Church's teaching that the social doctrine is an integral part of the New Evangelization.[16] This strategic shift involves a move away from conventional political advocacy on many issues across the full spectrum of public policy complemented by a move toward education, coupled with serious political organizing, on certain priority issues.

If the authority that the Church and its pastors once enjoyed is no longer available, and if the Church does not have the financial resources that many other advocacy lobbies enjoy, then conventional lobbying makes less and less sense as a model for the Church's public policy advocacy. Unless public officials are already sympathetic to the moral logic that shapes the Church's teaching on the life issues and on marriage, they are unlikely to listen to the bishops or their public policy advocates, because they have likely concluded that there is no point to listening and no cost to not listening. Furthermore, much of the ambient culture is instructing them *not* to listen and is threatening retribution if they do.

If Gospel truths and the moral reasoning that inform Catholic social doctrine are to be brought to bear on questions of first principles in the legislative process at the local and national levels, those responsible for the Church's public witness must restrategize their work and redeploy their resources. If the only things that many public officials understand are money and power, then Catholic public policy advocates—as well as bishops, priests, deacons, and lay catechists—must focus intensified energy on educating the Catholic people, so that the people of the Church, when first principles are at stake, are capable of bringing real pressure to bear on political leaders: political pressure and financial pressure. Evangelical Catholicism in the twenty-first century must also develop more sophisticated means of communicating the bishops' concerns to the bishops' people by explaining why these concerns are the Church's priority concerns; demonstrating how they touch on questions of democratic first principles; and giving Catholics the mechanisms to bring those concerns directly to legislators who need Catholic citizens' votes in order to remain in office.

The public witness of Evangelical Catholicism, in other words, requires political muscle. That strength is needed to prevent further encroachments from the culture of death, and, beyond that, to build free societies in which every child is welcomed in life and protected in law. That strength is needed to build free societies in which the elderly and the severely handicapped are regarded as men and women of immeasurable dignity and value, not "problems" to be "solved" with technological fixes. That strength is needed to build free societies that are hospitable to the stranger and committed to the rule of law; that live within their means; that do not burden future generations with unredeemable public debts—free societies in which the public and private sectors work together, as the social doctrine proposes, to provide quality education, health care, and a secure old age.

Political strength is also required to defend religious freedom within democracies, as well as throughout the world. The pressures on Catholic institutions to conform to the canons of the culture of death will intensify until the effectiveness of Catholic public policy advocacy matches the force of our convictions about the culture of life. These threats to religious freedom in the developed democracies have become evident through the life issues and the marriage issue, and no one should doubt that a season of persecution could be at hand. For the first chill winds of that season were already being felt in the early twenty-first century: when the truths the Church bears are described, with impunity, as examples of irrational bigotry in the mainstream media; when Catholic health-care professionals fear for their licenses to practice the arts of healing with a clear conscience; when the bishops who have the courage to speak truth to the power of political correctness are lampooned; when local tax authorities are used by legislative bodies to bring pressure on the Church; when campaign-finance laws are structured in such a way as to muzzle voices of religiously informed conscience; and when the Church is driven out of the work of foster care and adoption placement by legislation, regulations, or judicial decisions requiring "nondiscrimination" in placement with gay parents.[17]

Some will doubtless find irony here: the Catholic Church, a target of the continental European Enlightenment's theory of human rights, as defender of human rights; the Catholic Church, long identified with the *ancien régime* and ecclesiastical establishments, as proponent of religious freedom. History—and the story of the human quest for authentic freedom—have not ended; but culture—and thus history—have changed, such that the Catholic Church is now the world's premier institutional proponent of human rights and democracy. The Evangelical Catholicism of the twenty-first century will build on that dramatic evolution of the Church's role in public life to secure the foundations of the house of freedom, wherever they are imperiled.

Identity, Witness, and Advocacy

This agenda of deep reform in the Church's public policy advocacy depends, ultimately, on the bishops of the Church. Bishops' conferences that emphasize the integrity of Catholic identity have understood that a renewed sense of who Catholics are—including what Catholics stand for and why—is an essential feature of the New Evangelization. This stress on the imperative of clear Catholic identity is not a matter of winning an argument or of asserting power; it is a matter of giving effect to the teaching of the Second Vatican Council about the imperative of evangelization, which can only reach minds and hearts when it offers the fullness of Catholic truth with conviction as well as compassion.

As on so many other fronts, the transition from Counter-Reformation Catholicism to Evangelical Catholicism requires rethinking—in this case, rethinking (or perhaps better, rediscovering) the evangelical foundation of the Church's engagement with public policy. The Church of public witness, like the Church that celebrates the sacraments and ponders the Word of God, exists for the proclamation of the Gospel and the conversion of the world; everything and everyone in the Church is measured by that mission. The New Evangelization requires a Church sure of its identity and confident of the truths it bears, which include the truths of its social doctrine. So there must not be "identity Catholics" *here* and "social justice Catholics" *there*. If, as the papal magisterium has taught since the late twentieth century, the social doctrine is an integral part of the New Evangelization, then there is only one Catholicism, and in that Catholicism, clarity of Catholic identity and practice serves both the proclamation of the Gospel and the Church's work for justice in the public square.

The fulfillment of the Great Commission and the building of free and virtuous societies are integrally linked.

CHAPTER TWELVE

The Evangelical Catholic Reform of the Papacy

THE COUNTER-REFORMATION PAPACY, WHICH THE STERN AND AUTOCRATIC Pope Pius V helped define between 1566 and 1572, was essential to the reform of Catholicism after the Church-dividing crisis of the Reformation. It is difficult to imagine the reforms mandated by the Council of Trent being effectively implemented without strong leadership from the Roman center, which proved its worth even after the Reformation storm had abated. It is just as difficult to imagine a source other than that "center" unleashing the energies that evangelized the new worlds discovered by European explorers in the fifteenth and sixteenth centuries. But despite mid-twentieth-century assumptions about its permanence, the Counter-Reformation model was as time-bound as previous paradigms for exercising the Office of Peter. Indeed, the Counter-Reformation model began to fall into eclipse in the eighteenth and early nineteenth centuries, when popes such as Benedict XIV (1740–1758) and Pius VII (1800–1823) lived an exercise of the Petrine ministry that reached beyond the institutional defensiveness of the Counter-Reformation to engage intellectual and political modernity. Even so thoroughly defensive and autocratic a pope as Gregory XVI (1831–1846), who condemned the slave trade (anticipating the papacy as an office of global moral witness) and revitalized the Church's missionary activity, pointed the papacy beyond the Counter-Reformation model.

The last of the classic Counter-Reformation popes, Pius IX, began his thirty-two-year reign in 1846 as a reformer and died in 1878 as the symbol of a Church intransigently refusing to engage modernity in either the world of ideas or the world of affairs. At his demise, the worldly influence of the papacy, and perhaps even the institution of the papacy itself, was thought to be finished. Yet within two decades, Pius's successor, Leo XIII, created a new form of papal influence that set one of the foundations for the evangelical Catholic papacy of the twenty-first century: an exercise of influence that was born from the power of moral reason, argument, persuasion, and, above all, Christian witness.

A century after Pius IX's death seemed to mark the end of the papacy as a factor in world history, the cardinals elected a pope who, precisely through the power of evangelical witness, bent the course of history in a more humane direction through his pivotal role in the Revolution of 1989 and the collapse of European communism. On three occasions, that pope, John Paul II, and his successor, Benedict XVI, spoke to the world of power from the rostrum of the United Nations General Assembly as no other global leader could do, identifying and framing issues that humanity could not avoid and calling the world's political leadership to raise the horizon of its aspirations and enlarge its sense of the possible.

This remarkable transformation of the papacy, from the nadir of 1870 when Pius IX declared himself the "prisoner of the Vatican" to the triumph of John Paul II's 1996 walk through Berlin's Brandenburg Gate, was the result of a slow, steady retrieval of the biblical idea of the Office of Peter in the Church. John Paul II did not change history as a politician or diplomat; he changed history as a pastor, a teacher, and a witness. Indeed, the evangelical reform of the papacy is perhaps the clearest example of the truth that all genuine Catholic reform is a matter of "re-form," of reclaiming forgotten elements of the Church's Christ-given constitution and making them the foundation from which to develop new models of Catholic life and practice. Thus any consideration of the evangelical reform of the papacy in the twenty-first century must begin with a return to the first century, and Peter himself.

The Bishop of Rome as Christian Witness

Peter, the fisherman of Galilee, is among the most frequently encountered figures in the New Testament. At once impulsive and warm-hearted, cowardly and brave, insightful and thick-headed, he is a deeply human figure who embodies in a unique way the truth of which his great fellow-apostle, Paul, wrote to the Corinthians: that the "treasure" that is the revelation of God in Christ is held in "earthen vessels"—the weak and sinful people of the Church—"to show that the transcendent power belongs to God and not to us" [2 Corinthians 4.7].

Something of the character of the Petrine office in the Church can be gleaned from two gospel episodes in which Peter is the focus of the Lord's attention.

In the sixteenth chapter of Matthew, Jesus and the Twelve are walking through Caesarea Philippi, a market town in which various divinities were on offer, when the Master asks his followers a sharp question and receives an answer that changes Peter's life:

> "Who do men say that the Son of man is?" And they said, "Some say John the Baptist, others say Elijah, and others say Jeremiah or one of the prophets." He said to them, "But who do you say that I am?" Simon Peter answered, "You are the Christ, the Son of the living God." And Jesus answered him, "Blessed are you, Simon Bar-Jona! For flesh and blood has not revealed this to you, but my Father who is in heaven. And I tell you, you are Peter, and on this rock I will build my Church, and the powers of death shall not prevail against it. I will give you the keys of the kingdom of heaven, and whatever you bind on earth shall be bound in heaven, and whatever you loose on earth shall be loosed in heaven."[1]

In the last chapter of John's gospel, Peter, who did not prove himself a rock of fidelity during Jesus's trial but in fact denied him, only to repent in tears and then become one of the first witnesses to the Resurrection, is confronted by the Risen Lord by the Sea of Galilee. Here, after a breakfast that follows the miraculous drought of fish, a new challenge to Peter is laid down:

> When they had finished breakfast, Jesus said to Simon Peter, "Simon, son of John, do you love me more than these?" He said to him, "Yes, Lord; you know that I love you." He said to him, "Feed my lambs." A second time he said to him, "Simon, son of John, do you love me?" He said to him, "Yes, Lord; you know that I love you." He said to him, "Feed my sheep." He said to him the third time, "Simon, son of John, do you love me?" Peter was grieved because he said to him the third time, "Do you love me?" And he said to him, "Lord, you know everything: you know that I love you." Jesus said to him, "Feed my sheep. Truly, truly I say to you, when you were young, you girded yourself and walked where you would; but when you are old, you will stretch out your hands, and another will gird you and carry you where you do not wish to go. . . ." And after this he said to him, "Follow me."[2]

The scene at Caesarea Philippi suggests that the Office of Peter must express a profound faith: a deep conviction that Jesus is indeed Lord, and that in him, all that God has wished to reveal to the world of his divine life has been revealed. The post-Resurrection appearance at the Sea of Galilee suggests that this depth of faith must be complemented by an equal profundity of love—a radical love of the Lord that gives birth to a radical gift of self for the Lord's flock. By the charcoal brazier on the lakeshore, amid the fragments of their breakfast, the Risen Lord is not twitting Peter, as if his three denials during the interrogation of Jesus had to be repented by three specific assertions of his love. No, as Cardinal Karol Wojtyła pointed out in a challenging sermon preached at the Church of St. Stanisław in Rome a few days before his own election to the papacy, what is happening here is something far more challenging—even disturbing:

> The succession of Peter, the summons to the office of the papacy, always contains within it a call to the higher love, to a very special love. And always, when Christ says to a man, "Come, follow me," he asks him what he asked of Simon: "Do you love me *more* than do the others?" Then the heart of man must tremble. . . . A human heart must tremble, because in the question there is also a demand. You must love! You must love more than the others do, if the entire flock of sheep is to be entrusted to you, if the charge "Feed my lambs, feed my sheep" is to reach the scope which it reaches in the call and mission of Peter. . . . And so, in this summons, directed to Peter by Christ after his Resurrection, Christ's command, "Come, follow me," has a double meaning. It is a summons to service, and it is a summons to die.[3]

The Office of Peter, then, is both an office of vigilance over the symphony of truth the Catholic Church teaches and an office of supreme pastoral charity in which that symphony of truth is poured out in love. The Bishop of Rome, the successor of Peter, ensures that the Church has the arguments it must have about its understanding of that symphony of truth; the Bishop of Rome also ensures that those arguments are conducted in a way that befits those called to the more excellent way of Christian love.

These two core responsibilities of the Bishop of Rome, the Universal Pastor of the Church, have been visible in high relief in the four pontificates that drew the curtain on the Counter-Reformation papacy and accelerated the transition to the evangelical Catholic papacy. The transparent decency of John XXIII humanized the papacy and restored to the office its paternal warmth, even as the Church began to rediscover its universality and its evangelical self-confidence through the experience of an ecumenical council. Paul VI visibly suffered from the demands of Petrine love, which he sought to embody in a season of irrationality; he also paid the price of being the guardian of moral truth, particularly on the question of the appropriate means of regulating fertility. John Paul II's was the most consequential teaching pontificate in centuries; his service in the Office of Peter concluded with an unprecedented witness to the Paschal Mystery of Christ's suffering, death, and resurrection, which the Pope invited the world to encounter through the experience of his own suffering and death. Benedict XVI, master-teacher and catechist, wept with victims of sexual abuse and called the nations to a deeper understanding of the meaning of freedom.

In all of this, the Evangelical Catholicism of the late twenty-first century will look back and see the birth of a new model of papacy, drawn from the New Testament and what the Church knows of Peter from Scripture and tradition. Peter was many things in the first decades of the Church. He was one of the first to discover the empty tomb, and he was the subject of special attention by the Risen One. After receiving the gift of the Holy Spirit at Pentecost, he preached the first great Christian sermon and brought thousands of new believers into the Jerusalem Church. He converted the gentile centurion Cornelius, thus initiating the mission *ad gentes*, which was vastly expanded by St. Paul. During the debate over what the expanding Christian community would require of its gentile members, he was one of the centers of unity around which the debate was resolved. Ultimately, according to tradition verified by contemporary archaeological research, Peter went to Rome, where he died a martyr in Nero's circus and was buried in the nearby Vatican hill—where his grave immediately became a site of Christian pilgrimage and prayer.

What Peter was not, in all of this, was the CEO of a small, upstart religion seeking market-share in the consumer mall of Mediterranean spiritualities. Yet as the Counter-Reformation papacy evolved, the idea hardened that the Successor of Peter was first and foremost a manager: the CEO of Catholic Church, Inc. It is as sure a sign as any of the waning of Counter-Reformation Catholicism and the emergence of Evangelical Catholicism that this CEO model has been gradually undone in the late twentieth and early twenty-first centuries. It has been succeeded by a far more evangelically assertive model of the papacy, a model in which the

Bishop of Rome is, above all, the Church's first witness—the witness whose own witness strengthens the witness of all the brethren, as the Lord commanded Peter to do at the Last Supper: "Simon, Simon, behold, Satan demanded to have you, that he might sift you like wheat, but I have prayed for you that your faith may not fail; and when you have turned again, strengthen your brethren" [Luke 22.31–32].

It is this primary, evangelical function of the Office of Peter that led Paul VI to make the first tentative steps toward a missionary papacy in his world journeys. That turn toward papal mission was intensified by orders of magnitude in the globe-circling papacy of John Paul II. John Paul insisted, rightly, that his journeys were not "trips," some kind of papal tourism. Rather, they were religious pilgrimages in which the Universal Pastor of the Church came to local churches for two primary reasons: to bear witness to the faith, so that faith might be strengthened locally, and to lift up local sanctity (in his beatifications and canonizations throughout the world), so that the people of the Church might see that God is profligate in his gifts of grace and does not discriminate among their recipients, be they old Christians or new. That habit of papal pilgrimage continued with Benedict XVI, if at a slower pace necessitated by Benedict's age at his election. And it must continue in the evangelical Catholic papacy of the twenty-first century and beyond.

Where, then, will the Church look for such men? What qualities are important in an evangelical Catholic pope?

Preparation for the Impossible

The first thing to be discerned about any possible candidate for the papacy is whether he wants the job: for if he does, his desire disqualifies him, not so much for a lack of humility as for a lack of prudence, even sanity. No sane man seeks the burden of the papacy. No man who knows the demands made on a pope—which range from sheer physical stamina to a deep spiritual capacity to bear the wounds of the entire Church without being bled to death by them—will seek the office. The office seeks the man.

There are different views of the work of the Holy Spirit in a conclave. Between the death of John Paul II and the election of Benedict XVI, Cardinal Ennio Antonelli gave an interview in which he said that God had already chosen the next pope; the cardinal-electors' task was to discern who God's choice was. Interestingly enough, Cardinal Joseph Ratzinger, on whom the choice would fall in that conclave, held a more minimalist view of the Spirit's role: the task of the Holy Spirit, he once said, was to ensure that the cardinals did not elect a pope who would utterly destroy the Church. But regardless of where theologians align themselves along the spectrum defined by Antonelli and Ratzinger on the question of the divine role in a papal election, the Church's experience of the papacy in late modernity and early postmodernity suggests a certain set of qualifications for the Office of Peter.

In the final analysis, the task is so difficult as to verge on the impossible, and as Cardinal Wojtyła noted in 1978, the summons to Peter's Chair is a summons to death, in various senses of that word. But for all the impossible demands that the office lays on its occupant, the Church is not without resources of experience and insight in defining a profile of desirable qualities to be sought in the evangelical Catholic popes of the twenty-first century and beyond.

A profound and transparent faith

In *The Shoes of the Fisherman*, novelist Morris West imagined a conversation between an Italian cardinal canvassing his fellow-electors on the first night of a conclave and a mystically inclined cardinal from one of the Eastern Catholic Churches. The Italian is trying to convince his brother-cardinal that a new man among them, a Ukrainian recently released from a Soviet labor camp, is God's choice for the Office of Peter. The Eastern cardinal's response is wise as well as instructive:

"Always," said Rahamani the Syrian in his pliant, courteous fashion, "always you search a man for the one necessary gift—the gift of cooperation with God. Even among good men this gift is rare. Most of us, you see, spend our lives trying to bend ourselves to the will of God, and even then we often have to be bent by a violent grace. The others, the rare ones, commit themselves, as if by an instinctive act, to be tools in the hands of the Maker. If this new man is such a one, then it is he whom we need."[4]

The evangelical Catholic popes of the twenty-first century and beyond must be men of deep faith who have the ability to propose the symphony of Catholic truth, by word and example, as a compelling alternative to the other visions of human goods that shape (and misshape) the postmodern world. A reclusive man, a man who wears his doubts and his sense of ambiguities on his sleeve, a man who is shy about the world media, or a man whose commitment to "dialogue" typically trumps his commitment to evangelization is thus lacking one important quality to be sought in the popes of the evangelical Catholic future. Confidence in the symphony of truths that the Church teaches need not make a man arrogant (another disqualifying personal characteristic for a potential pope, it should be said); intellectual security can and should go hand in hand with humility, and with a palpable sympathy for the struggles with belief that many men and women undergo. Still, the world has come to expect (and even desire) popes who speak forthrightly, because what they teach is an expression of what the Catholic Church believes, on which they have staked their lives. The world may not always approve of what popes say. But the world knows, even if it rarely admits, that the human condition would be impoverished if popes began to speak in the ambiguous categories of liberal Protestantism or became neutral discussion-moderators in interreligious dialogue.

Natural resilience, amplified by grace

In addition to being richly endowed with the supernatural gift of faith, and with the human gifts of intellect and personality necessary to make that faith into an evangelically attractive proposal, the evangelical Catholic popes of the twenty-first century and beyond must be men of human resilience—able, like John Paul II, to draw from the wellspring of their prayer a superabundance of energy, patience, compassion, and endurance. The crushing burden of the papacy is not simply, or even primarily, a matter of schedule (which can always be adjusted); it is a matter of the spirit, and of the dark side of the human condition. In another novel, *The Devil's Advocate*, Morris West wrote of the pope as a man who "carried . . . the sins of the world like a leaden cope on his shoulders."[5] Popes know far too much for any one human being to bear: they know the wickedness and evil in the world in macrocosm (as they are regularly briefed on it by Vatican officials and papal nuncios), and they know human sorrow in microcosm (from the prayer requests that pour into the papal apartment from all over the world, every day). This weight of knowledge cannot be borne alone and requires a special grace of strength, which the Lord promised to Peter. That grace, however, builds on a human foundation of physical and psychological hardiness and resilience. This suggests that, save for rare occasions, the Evangelical Catholicism of the future will be best served by popes who are elected when they are still physically vigorous men, capable of taking a terrible pounding while still turning a face of hope to a Church seeking guidance—and to a world in need of conversion.

Pastoral experience

John Paul II's contribution to the retrieval and renewal of the papacy as an office of evangelical witness was made possible in large part by the fact that he came to Peter's Chair with a vast amount of pastoral experience as a priest and bishop. That "he knew our lives from inside," as one of his oldest lay friends put it, was a great benefit to his papacy, as was his experience as the effective leader of a local church. Indeed, virtually every one of the major initiatives of John Paul II's papacy, from World Youth Days and his extensive schedule of pastoral pilgrimages to the Theology of the Body and his teaching on marriage and the family, can be traced back to his experience as archbishop of Kraków. That experience was, if you will, the testbed for his pontificate. And while the specifics of that experience were unique and unrepeatable, the general model makes eminent sense for the future: with rare exceptions, the Church is best served by popes who have already demonstrated a capacity for evangelically effective pastoral leadership—including experience in meeting the challenges posed by the cultured despisers of religion.

Good judgment in people

Proven judgment in assessing people and deploying their gifts well for the good of the whole is an essential quality in the evangelical Catholic popes of the future. A pope may be brilliant, holy, and a good teacher; but if he has bad judgment in the people he appoints to high office, in the Holy See and to bishops' chairs around the world, his pontificate will not have the evangelical impact it must have. Precisely because the popes of Evangelical Catholicism cannot be micromanaging chief executives, they must have good judgment in the men they select to lead local churches as bishops. They must also show shrewd judgment in choosing men to manage the machinery of the Church's central administration, so that the work undertaken in Rome helps to sanctify the Church and convert the world. A man given to softness in judgment about people, seeing virtues where they do not exist and imagining qualities that are not there, is ill-suited to the demands of the papacy, which, in terms of internal management, is an office in which the primary task is the wise selection of collaborators who will facilitate, not impede, the pope in his unique responsibility for governance.

Openness and curiosity

Parallel to this quality of good judgment in people is the quality of openness to a wide range of inputs. A pope who relies exclusively on conventional ecclesiastical sources of information—the nunciatures around the world and the bishops' conferences, whose reports are usually filtered through the Roman Curia—is going to learn some things. But he is not going to learn all that he should; and he may not learn the things he most needs to know, including the truth about his own misperceptions and misjudgments. The constant flow of guests into the papal apartment during the pontificate of John Paul II reflected that great pope's lifelong habit of learning from conversation; future popes need not emulate John Paul's example in all details, but they would do well to learn from his willingness, indeed eagerness, to go outside the normal ecclesiastical channels of information to afford himself as broad an array of information as possible. Only in that way will a pope have a detailed sense of how Evangelical Catholicism is faring in an often-challenging world.

Strategic vision

The great popes of late modernity and early postmodernity were men of the long view, whose depth of faith allowed them to plant seeds for the future, confident that what was well-planted could be trusted to grow in its own, and God's, time. That depth of faith must be complemented by strategic vision. And in the Evangelical Catholicism of the future, the strategic vision required of popes will have to be tri-focal: the popes of the twenty-first century and beyond must nurture and guide the tremendous growth of the Church in the Third World, while concurrently developing strategies for the reconversion of the post-Christian and spiritually bored West and for meeting the challenge of jihadist Islam. Men whose primary skills lie in the management of existing situations are thus lacking in one important quality for an evangelical Catholic pope: the ability to create new situations by seeing opportunities and openings where others see only obstacles.

Courage

As the Catholic Church understands it, fortitude, or what is typically called "courage," is one of the gifts of the Holy Spirit that "complete and perfect the virtues of those who receive them," fortitude also being one of the cardinal virtues.[6] Christian courage is deeply bound to faith, the faith that takes quite literally the Lord Jesus's teaching at the Last Supper: "In the world you have tribulation; but be of good cheer, I have overcome the world" [John 16.33]. A timid man, who sees ambiguities and dilemmas but does not have the courage to see beyond ambiguity and difficulty, is ill-fit for the papacy. So is a man easily shaken by failure.

The courage required of popes was unmistakably evident in the first centuries of the Church, when to become the Bishop of Rome was to receive a sentence of martyrdom. That kind of courage, resting on the rock of Peter's faith, may or may not be required of popes in the Evangelical Catholicism of the future. What is certain is that the popes of the Church that is being born in the early decades of the twenty-first century must be men of courage in the face of the kind of postmodern indifference that can lead to active hostility, and ultimately to what Pope Benedict XVI rightly called the "dictatorship of relativism."

Popes must also have the courage to be disciplinarians, particularly at times when the good of the Church requires the unambiguous clarification of doctrine or the removal from office of senior Vatican officials or local bishops. The Catholic Church is not a high school, and the pope is not its prefect of discipline; local bishops are primarily responsible for the integrity of Catholic faith, practice, and identity in their dioceses. But there are certain disciplinary problems in the Church that only popes can address. The requisite willingness to do what is hard and take the criticism that inevitably follows is thus an essential quality in a pope, who will see in such actions necessary means to furthering the Church's mission of evangelization.

Languages

Competence in multiple languages is no guarantor of a more wide-ranging human competence; a man who cannot make sense, or lead, in one language is unlikely to do so in several. Nonetheless, a gift for languages is one quality that the Evangelical Catholicism of the future would like to see in its chief shepherds. Given the demographics of world Catholicism in the twenty-first century, this means that a pope who cannot function liturgically and homiletically in English and Spanish is going to be at a serious disadvantage. And until the Roman Curia changes its ingrained habits and institutional culture, a working knowledge of Italian is also an important attribute for a pope.

The irrelevance of nationality

Considering the expectations that both Church and world have of the popes of the twenty-first century, and the qualities necessary for an effective exercise of the Petrine ministry, it should be obvious that nationality ought to mean nothing in choosing a pope. Evangelical Catholicism is not the preserve of any one nationality, ethnicity, or race, and neither is the evangelical Catholic papacy of the future. It will be difficult enough to find men who have, in some measure, the qualifications just discussed. It would be irresponsible of the cardinal-electors to preemptively constrain themselves and limit their choices by dismissing some nationalities, races, or ethnicities, or by giving pride of place to others. Those who imagine that any nationality has a proclivity for the papacy have demonstrated by that very assumption that they have not grasped the essentials of the Evangelical Catholicism of the future; their counsel should be treated with the skepticism it deserves.

An Evangelical College of Cardinals

The College of Cardinals has evolved over time, and no doubt will continue to evolve in the Evangelical Catholicism of the twenty-first century and beyond. From Pius XII through John Paul II, popes tried to internationalize what had once been a dominantly Italian body; efforts were also made to give the cardinals a more active role as papal counselors, in a contemporary expression of the College's origins in the presbyterate of the Diocese of Rome. John Paul's efforts along these lines were not noticeably successful; the consistory he called to discuss and lay plans for the Great Jubilee of 2000 showed such a marked lack of enthusiasm for the project that the Pope took over the planning himself, with exceptional results.[7] Despite this unhappy experience, however, the idea of the College as a body of papal counselors who meet regularly to consider the condition of the world Church from a variety of vantage points is sound. Thus one might imagine biennial or triennial consistories called to measure the advance of the New Evangelization throughout the world. Such regular meetings of the College, outside the consistories in which new cardinals are created, would also allow the future papal electors an opportunity to get to know one another better, which would presumably allow them to function more effectively as an electoral college when they gather for their most solemn responsibility, the election of a new Bishop of Rome.

If the College of Cardinals is a body of papal counselors in more than name, then it is obvious that the College's members should reflect the diversity of local Church experiences within the world Church. The trend toward a re-Italianization of the College during the pontificate of Benedict XVI was thus a step backward, and one that ought to be reversed in future pontificates. When the Church of Italy shows itself a leader in the New Evangelization, then it may claim, with justification, a significant number of members of the College of Cardinals; the same holds true for other countries with traditionally large numbers of cardinals, who in the early twenty-first century preside over what seem to be dying or moribund local churches. Conversely, the local churches of the global South, where Catholicism is growing rapidly, have reason to expect that their experience will be better represented in the College of Cardinals of the future. The size of the College of Cardinals—which was limited by Paul VI and John Paul II to a maximum of 120 papal electors—seems about right; more than 120 electors would make for an awkward conclave process. But the distribution of electors ought to reflect the realities of the Evangelical Catholicism of the present and future, rather than what some Italians imagine as their rightful dominance of the College.

The traditional hierarchy within the College of Cardinals should be reexamined in light of the vision of Evangelical Catholicism and the face that the Church wishes to present to the world. Traditionally, the cardinals are divided into three "orders": cardinal bishops (who are the titular heads of the suburbicarian sees around Rome), cardinal priests (usually residential bishops in their own countries), and cardinal deacons (usually cardinal-officials of the Roman Curia). The dean of the College is the senior cardinal bishop. According to John Paul II's 1996 apostolic constitution on the election of "The Shepherd of the Lord's Whole Flock" (*Universi Dominici Gregis*), the dean has three crucial duties on the death of a pope: he presides over the daily congregations of cardinals between the pontiff's death and the sealing of the conclave to elect his successor; he is the principal celebrant at the deceased pontiff's funeral Mass; and he celebrates the Mass *pro eligendo Romani Pontificis* [for the election of the Roman Pontiff] just before the cardinals are sealed into the conclave to begin balloting. This arrangement worked quite well during the 2005 interregnum; Cardinal Joseph Ratzinger, by all accounts, did a fine job of guiding the cardinals' discussions throughout the interregnum; he was a masterful celebrant and homilist at John Paul II's funeral Mass; and he preached a notable homily on the dangers of the "dictatorship of relativism" at the Mass *pro eligendo Romani Pontificis*. His brilliant work during the interregnum solidified the "consensus of esteem" that led to his quick election as Pope Benedict XVI.

As Pope Benedict's pontificate lengthened, however, a new situation arose: the cardinal dean was Angelo Sodano, former secretary of state to John Paul II. Sodano lost his right to vote in a future conclave when he turned eighty on November 23, 2007; the vice-dean, Cardinal Roger Etchegaray, was even older, having been born five years before Sodano. Unlike Cardinal Bernardin Gantin, who voluntarily stepped down as dean of the College when he turned eighty (thus making it possible for Ratzinger, then vice-dean, to become dean), Cardinal Sodano showed no inclination to voluntarily relinquish the deanship in the years after his eightieth birthday—and in any event he would have been succeeded (unless he, too, stepped down) by the even older Etchegaray, neither of whom would have a vote in the conclave to elect a successor to Benedict XVI.

For both evangelical and practical reasons, this situation ought not happen again. The funeral Mass of a pope is one of the Church's great catechetical opportunities on a global scale, and it seems counterintuitive, and likely counterproductive, for it to be led by an octogenarian cardinal who is superannuated *de facto* if not *de iure*. Similarly, it makes little sense for a cardinal who lacks a conclave vote to preside over the daily meetings of the College of Cardinals during a papal interregnum. The participation of the nonvoting cardinals in those meetings can bring the benefit of vast and differentiated experience to bear on the College's assessment of the state of the Church and its evangelical mission during the interregnum. But the cardinal who presides over such deliberations and sets the tone for them ought to also be a cardinal who will share the responsibilities of a cardinal-elector. And as the Church cannot always rely on humility like Cardinal Gantin's to resolve these anomalies, both the dean and vice-dean of the College should be required to relinquish their positions when they reach their eightieth birthdays and thus lose their conclave votes, if they have not already stepped aside.

Reforming the Roman Curia

Most of what the world thinks it knows of the Roman Curia is, in fact, mistaken. The world imagines that the Curia is a huge bureaucracy; the fact is that the global community of the Catholic Church, some 1.2 billion people, is served by a central administration that employs 3,000 or so people, of whom perhaps 40 have real operational responsibilities or decision-making roles. The world thinks the Church's central administration disposes of vast amounts of wealth; but the Curia not infrequently runs a deficit, and much of the Church's support for Third World Catholicism comes from German Catholic development agencies (funded by German taxes), not from Rome.

The reform of the Roman Curia in the twenty-first century and beyond will begin from one, basic premise: the vigor of Evangelical Catholicism primarily depends on the holiness, the missionary zeal, and the vision of the entire Church, not on the functioning of various offices in Rome. That understanding, however, will be complemented by clarity on a related point: structure counts, and the Church's central administrative structures should advance, not impede, the Church's pursuit of the universal call to holiness and the Church's exercise of the universal responsibility of mission, just as those structures ought to support, not impede, the pope's ministry as Universal Pastor of the Church.

That was not always the case in the first decades of the twenty-first century, when the Curia not infrequently caused acute embarrassment to Benedict XVI, putting obstacles in the way of his evangelical, catechetical, and pastoral efforts, and ill-serving the Pope's attempts to reframe the global agenda of debate on the crucial issues facing humanity. That these failures ran parallel to a re-Italianization of the Curia suggested that the Curia, as an instrument intended to facilitate the pope's mission as Supreme Pontiff and Universal Pastor, ought to draw on the full range of talent available from throughout the world Church, rather than from the shallower talent pool of any one country.

Serious curial reform was one of the priorities that the cardinals of 2005 identified for the next pontificate, when they met after the death of John Paul II. That reform did not take place under Benedict XVI, and in some respects the situation worsened. Evangelical witness is and must be the priority of any pope. But the popes after Benedict XVI will have to attend to the long-delayed reform of the Roman Curia, precisely so that they, and the Church, are better served in their efforts at evangelism. Some of the elements of that reform can be sketched briefly, in alphabetical order.

Attitude and culture

The Church is ill-served when too many members of the Roman Curia, at all levels, are ambitious clerics who want a job in Rome as a means to climb the ecclesiastical career ladder. As a general rule, those who want to work in the central administration of the Church are least fit for that role. If curial life and culture are dominated by clerical ambition, attitudes become warped, the business of management is made more difficult, and the People of God are treated as if they were cattle, not sheep to be nourished and shepherded.[8]

The traditional thirty-six-hour curial workweek, spread across six days, is a reflection of ancient custom, not organizational efficiency. The Roman Curia ought to work forty hours a week, over five days, like most of the rest of the world with which it must deal.

A reform of work schedule and institutional culture might also help address the problems caused by the languid pace of the curial response to crisis, as when the Church in Ireland goes into free fall because of revelations of decades of crime and cover-up, or when the founder of the Legionaries of Christ is found to have been a sociopath who lived a dissolute life while deceiving the Church as to his true purposes. There is merit in the typical (and, let it be said, Italianate) curial tendency to minimize crisis, on the grounds that everything has been seen before and that no good purpose is served by getting into a flap. On the other hand, there are situations that demand a rapid, decisive, and effective response, not because the media is in an uproar, but because the good of the entire Church demands it. Addressing with stern and effective measures the meltdown of Irish Catholicism in the face of clerical abuse and episcopal malfeasance would seem to have been a case in point; so would the imperative of a rapid response to the crisis of the Legionaries of Christ. Neither happened when these crises broke, thus underscoring the importance of a deep reform of the culture of the Roman Curia and its habits of work.

Communication

Vatican communications were in such a shambles during the first four years of the pontificate of Benedict XVI that some action was finally taken to repair the damage. Still, far more remains to be done if the communications process for which the Roman Curia is responsible is to become an aid to the Church's evangelical mission. The opening of a Vatican Web hub was a step in the right direction, but the various instruments to which that hub directs people are in need of significant reform. Vatican Radio should cease imitating the BBC and CNN, and focus its reporting and commentary on the life of the Church, rather than on elections in small countries and international meetings of no real consequence. *L'Osservatore Romano* should be internationalized, rather than continuing as an Italian daily with limited resources. Were the Vatican's semi-official newspaper to draw its personnel and talent from all over the world Church, *L'Osservatore Romano* might even begin to be taken seriously by the senior officials of the Holy See, whose indifference to it was one obstacle to its reform in the first decades of the twenty-first century.

The Curia must also recognize that, although Italian remains its *lingua franca* (until such time as, like every other international center of consequence, English becomes the working language), Italian is not spoken or read by the overwhelming majority of the world's Catholics. Thus no major papal or Vatican statement should ever be issued unless English and Spanish translations are available at the time the document is released and presented in a press conference.

Competence

Bishops should understand that the release of talented priests for service in the Roman Curia, while often a hardship for the local church, is often a great gift to the universal Church. Openness on the part of bishops to permitting priests to take positions in Rome for a period, or to allowing their priests to join the diplomatic service of the Holy See, is also an essential part of the internationalization of the Church's central administration.

Conversely, the pope and his most-senior collaborators must understand that service in the papal diplomatic corps does not necessarily qualify a man for any middle-management or senior leadership position in the Roman Curia, which was often the operating assumption in the last decades of the twentieth century and the first decades of the twenty-first. The movable parts among senior churchmen are not all interchangeable; high curial office ought not be an automatic reward for diplomatic services rendered; nationality should, again, be irrelevant when identifying senior officials.

Curial reform also requires that incompetence in curial office should be neither rewarded nor ignored: as when Benedict XVI was embarrassed—and vilified in the world press—because no one in the relevant curial offices had the wit to check Google and discover that a Lefebvrist bishop, whose excommunication the Pope was about to lift, was a Holocaust-denying lunatic; or when neither the nuncio in Poland nor the Congregation for Bishops discovered, before the appointment was made, that the newly named archbishop of Warsaw had a history of collaboration with the Polish communist secret police; or when the cardinal secretary of state sent a fulsome letter of praise to a Polish priest whose radio station regularly engaged in blatantly partisan politics and indulged in occasional anti-Semitic innuendo; or when curial incomprehension of the facts of political life in Castroite Cuba led to a less-than-satisfactory papal pilgrimage to that hard-pressed island.

A reformed Curia would also not be used by the highest authorities of the Church to attempt bureaucratic solutions to problems that ought to be resolved by appropriate disciplinary action. The establishment in 2010 of a new Pontifical Council for the New Evangelization was intended, inter alia, to "solve" the problem caused by the gross errors made by a prominent Italian bishop in commenting on a difficult case of pregnancy following rape—a perfect example of how things ought *not* to be done in the Evangelical Catholicism of the future.[9]

Ideas

Like any other bureaucracy, the Roman Curia has developed default positions over time: ideas that have gotten embedded in the institution's modus operandi and that are rarely, if ever, examined critically. In the first decades of the twenty-first century, following a pattern set in the aftermath of the Second Vatican Council, these default positions in the sections of the Curia responsible for the Church's interface with world affairs tended to mirror the default positions of other European international or transnational bodies: a preference for ever-larger aggregations of power at the international level (to the point where one senior curial official in 2012 said that any Catholic opponent of a world political authority was a bad Catholic); a settled distaste, bordering on avoidance, for recognizing the realities of jihadist Islam and its effects on both religious freedom and world politics; and a disinclination to think that armed force might ever be a useful and morally appropriate instrument of statecraft.[10]

If the structural reform of the Curia suggested below is undertaken, such that most of the Pontifical Councils established since Vatican II become in-house curial think tanks, one of their tasks ought to be to reexamine these and other default positions in the Roman Curia according to the vision of Evangelical Catholicism and the new pattern of Catholic advocacy on public policy issues outlined in the previous chapter.

Structure

The post–Vatican II structure of the Roman Curia, in which the Secretariat of State sits atop both Congregations (curial bodies with administrative jurisdiction, such as the Congregation for Bishops and the Congregation for the Clergy) and Pontifical Councils (which do not have jurisdiction, such as the Pontifical Council for the Laity and the Pontifical Council for Justice and Peace), ought to be reexamined in light of the theological vision of Evangelical Catholicism and the requirements of sound management practice.

One fundamental change, bruited during the 2005 interregnum, would transform the First Section of the Secretariat of State (which deals with the internal affairs of the Church) into an executive office of the pope, with the Secretariat's Second Section (which manages the Holy See's diplomatic relations with states) becoming an independent body, as it once was. Thus the apex of the curial structure would no longer be a bureaucratic body (although work from the rest of the Curia would continue to flow through the reformed executive office of the pope), and the Congregation for the Doctrine of the Faith, a theological body, would resume its place as first among the curial departments ("dicasteries," in Vatican-speak).

It was also suggested in 2005 that, as part of this reform, the Pontifical Councils would revert to being the in-house think tanks they were originally intended to be, rather than the advocacy agencies they had become. As such, the Pontifical Councils would no longer have to be led by cardinals, and the number of places in the College of Cardinals absorbed by the Curia would necessarily decrease. Such a reconfiguration of the Pontifical Councils would also solve a problem that became serious at several points during the pontificate of Benedict XVI, namely, the tendency of some Pontifical Councils to issue statements or documents that had no authority other than that of their authors, but were immediately presumed by much of the Church and virtually all of the world media to be expressions of either the Pope's views and/or the Church's teaching. In a reformed Curia, Pontifical Councils would share the products of their reflection within the Curia, and perhaps among the bishops' conferences, but would not speak publicly in the name of anyone.[11]

A further advantage of such a reconfiguration would be that it would give these agencies time to reconsider the default positions that had become bureaucratically hardened within the Pontifical Councils over the last decades of the twentieth century and the first decades of the twenty-first. Thus the Pontifical Council for Justice and Peace, reconfigured as an intracurial think tank on the Church's relations with states and the Church's address to world politics, could reexamine some of the default positions noted just above. Similarly, the Pontifical Council for Promoting Christian Unity could reexamine its long-standing commitment to various bilateral dialogues with liberal Protestant bodies that seemed to be achieving very little, while opening new lines of conversation with the evangelical, fundamentalist, and Pentecostal Protestants who were manifestly the growing Protestant communities of the twenty-first century and beyond.[12]

There are, to be sure, many ways to imagine a reconfigured Roman Curia. That its reform is an imperative, few would doubt. In any reconfiguration, one essential question should remain at the center of reflection: How can the Roman Curia more effectively serve the Servant of the Servants of God, the Bishop of Rome, and the entire world Church, in the task of fulfilling the Great Commission?

As with every other facet of the deep reform of the Church, the reform of the Roman Curia ought to be measured by the twin criteria of truth and mission: Does this structure reflect the truths of Catholic faith and facilitate the universal call to holiness? Does this structure advance the mission of the Church and the conversion of the world?

Epilogue

Holiness
and Mission

EVERY CHRISTIAN EXPERIENCES THE TEMPTATION TO WHICH PETER succumbed after Jesus was arrested in Gethsemane: the temptation to follow the Lord "at a distance."[1] Keeping a safe distance from the Lord Jesus is a way of hedging our bets, of being "reasonable" about our discipleship, of not looking too fanatical about this business of faith.

The Lord Jesus, however, did not ask that we keep our distance. His call to the first disciples, like his call to those who would be his disciples in the twenty-first century and the third millennium, is simple and unambiguous: "Follow me, and I will make you fishers of men" [Matthew 4.19]. "Follow me," and you will find the holiness that is your heart's deepest desire. "Follow me," and be sent into mission.

In its Dogmatic Constitution on the Church, the Second Vatican Council spoke eloquently about the universality of the call to holiness. The Lord himself, the Council Fathers recalled, "preached holiness of life . . . to each and every one of his disciples without distinction . . . : 'You, therefore, must be perfect, as your heavenly Father is perfect'" [Matthew 5.48]. Baptized into sanctity, Christians are instructed by St. Paul to live "as is fitting among saints" [Ephesians 5.3] and to grow, "as God's chosen ones, holy and beloved, [into] compassion, kindness, lowliness, meekness, and patience" [Colossians 3.12]. Scripture thus makes clear "that all Christians in any state or walk of life are called to the fullness of Christian life and to the perfection of love," so that "following in [Christ's] footsteps and conformed to his image, doing the will of God in everything, they may wholeheartedly devote themselves to the glory of God and to the service of their neighbor."[2]

Holiness is not an option for those who take Baptism seriously. Holiness is an obligation, to be pursued not "at a distance," but through an ever-closer embrace of "the Lamb of God, who takes away the sins of the world" [John 1.29].

Thus the first task of Evangelical Catholicism is to foster the holiness of all the people of the Church. That task, in turn, leads directly to mission.

As John Paul II wrote in *Redemptoris Missio*, "the universal call to holiness is closely linked to the universal call to mission." Moreover, the acceptance of that evangelical responsibility is itself a means of sanctification, for "the Church's missionary spirituality is a journey toward holiness." Thus the true evangelist, the true disciple-in-mission, is the saint, the "person of the Beatitudes." The Lord himself made this clear in the way he prepared the first disciples for mission: "Before sending out the Twelve to evangelize, Jesus . . . teaches them the paths of mission: poverty, meekness, acceptance of suffering and persecution, the desire for justice and peace, charity—in other words, the Beatitudes, lived out in apostolic life." And as it was then, so it must be in the third millennium of Christian witness: "In a world tormented and oppressed by so many problems, a world tempted to pessimism, the one who proclaims the 'Good News' must be a person who has found true hope in Christ."[3]

In the last decades of Counter-Reformation Catholicism, Pope Pius XI—the pope who confronted fascism, Nazism, communism, and murderous Mexican anticlericalism—drew the Church's attention to an evangelical paradox: it ought to be a cause for thanksgiving that God had ordained that Catholics live among these challenges, for it was no longer permitted that anyone be mediocre. In the first decades of the first flowering of Evangelical Catholicism, Pope John Paul II picked up his predecessor's theme and, in his apostolic letter closing the Great Jubilee of 2000, wrote to the world Church that "it would be a contradiction to settle for a life of mediocrity, marked by a minimalist ethic and a shallow religiosity."[4] Thus the Evangelical Catholicism of the future must dig deeply into the sources of sanctification, in Word and Sacrament. And it must, like the disciples on the Sea of Galilee, "put out into the deep . . . for a catch" [Luke 5.4]. The Evangelical Catholicism of the third millennium must live the truth of its spousal relationship to Christ the Bridegroom by inviting the world, through mission, to the Wedding Feast of the Lamb.

All true reform in the Church of the twenty-first century and beyond is thus ordered to holiness and mission. The Church is *semper reformanda*, always in need of reform, "not [to] be conformed to this world" [Romans 12.2], but to be purified in holiness for mission. The Church is *semper reformanda* not as a matter of good management practice, but so that its essential structures support the universal call to holiness and the universal call to mission.

Reflecting on the Great Jubilee of 2000, John Paul II wrote that, if the Church's year-long celebration of the two thousandth anniversary of the Incarnation had "been a genuine pilgrimage, it will have stretched our legs for the journey ahead."[5] The same might be said of the decades between the pontificates of Pope Leo XIII and Pope Benedict XVI: those years have been a pilgrimage from Counter-Reformation Catholicism to Evangelical Catholicism. And the journey is not over, for the deep reform of the Church that is embodied in this transition from one historical mode of Catholicism to another is not yet complete. The pursuit of holiness remains. The call to mission remains.

There are still Emmaus roads to be walked. And along them the evangelical Catholics of the future, having met the Risen One in Word and Sacrament, will still proclaim, to those with ears to hear, "We have seen the Lord!" [John 20.25].

Acknowledgments

THIS BOOK IS THE PRODUCT OF SOME THIRTY YEARS OF REFLECTION ON THE future of the Catholic Church. During those three decades, I have had the privilege of discussing the deep reform of the Church with Catholics in virtually every state of life and in a wide variety of circumstances around the world. It would be impossible to name all those to whom I owe a debt of gratitude for insight, correction, and inspiration—an impossibility for which some of my interlocutors may well be grateful. But it would be unthinkable not to note the contributions to my thinking of the two men to whom I have dedicated *Evangelical Catholicism*.

My friendship with Father Jay Scott Newman began during his student days in Rome. In the two decades since we walked up the Aventine and through the Palatine, we have talked about virtually everything written in this book. Moreover, Father Newman's various pastorates in South Carolina have shown me Evangelical Catholicism in action. There is little in this book that bears on parish life that has not proven itself in parish life, thanks to Father Newman.

Russell Hittinger and I have been discussing the pivotal role of Pope Leo XIII in the development of twentieth- and twenty-first-century Catholicism for a decade and a half, primarily during the summer weeks in Kraków when both of us have taught in the *Tertio Millennio* Seminar on the Free Society. Professor Hittinger's seminal intellectual work on the teaching and legacy of Leo XIII have been the essential background to my suggestion that the deep reform of the Church has been underway since Leo's historic pontificate, which set in motion the transition from Counter-Reformation Catholicism to Evangelical Catholicism.

And as both Dr. Hittinger and Father Newman share my interest in the Civil War, we have had the happy opportunity to talk through a fair amount of what appears here on several field trips together, tracing the paths of the Army of Northern Virginia and the Army of the Potomac in the mid-nineteenth century while pondering the Catholic Church of the twenty-first.

Thus it is both a duty and a pleasure to dedicate this book to two close friends and collaborators.

I am very happy to have been brought back to Basic Books by Lara Heimert and John Sherer, to whom I extend my thanks for their warm welcome on my return—a process facilitated by my longtime agent and friend, Loretta Barrett. Lara Heimert's acute editorial suggestions helped me write a tighter book with more critical edge. Katherine Streckfus is a magnificent copy editor; readers should be grateful for her many acute suggestions, as I surely am.

Several of the themes in the book were tested in the pages of *First Things*, which was also home to an earlier version of Chapter 11. My thanks go to my colleagues of the *First Things* board and to Dr. R. R. Reno, the magazine's editor, for their encouragement. I was also able to preview some of the book's arguments in lectures at Assumption College in Worcester, Massachusetts, at the FASTA University in Mar del Plata, Argentina, and at the offices of the Episcopal Conference of Argentina in Buenos Aires; my thanks to those who brought me to those venues and to those whose questions sharpened the argument in various ways.

The Ethics and Public Policy Center has been my professional home since 1989, and it is a pleasure to acknowledge the friendship, support, and wise counsel of my EPPC colleagues. A special word of thanks must go to Edward Whelan, EPPC's president, and to my colleague in EPPC's Catholic Studies Program, Stephen White. Our philanthropic partners make the work possible, and they, too, deserve a public word of appreciation.

I am, of course, solely responsible for the arguments and proposals here.

—G.W.

JUNE 29, 2012

Solemnity of Saints Peter and Paul, Apostles

Notes

Prologue

1. After the Bible, Pius XII was the single most cited source in the footnotes of the documents of Vatican II. As its title suggested, the 1943 encyclical *Mystici Corporis Christi* [The Mystical Body of Christ] proposed a more richly biblical idea of the Church's identity than was customary in Counter-Reformation Catholicism, which typically thought of the Church in legal-juridical terms as a "perfect society" [*societas perfecta*]. Pius also advanced the liturgical movement with the 1947 encyclical *Mediator Dei* (and still more with his subsequent reform of the rites of Holy Week) and gave a nudge to Catholic biblical studies in the 1943 encyclical *Divino Afflante Spiritu.* Pius's critique of certain forms of postwar Catholic theology in the 1950 encyclical *Humani Generis,* the tendency of the Catholic "progressive" party to juxtapose Pius XII with John XXIII (which fits that camp's interpretation of Vatican II as a Council of "rupture"), and the controversies over Pius XII's wartime role have all tended to obscure his significance as a reformer and one of the most significant influences on the Council.

2. *Evangelii Nuntiandi* [The Preaching of the Gospel] was given real effect by Paul VI's second successor, John Paul II, whose election in October 1978 may have been influenced to some degree by Paul's powerful call to the Church to regather itself for its evangelical mission after a decade of internal strife. A further connection between these two popes, through this important apostolic letter, may be found in the fact that *Evangelii Nuntiandi* was drafted by the Brazilian Dominican Lucas Moreira Neves, who played a major role in the pontificate of John Paul as prefect of the Congregation for Bishops.

3. See J.H.H. Weiler, *Un'Europa Cristiana? Un saggio esplorativo* (Milano: Biblioteca Universale Rizzoli, 2003).

Chapter One

1. For an overview of John Paul II's papal accomplishment, see George Weigel, *The End and the Beginning: Pope John Paul II—The Victory of Freedom, the Last Years, the Legacy* (New York: Doubleday, 2010), 430 ff.

2. See John Paul II, *Novo Millennio Ineunte* [Entering the New Millennium], January 6, 2001.

3. See Henri de Lubac, S.J., *The Drama of Atheist Humanism* (San Francisco: Ignatius Press, 1995), and Owen Chadwick, *The Secularization of the European Mind in the Nineteenth Century* (Cambridge: Cambridge University Press, 1990).

4. Had Manning's suggestion been followed, there would have been many ironies in the fire, indeed.

5. See Leo XIII, *Aeterni Patris* (1879).

6. See Leo XIII, *Providentissimus Deus* (1893), the document generally regarded as the charter of modern Catholic biblical studies. Leo's creation of the Pontifical Biblical Commission in 1902 was another, and perhaps even more important, accelerator of modern Catholic biblical scholarship.

7. In 1883, Leo opened the Vatican archives and library to all qualified researchers in the calm conviction that historical truth would serve the cause of the Church and its mission.

8. Leo discussed the Church's relationship to political modernity in *Immortale Dei* (1885), *Libertas* (1888), and numerous other magisterial texts; for a discussion of Leo's political theory, see Russell Hittinger, "Pope Leo XIII (1810–1903)," in *The Teachings of Modern Roman Catholicism on Law, Politics, and Human Nature,* John Witte, Jr., and Frank S. Alexander, eds. (New York: Columbia University Press, 2007), 39–75.

9. In *Longinqua Oceani*, an 1895 encyclical marking the centenary of the Catholic hierarchy in the United States, Leo set in motion the intellectual process that would lead to Vatican II's Declaration on Religious Freedom [*Dignitatis Humanae*], by teaching that the American church-state system, in which the state claimed no theological competence, *tolerari potest* [could be tolerated]. For a discussion of this important moment in the modern papal magisterium (which was in some respects prepared by the sermon extolling the American arrangement preached by Baltimore's Cardinal James Gibbons in his Roman titular church of S. Maria in Trastevere in 1887), see Gerald P. Fogarty, S.J., *The Vatican and the American Hierarchy from 1870 to 1965* (Wilmington, DE: Michael Glazier, 1985).

10. See John Henry Newman, "Note on Liberalism," in *Apologia pro Vita Sua*, Ian Ker, ed. (New York: Penguin Books, 1994), 252–262.

11. Peter L. Berger, *Adventures of an Accidental Sociologist: How to Explain the World Without Becoming a Bore* (Amherst, NY: Prometheus Books, 2011), 248.

12. Joseph Ratzinger, *Images of Hope: Meditations on Major Feasts* (San Francisco: Ignatius Press, 2006), 71–73. "Icon," here, refers to a reality-in-the-world that makes a spiritual reality present and, as it were, tangible.

13. The Church of the twenty-first century reads excerpts from the *Jerusalem Catecheses* in the Office of Readings for Thursday, Friday, and Saturday of the Octave of Easter.

14. The impact of holiness of mission was neatly and elegantly described by Blessed John Henry Newman, a prophet of Evangelical Catholicism, in an 1857 homiletic reflection on Christians who are called to be saints "in the world" for the sake of the world's conversion:

> They do not put away their natural endowments, but use them to the glory of God. . . . The world is to them a book, to which they are drawn for its own sake, which they read fluently, which interests them naturally—though, by reason of the grace which dwells within them, they study it and hold converse with it for the glory of God and the salvation of souls. Thus they have the thoughts, feelings, frames of mind, attractions, sympathies, antipathies of other men, so far as these are not sinful, only they have these properties of human nature purified, sanctified, and exalted; and they are only made more eloquent, more poetical, more profound, more intellectual, by reason of their being more holy. [John Henry Newman, "St. Paul's Characteristic Gift," in *Sermons Preached on Various Occasions* (London, 1857), 92–93.]

Chapter Two

1. *Dei Verbum*, 2.

2. Ibid., 1.

3. In this respect, John Henry Newman, beatified by Pope Benedict XVI in 2010, is, once again, a forerunner of Evangelical Catholicism. As Edward Short wrote, "Newman was not a religious seeker; he was a religious finder. As he told an unknown correspondent in 1874, '*Means* always cease when the *end* is obtained. You cease walking when you have got home—

if you went on walking, you would get all wrong. *Inquiry* ends, when at length you *know* what you were inquiring about. When the water boils, you take the kettle off the fire; else, it would boil away. So it is with private judgment; till you have found the truth, it is the only way you have of arriving at it—but when you have got the truth, there is nothing to inquire about.'" Save, of course, to deepen one's understanding of the truth that has been given; but that is what theology, disciplined by the truths of Scripture and apostolic tradition, is for. [Short, *Newman and His Contemporaries* (London: T&T Clark International, 2011), 7.]

4. Cited in Short, *Newman and His Contemporaries*, 332.

5. Emphasis added.

6. Leo XIII, *Annum Sacrum*, 8. The "Holy Year" of the encyclical's title is the impending Jubilee year of 1900.

7. See Peter H. Wilson, *The Thirty Years War: Europe's Tragedy* (Cambridge: Belknap Press of Harvard University Press, 2009), for an important study of this period in European history that stresses the political, economic, and dynastic roots of the conflict: a challenge to the claim that the Thirty Years' War was essentially a "war of religion."

8. See Timothy Snyder, *Bloodlands: Europe Between Hitler and Stalin* (New York: Basic Books, 2010).

9. See George Weigel, *The Cube and the Cathedral: Europe, America, and Politics Without God* (New York: Basic Books, 2005).

10. On the meaning of the Divine Mercy for John Paul II, see George Weigel, *The End and the Beginning: Pope John Paul II—The Victory of Freedom, the Last Years, the Legacy* (New York: Doubleday, 2010), 227–230, 438.

11. For an important, pre–Vatican II discussion of this problem, see Karl Rahner, S.J., "Current Problems in Christology," in Rahner, *Theological Investigations I: God, Christ, Mary and Grace* (Baltimore: Helicon Press, 1961), 149–200.

12. Aleksandr Solzhenitsyn, "Men Have Forgotten God," *National Review*, July 22, 1983, 872–876. Solzhenitsyn delivered the Templeton Prize Lecture in London on May 10, 1983.

13. Leo XIII, *Annum Sacrum*, 6.

14. See Matthew 4.17, Mark 1.14.

15. See Acts 2.46–47.

16. See Matthew 25.34ff. and parallels.

17. As indicated further below, this idea of "degrees of communion" was introduced to the Catholic discussion not by Roman curial enforcers, but by the Fathers of the Second Vatican Council in the Decree on Ecumenism [*Unitatis Redintegratio*], 19–23.

18. See *Dei Verbum*, 11.

19. Ibid., 7.

20. Ibid.

21. Ibid., 10.

22. Ibid., 24.

23. Schillebeeckx's book was first published in Dutch in 1959 and in English in 1963.

24. Cf. John 6.54–58.

25. Thus Canadian theologian Douglas Farrow, explicating the Eucharistic theology of the second-century theologian Iranaeus of Lyons, wrote:

> This Eucharist, continues Iranaeus, sets forth before all people an *indicium libertatis*, a token or proof of liberty. Not simply because it can be and is offered throughout the whole world—so that in every place, and not only in Jerusalem, people should have access to heaven—but because it is offered by those who are really free; free not only from Egypt, but from a defiled conscience and spiritual

oppression, from political impotence and social fragmentation, from the fear of death and the threat of Sheol. By bringing our human nature, once for all, into the presence of the Father [through the Resurrection and Ascension], Christ liberates us for life in the Spirit . . . [and empowers us] to receive the gifts of which we are otherwise incapable, including the gift of immortality. [Douglas Farrow, *Ascension Theology* (London: T&T Clark International, 2011), 68.]

26. On this point, see Servais Pinckaers, O.P., *The Sources of Christian Ethics* (Washington, DC: Catholic University of America Press, 1995), and Pinckaers, *Morality: The Catholic View* (South Bend, IN: St. Augustine's Press, 2001).

27. Aldous Huxley, *Brave New World* (New York: Bantam Books, 1968), 119–120.

28. Robert Bolt, *A Man for All Seasons* (New York: Vintage Books, 1962), 81.

29. According to Douglas Farrow, the Paschal Mystery of Jesus Christ—his death, Resurrection, and Ascension—is a drama of

perfecting grace, completing what was begun when the Spirit, who long ago brooded over the waters and brought forth life on earth, hovered over Mary, who brought forth a son. Not only does it fully erase the alienation between God and man introduced by the fall, it fully establishes the communion between God and man at which God was already aiming in creation itself. Indeed, it is the act by which God in principle—or rather in person—completes the formation of man and perfects his image in man. In bearing our humanity home to the Father, Jesus brings human nature as such to its true end and to its potential in the Holy Spirit. He causes it to be entirely at one with God, and so to become the object (and for other creatures, the mediator) of God's eternal blessing. [Farrow, *Ascension Theology*, 122.]

30. See Hans Urs von Balthasar, *The Threefold Garland* (San Francisco: Ignatius Press), 99–105; Balthasar, *Credo: Meditations on the Apostles' Creed* (New York: Crossroad, 1990), 51–54; Balthasar, *In the Fullness of Faith: On the Centrality of the Distinctively Catholic* (San Francisco: Ignatius Press, 1988), 20–23.

31. Richard John Neuhaus, *The Catholic Moment: The Paradox of the Church in the Post-Modern World* (New York: Harper and Row, 1987).

Chapter Three

1. As the Council Fathers wrote in the Dogmatic Constitution on the Church, although "the sole Church of Christ which in the Creed we profess to be one, holy, catholic, and apostolic . . . subsists in the Catholic Church, which is governed by the successor of Peter and by the bishops in communion with him," nonetheless "many elements of sanctification and of truth are found outside its visible confines" [*Lumen Gentium*, 8]. This point was reiterated in the Council's Decree on Ecumenism, which takes the point even further in terms of understanding the Catholic Church's relationship to other Christian communities within the one Church of Christ:

Men who believe in Christ and have been properly baptized are put in some, though imperfect, communion with the Catholic Church. . . . Moreover, some, even very many, of the most significant elements and endowments which together go to build up and give life to the Church itself, can exist outside the visible boundaries of the Catholic Church: the written Word of God; the life of grace; faith, hope, and charity, with the other interior gifts of the Holy Spirit. . . . All of these, which come from Christ and lead back to him, belong by right to the one Church of Christ. [*Unitatis Redintegratio*, 3.]

2. See *Catechism of the Catholic Church*, 813–819.

3. See Revelation 21.9ff; on the holiness of the Church, see *Catechism of the Catholic Church*, 823–829.

4. *Lumen Gentium*, 1.

5. On the catholicity or universality of the Church, see *Catechism of the Catholic Church*, 832–856 and especially 849–856, which stresses that mission is "a requirement of the Church's catholicity."

6. On the apostolic character of the Church, see *Catechism of the Catholic Church*, 857–865.

7. The profile that follows, like much of the material above, has been deeply influenced by the thought, writing, preaching, and work of Rev. Jay Scott Newman, pastor of St. Mary's Church in Greenville, South Carolina. Father Newman's letters to his parish on the meaning of Evangelical Catholicism are the intellectual scaffolding of this chapter, although I have developed the distinctive "characteristics" of Evangelical Catholicism in a somewhat different way than his.

8. The following sequence from *Baltimore Catechism #2* illustrates this approach:

62. Q. What do you believe of Jesus Christ?
A. I believe that Jesus Christ is the Son of God, the second Person of the Blessed Trinity, true God and true man.

63. Q. Why is Jesus Christ true God?
A. Jesus Christ is true God because he is the true and only Son of God the Father.

64. Q. Why is Jesus Christ true man?
A. Jesus Christ is true man because he is the Son of the Blessed Virgin Mary, and has a body and soul like ours.

65. Q. How many natures are there in Jesus Christ?
A. In Jesus Christ there are two natures, the nature of God and the nature of man.

66. Q. Is Jesus Christ more than one person?
A. No, Jesus Christ is but one Divine Person.

67. Q. Was Jesus Christ always God?
A. Jesus Christ was always God, as he is the second Person of the Blessed Trinity, equal to his Father from all eternity.

68. Q. Was Jesus Christ always man?
A. Jesus Christ was not always man, but became man at the time of his Incarnation.

69. Q. What do you mean by the Incarnation?
A. By the Incarnation I mean that the Son of God was made man.

70. Q. How was the Son of God made man?
A. The Son of God was conceived and made man by the power of the Holy Ghost, in the womb of the Blessed Virgin Mary. [*Baltimore Catechism #2* (London: Baronius Press, 2006), 21–22.]

While these formulas succinctly and accurately convey the essence of the authoritative teaching of three ecumenical councils (Nicaea I, Ephesus, and Chalcedon), their inability to engender conversion among modern nihilists was neatly captured by Evelyn Waugh in the famous scene in *Brideshead Revisited*, in which Father Mowbray, a noted pastor to potential converts, finds it impossible to break through the religious vacuity and lack of natural piety of Rex Mottram. "He's the most difficult convert I have ever met," Father Mowbray tells Lady Marchmain. "I gave him the catechism to take away. Yesterday I asked him whether Our Lord had more than one nature. He said: 'Just as many as you say, Father.' . . . Lady Marchmain, he doesn't correspond to any degree of paganism known to the missionaries" [Evelyn Waugh, *Brideshead Revisited* (London: Penguin Classics, 2000), 185]. This modern dissolution of what Father Mowbray called "natural piety," which has become an even more severe cultural problem as modernity gave way to postmodernity, is one facet of the cultural challenge that requires the replacement of Counter-Reformation Catholicism by Evangelical Catholicism.

9. As the Fathers of Vatican II put it in *Gaudium et Spes* [The Pastoral Constitution on the Church in the Modern World], "the Lord Jesus, when praying to the Father 'that they may all be one . . . even as we are one' [John 17.21–22], has opened up new horizons . . . by implying that there is a certain parallel between the union existing among the divine persons and the union of the sons of God in truth and love. It follows, then, that if man is the only creature on earth that God wanted for his own sake, man can fully discover his true self only in a sincere giving of himself" [*Gaudium et Spes,* 24].

10. The question of Jesus's self-awareness as the Anointed One of God has become problematic for many twenty-first-century Christians because of the skepticism engendered by inept preaching based on forms of the historical-critical method of biblical interpretation. Yet according to the English exegete N. T. Wright (using the Tetragrammaton, YHWH, as the name of the God of Israel), a serious historical case can be made for Jesus's self-awareness as Messiah: "Jesus believed it was his vocation to be the embodiment of that which was spoken of in the Jewish symbols of Temple, Torah, Word, Spirit and Wisdom, namely, YHWH's saving presence in the world, or more fully, in Israel and for the world. He believed it was his task to accomplish that which only YHWH could achieve: the great new exodus, through which the name and character of YHWH would be fully and finally revealed, made known" [N. T. Wright, *The Challenge of Jesus: Rediscovering Who Jesus Was and Is* (Downers Grove, IL: InterVarsity Press, 1999), 122–123].

In another book, Wright, arguing on the basis of accepted historical method, made this point even more sharply: "I propose, as a matter of history, that Jesus of Nazareth was conscious of a vocation: a vocation given him by the one he knew as 'father,' to enact in himself what, in Israel's scriptures, God had promised to accomplish all by himself. He would be the pillar of cloud and fire for the people of the new exodus. He would embody in himself the returning and redeeming action of the covenant God" [N. T. Wright, *Jesus and the Victory of God* (Minneapolis: Fortress Press, 1996), 651–653]. Wright's exegesis in *Jesus and the Victory of God* and *The Resurrection of the Son of God* (Minneapolis: Fortress Press, 2003) is an important bulwark to the truth-claims advanced by Evangelical Catholicism.

11. C.S. Lewis, *Mere Christianity* (London: Collins, 1952), 54. Lewis's "trilemma" is not universally accepted, but it certainly sharpens the issue.

12. On this point, see John Paul II, *Ecclesia in Europa* [The Church in Europe], 76.

13. As the Fathers of the Second Vatican Council taught,

> among the important duties of bishops that of preaching the Gospel has pride of place. For the bishops are heralds of the faith, who draw new disciples to Christ; they are authentic teachers, that is, teachers endowed with the authority of Christ, who preach the faith to the people assigned to them, the faith which is destined to

inform their thinking and direct their conduct; and under the light of the Holy Spirit they make that faith shine forth, drawing from the storehouse of revelation new things and old [cf. Matthew 13.52]; they make it bear fruit and with watchfulness they ward off whatever errors threaten their flock [cf. 2 Timothy 4.14]. [*Lumen Gentium*, 25.]

See also the Council's Decree on the Pastoral Office of Bishops in the Church: "By virtue . . . of the Holy Spirit who has been given to them, bishops have been constituted true and authentic teachers of the faith and have been made pontiffs and pastors" [*Christus Dominus*, 2].

14. On the teaching authority of the pope and bishops, see *Lumen Gentium*, 25.

15. *Ex umbris et imaginibus in veritatem* was the motto Newman had inscribed on his gravestone.

16. *Baltimore Catechism #4*, 136.

17. Farrow, *Ascension Theology* (London: T&T Clark International, 2011), 65–66.

18. Ibid., 68.

19. See ibid.

20. Pope Benedict XVI, Address to the Fifth General Conference of the Bishops of Latin America and the Caribbean: Aparecida, Brazil, May 13, 2007.

21. At St. Patrick's Catholic Church in London's Soho district, for example, an international request line for prayers is staffed for hours each night by young people. They take calls for help before the Blessed Sacrament in a chapel reserved for Eucharistic adoration.

22. The related challenge is that there are men and women outside the legal/canonical boundaries of the Catholic Church—men and women who adhere to other Christian communities— who are in fact in fuller communion with the Catholic Church doctrinally, spiritually, and morally than those just-inside-the-boundaries Catholics.

23. See George Weigel (with Elizabeth Lev and Stephen Weigel), *The Station Churches of Rome: An Itinerary of Conversion* (New York: Basic Books, 2013).

24. See *Unitatis Redintegratio*, 19–23.

25. See Peter L. Berger, *A Rumor of Angels: Modern Society and the Rediscovery of the Supernatural* (Garden City, NY: Doubleday Anchor Books, 1970).

26. On this point, see Joseph Ratzinger, *The Spirit of the Liturgy* (San Francisco: Ignatius Press, 2000), 22–23.

27. On this point, see Farrow, "The Politics of the Eucharist," in *Ascension Theology*, 90–120.

28. For some of the difficulties experienced in the United States, see Gerald P. Fogarty, S.J., *American Catholic Biblical Scholarship: A History from the Early Republic to Vatican II* (New York: Harper and Row, 1989). Leo XIII's 1893 encyclical attributes all of Revelation to the loving design of the "God of all Providence" in the letter's title.

29. See Joseph Ratzinger / Pope Benedict XVI, *Jesus of Nazareth: Part Two—From the Entrance into Jerusalem to the Resurrection* (San Francisco: Ignatius Press, 2011), xiv–xv.

30. There were many books that could have been in the Bible and were not included in the canon; thus the very process of forming the canon casts light on the canon's various parts.

31. This was the pastoral planning method used by Cardinal Karol Wojtyła during his years as archbishop of Krakow; see George Weigel, *Witness to Hope: The Biography of Pope John Paul II* (New York: HarperCollins, 1999), 187–188.

32. John Henry Newman, "Meditations on Christian Doctrine: Hope in God—Creator [March 6, 1848]," in *Prayers, Verses, and Devotions* (San Francisco: Ignatius Press, 1989), 338–339.

33. The simpler *Baltimore Catechisms* tended to reinforce this functionalist notion of priesthood, for, although the *Catechism* noted the "grace" conferred by the sacrament of Holy Orders,

it preceded that affirmation by stating that "Holy Orders is a Sacrament by which bishops, priests, and other ministers of the Church are ordained and receive the power . . . to perform their sacred duties" [*Baltimore Catechism #2*, 279].

34. See Russell Shaw, *To Hunt, to Shoot, to Entertain: Clericalism and the Catholic Laity* (San Francisco: Ignatius Press, 1993).

35. See John Paul II, *Redemptoris Missio*, 37.

36. On this point, see Robert Louis Wilken, "The Church as Culture," *First Things* 142 (April 2004): 31–36. See also George Weigel, "Diognetus Revisited, or, What the Church Asks of the World," in Weigel, *Against the Grain: Christianity and Democracy, War and Peace* (New York: Crossroad, 2008), 64–84.

37. On the time-specific character of much of the cultural analysis in *Gaudium et Spes*, see George Weigel, "Rescuing *Gaudium et Spes*: The New Humanism of John Paul II," *Nova et Vetera* 8, no. 2 (2010): 251–267.

38. As noted above, the neologism "Christophobia" was first used in a twenty-first-century context by the distinguished comparative constitutional law scholar Joseph Weiler (himself an Orthodox Jew), during the 2003–2004 debate over the European Constitutional Treaty. A summary of Weiler's position is in George Weigel, *The Cube and the Cathedral: Europe, America, and Politics Without God* (New York: Basic Books, 2005), 72–77.

39. See Kenneth Clark, *Civilisation* (New York: Harper and Row, 1969), 1–32.

40. See Weigel, *The Cube and the Cathedral*, 102–105.

41. Wilken, "The Church as Culture," 35.

42. On this point, see Aidan Nichols, O.P., *Criticising the Critics: Catholic Apologias for Today* (Oxford: Family Publications, 2010), 69–87.

43. John Paul II, *Redemptoris Missio*, 62. See also Weigel, *Witness to Hope*, 633–635.

44. On "permanent mission," see the Message of the Fifth General Conference of the Bishops of Latin America and the Caribbean, 17.

45. On *Vita Consecrata* [The Consecrated Life], see Weigel, *Witness to Hope*, 783–785.

46. *Lumen Gentium*, 17.

Chapter Four

1. Ravasi's brief exegesis of Matthew 14.22–33 may be found in *Messale Quotidiano: domeni-cale—festivo e feriale* (Milano: Edizioni San Paolo, 1994), 1447–1448.

In 2002, in a small book written in response to the abuse scandals that were then roiling the Church in the United States, I told the following tale from the epicenter of the crisis; the story, and the comments I made on it, remain salient:

> In March 2002, Betsy Conway, a Sister of St. Joseph in the archdiocese of Boston, was quoted by syndicated columnist Michael Kelly as saying, "This is our Church, all of us, and we need to take it back." Michael Kelly agreed. Both he and Sister Betsy [were] mistaken.
>
> The Church is Christ's, not ours. It was not created by us, or by our Christian ancestors, or by the donors to the diocesan annual fund, but by Jesus Christ—a point the Lord made abundantly clear himself in the gospels: "You did not choose me, but I chose you" [John 15.16]. As one Jesuit priest, a close student and sharp critic of the corruptions of his own community, wrote to friends in response to Kelly's column, "The Church is not ours to take back because it never belonged to us, and the instant we make it 'our own' we are damned. No merely human institution, no matter how perfectly pure and gutsy and dutiful its members, can

take away even a venial sin. That is the point St. Paul takes sixteen chapters to get across to the Romans." [Weigel, *The Courage To Be Catholic* (New York: Basic Books, 2002), 228.]

2. William Walsham How, "For All the Saints," v. 8.

3. *Caritas in Veritate*, published in 2009, was the title of Benedict XVI's third encyclical.

4. Murray wrote six articles on Leo XIII's political theory between 1952 and 1955. See John Courtney Murray, S.J., "The Church and Totalitarian Democracy," *Theological Studies* 13 (December 1952): 525–563; "Leo XIII on Church and State: The General Structure of the Controversy," *Theological Studies* 14 (March 1953): 1–30; "Leo XIII: Separation of Church and State," *Theological Studies* 14 (June 1953): 145–214; "Leo XIII: Two Concepts of Government," *Theological Studies* 14 (December 1953): 551–567; "Leo XIII: Two Concepts of Government: Government and the Order of Culture," *Theological Studies* 15 (March 1954): 1–33; and "Leo XIII and Pius XII: Government and the Order of Religion," in John Courtney Murray, S.J., *Religious Liberty: Catholic Struggles with Pluralism*, J. Leon Hooper, S.J., ed. (Louisville, KY: Westminster/John Knox Press, 1993), 49–125.

5. See George Weigel, *Witness to Hope: The Biography of Pope John Paul II* (New York: HarperCollins, 1999), 562–564, for a discussion of the crisis moment, which came in 1988.

6. See George Weigel, "Rome's Reconciliation," *Newsweek*, January 25, 2009.

7. A far more sophisticated question-and-answer format was adopted for *YouCat*, the *Youth Catechism of the Catholic Church*, which was adapted from the *Catechism of the Catholic Church* and published in 2011. *YouCat* complements its questions and answers with discussions, biblical and patristic citations, and brief passages from the saints, thus enriching its catechesis from multiple sources.

8. See *Gaudium et Spes*, 22 and 24.

9. George Weigel, *The Cube and the Cathedral: Europe, America, and Politics Without God* (New York: Basic Books, 2005), 73–74.

10. On the rapid marginalization of the Pastoral Constitution's reading of the signs of the times, see George Weigel, "Rescuing *Gaudium et Spes*: The New Humanism of John Paul II," *Nova et Vetera* 8, no. 2 (2010): 251–267.

11. Matthew 13.24–30.

Chapter Five

1. The key votes on the questions of the nature of the episcopate, the bishops as a "college," and the relationship of the college to the Bishop of Rome (which led to no small controversy and a fair amount of ecclesiastical elbow-throwing at the Council) are noted in John W. O'Malley, S.J., *What Happened at Vatican II?* (Cambridge: Belknap Press of Harvard University Press, 2008), 184. The Dogmatic Constitution on the Church is often known by its Latin title, *Lumen Gentium*, referring to Christ, the "Light of the Nations." The Latin title of the Decree on the Pastoral Office of Bishops in the Church, *Christus Dominus*, replicates the decree's first words, "Christ the Lord."

2. See *Lumen Gentium*, 18–29; *Christus Dominus*, 2.

3. The title of Father Thomas Reese's study of the U.S. bishops' conference, *A Flock of Shepherds* (New York: Sheed and Ward, 1992), inadvertently captures many of these problems. Shepherds lead flocks. When shepherds become members of a flock, something essential in the nature of a shepherd, and in the nature of shepherding, has been lost.

4. Candidates for the episcopate in Africa and Asia are vetted through the Congregation for the Evangelization of Peoples (*Propaganda Fidei*), rather than through the Congregation for Bishops.

5. Details of the many strategems by which Polish communist authorities sought to impede the episcopal ministry of Karol Wojtyła and destroy his reputation may be found in "*Defensor Civitatis*," Chapter 2 of George Weigel, *The End and the Beginning: Pope John Paul II—The Victory of Freedom, the Last Years, the Legacy* (New York: Doubleday, 2010).

6. See *Lumen Gentium*, Chapter 5.

7. For a more detailed account of Wojtyła's theory and practice of episcopacy in Kraków, see George Weigel, *Witness to Hope: The Biography of Pope John Paul II* (New York: Harper-Collins, 1999) Chapter 6, "Successor to St. Stanisław."

8. This minimum age of fifty reflected, at least in part, the U.S. Church's unhappy experience with bishops appointed in their late thirties and early forties in the immediate post–Vatican II years, many of whom turned out to be problematic in various ways. But that was then and this is now. Those were men formed (or malformed) in the confusions of their time; their equivalents today have been through a very different formation process and have lived a different experience of priesthood.

9. That sense of detachment from the real world of the evangelical mission and its difficulties (which are, to put it gently, extreme in Europe in the early twenty-first century) was neatly captured in a June 2011 press release from the Council of European Bishops' Conferences announcing the subjects of a forthcoming Council meeting in Vilnius, Lithuania. The press release noted that the agenda of discussion would include "the relationship between culture and quality of faith" in "Church perspective"; "spiritual life and belonging to the Church today in the midst of the quick rhythms of life and stress"; and "the Church's structures and charisms." As one observer noted, "that would sure make me want to surrender my life in the obedience of faith to the Way of the Cross."

10. St. Gregory the Great, *Homily on Ezekiel*, in the Office of Readings for the liturgical memorial of Gregory the Great, Pope and Doctor of the Church.

11. This biblical and theological context, not debates over the proper interpretation of the canon law on the proper reception of holy communion, ought to frame the future discussion over Catholic politicians publicly receiving the Eucharist when they are manifestly in a defective state of communion with the Church, either because of personal lifestyle or public action. Among intelligent bishops who are reading the same canons, there is clear disagreement over what the current canons require. This suggests that, however important canonical clarification may be, the issue is deeper than it may appear and involves the bishop's responsibility for the integrity of the sacramental system in his diocese.

12. See "The Bishop Morris Affair," *Catholic World Report*, July 2011, 32–33. The difficulty in bringing the Morris affair to a conclusion, and indeed the confusions about what precisely had happened in Toowoomba from a canonical point of view, suggest that a reform of canon law to deal with the instances of episcopal failure described here may be necessary. For a description of some of the canonical loose ends in the Toowoomba case, see Edward Peters, "What's Up Down Under?" February 8, 2012, http://canonlawblog.wordpress.com.

13. See James Kitfield, *Prodigal Soldiers: How the Generation of Officers Born of Vietnam Revolutionized the American Style of War* (Herndon, VA: Potomac Books, 1997).

14. See, for example, Robin Lane Fox's discussion of the early episcopate in *Pagans and Christians* (New York: Alfred A. Knopf, 1987).

Chapter Six

1. For a fuller discussion of these points, see George Weigel, *The Courage To Be Catholic* (New York: Basic Books, 2002), 147–196.

2. See the *Catechism of the Catholic Church*, 1142, 1548.

3. Throughout this chapter, the focus is on the diocesan priesthood; priests in religious communities of men will be discussed later in the book.

4. See Thomas McGovern, *Priestly Celibacy Today* (Princeton, NJ: Scepter Publishers, 1998). For new insights into the historical origins of the discipline of celibacy in the Latin rite, see Alfons Maria Cardinal Stickler, *The Case for Clerical Celibacy: Its Historical Development and Theological Foundation* (San Francisco: Ignatius Press, 1995), and Christian Cochini, S.J., *The Apostolic Origins of Priestly Celibacy* (San Francisco: Ignatius Press, 1990). Thomas McGovern discusses the relationship between celibacy and other issues of the priest's self-understanding in *Priestly Identity: A Study in the Theology of Priesthood* (Dublin: Four Courts Press, 2002).

5. The charter for the evangelical Catholic reform of seminaries may be found in John Paul II's 1992 postsynodal apostolic exhortation, *Pastores Dabo Vobis* [I Will Give You Shepherds].

6. A more developed presentation of this masterpiece of apologetics may be found in the film series' companion book, *Catholicism: A Journey to the Heart of the Faith* (New York: Image, 2011).

7. See Joseph Ratzinger / Pope Benedict XVI, *Jesus of Nazareth: Part Two—Holy Week: From the Entrance into Jerusalem to the Resurrection* (San Francisco: Ignatius Press, 2011), xiv–xv.

8. See, for example, the volumes of the Brazos Theological Commentary on the Bible.

9. See George Weigel, *Witness to Hope: The Biography of Pope John Paul II* (New York: HarperCollins, 1999), 88–121, for the story of the early years of this network of friendship, and George Weigel, *The End and the Beginning: Pope John Paul II—The Victory of Freedom, the Last Years, the Legacy* (New York: Doubleday, 2010), 373–374, for the poignant story of these friendships in their golden years.

Chapter Seven

1. Joseph Ratzinger, *The Spirit of the Liturgy*, translated by John Saward (San Francisco: Ignatius Press, 2000), 28.

2. *Sacrosanctum Concilium*, 7.

3. Interestingly enough, Islamic polemicists criticized Christians for this practice, claiming that it represented a return to pagan sun-worship.

4. Citations from Father Lang are taken from U. M. Lang, *Turning Towards the Lord: Orientation in Liturgical Prayer* (San Francisco: Ignatius Press, 2004).

5. See Denis R. McNamara, *Catholic Church Architecture and the Spirit of the Liturgy* (Chicago: Hillenbrand Books, 2009).

6. March 25 is also the anniversary of the first Mass in the original thirteen colonies, which was celebrated in 1634 by Father Andrew White, S.J., on St. Clement's Island in what became the proprietary colony, and still later the state, of Maryland.

7. See Paul Vitz and Daniel C. Vitz, "Messing with the Mass: The Problem of Priestly Narcissism Today," *Homiletic and Pastoral Review*, November 2007.

8. *Sacrosanctum Concilium*, 116.

9. One model of the kind of hymnal that would support the reform of the reform described here is the St. Michael Hymnal, developed by St. Boniface parish in Lafayette, Indiana.

10. This process of biblical catechesis would be immeasurably advanced in the United States if the bishops would not only authorize the use of translations other than the supremely clunky Revised New American Bible, but actually ban the RNAB from liturgical use. The argument that royalty income from the use of the RNAB (for which the U.S. Conference of Catholic Bishops holds the copyright) is essential to the conference's work is not worthy of a bishops' conference that takes the Church's worship with the seriousness it deserves.

11. How anyone can imagine that the abundant use of lace in liturgical vestments advances the reform of the priesthood as a manly vocation is one of the minor mysteries of early twenty-first-century Catholic life.

Chapter Eight

1. John Paul II, *Vita Consecrata*, 14.

2. Ibid., 19 (emphases in original).

3. See ibid., 104.

4. See ibid., 23, 34.

5. The "Law of the Gift" was a key idea in Karol Wojtyła's philosophical anthropology and personalist ethics. For one example of his thinking on this point, see "The Personal Structure of Self-Determination," a lecture Wojtyła delivered in 1974 at an international Thomistic congress, in Karol Wojtyła, *Person and Community: Selected Essays*, translated by Theresa Sandok, O.S.M. (New York: Peter Lang, 1993), 187–195.

6. See *Vita Consecrata*, 91.

7. See ibid., 87.

8. See ibid., 88.

9. Ibid., 16.

10. The LCWR traces its origins to the Conference of Major Superiors of Women (CMSW), founded in 1956 at the encouragement of the Holy See. The CMSW changed its name to Leadership Conference of Women Religious in 1971, but there were more and graver changes afoot in the LCWR congregations at that time than a change in the name of their umbrella organization.

11. Sister Mary Dominic Pitts, O.P., "The Threefold Response of the Vows," in *The Foundations of Religious Life: Revisiting the Vision* (Notre Dame, IN: Ave Maria Press, 2009), 107.

12. Ibid.

13. Sandra Schneiders, I.H.M., "Self-Determination and Self-Direction in Religious Communities," in *Women in the Church I*, Madonna Kolbenschlag, ed. (Washington, DC: Pastoral Press, 1987), 166. For a sharp and, to some minds, devastating critique of Schneiders's theology of the religious life, see Sister Mary Prudence Allen, R.S.M., Ph.D., "Communion in Community," in *The Foundations of Religious Life*, 112–154 and notes. The seriousness and judiciousness of Dr. Schneiders's biblical scholarship struck some observers as being in sharp contrast to her theology of the religious life.

14. For an exploration of the paths by which religious life among American communities of religious women was deconstructed (including an important examination of grave problems in the pre–Vatican II formation of sisters), see Ann Carey, *Sisters in Crisis: The Tragic Unraveling of Women's Religious Communities* (Huntington, IN: Our Sunday Visitor, 1997). Carey's book was based on extensive research in the LCWR archives, although her conclusions were dismissed by LCWR leaders.

15. See Joseph M. Becker, S.J., *The Re-formed Jesuits: A History of Change in Jesuit Formation During the Decade 1965–1975*, 2 vols. (San Francisco: Ignatius Press, 1992, 1997), for a description of how these dramatic changes were rapidly effected.

16. Further details are provided in George Weigel, *Witness to Hope: The Biography of Pope John Paul II* (New York: HarperCollins, 1999), 425–430 and 468–470.

17. Paul Shaughnessy, S.J., "Are the Jesuits Catholic?" *Weekly Standard*, June 3, 2002, reviewing Peter McDonough and Eugene C. Bianchi, *Passionate Uncertainty: Inside the American Jesuits* (Berkeley: University of California Press, 2002).

18. In the wake of the assassination attempt on John Paul II, one not very discreet Jesuit, the Irishman Cyril Barrett, was heard to "bellow" in a London restaurant, "The only thing wrong

with the bloody Turk was that he couldn't shoot straight." When Father Barrett died, this remark was cited as an example of his "detestation of institutional narrowness." See James Hitchcock, "The Failure of Liberal Catholicism," *Catholic World Report*, May 2011.

19. Ibid.

20. Cited in Ann Carey, "Post-Christian Sisters," *Catholic World Report*, July 2009, 22.

21. Dr. Schneiders's letter on the visitation was originally intended for friends, but inevitably got into the blogosphere. It was then published in the *National Catholic Reporter*'s online edition with Dr. Schneiders's permission. The false accusation of "dishonesty" in the post-2002 investigation of U.S. seminaries, which aimed, among other things, to resolve lingering problems of homosexual culture and activity in some seminaries, and the reference to "questions they shouldn't ask," inevitably invited concerns about what, beyond issues of orthodoxy and prayer life, the sisters represented by Dr. Schneiders wished to keep "reserved." As for strategies of "nonviolent resistance," some might argue that the more accurate description of the approach to inquiries from the Holy See typically taken by these communities of religious women and by the LCWR would be "stonewalling."

22. John L. Allen, Jr., "Vatican Must Hear 'Anger and Hurt' of American Nuns, Official Says," *National Catholic Reporter Today*, December 7, 2010. The formal title of what most call the "Congregation for Religious" is the Congregation for Institutes of Consecrated Life and Societies of Apostolic Life.

23. Cindy Wooden, "Vatican Aims to Regain Trust of U.S. Religious Women, Official Says," Catholic News Service, August 10, 2011.

24. In April 2012, as the result of a doctrinal assessment conducted by the Congregation for the Doctrine of the Faith [CDF], the Vatican took the LCWR—not its member-congregations, but the trade association itself—into a form of receivership, appointing Archbishop J. Peter Sartain of Seattle to oversee a reform of the organization's statutes and program, in which the congregation found serious (and amply documented) doctrinal difficulties. The disinclination of the LCWR to concede that there were any doctrinal problems with its program, or with the conception of the consecrated life manifest in that program and in LCWR publications, did not bode well for a quiet resolution of the conflict between the LCWR and the central authority of the Catholic Church—an authority the LCWR, at its August 2012 annual assembly, seemed to tacitly reject as the final arbiter of authentically Catholic consecrated life.

25. That the Holy See changed the Legion's constitutions in the wake of the revelation of Maciel's sins and crimes would also seem to suggest that the legal answer implied in the constitutions' being given the Holy See's approval was not definitive; but that was a matter for the canon lawyers to sort out.

26. See, for example, Sandra M. Schneiders, I.H.M., *Prophets in Their Own Country: Women Religious Bearing Witness to the Gospel in a Troubled Church* (Maryknoll, NY: Orbis Books, 2011); *Finding the Treasure: Locating Catholic Religious Life in a New Ecclesial and Cultural Context* (Mahwah, NJ: Paulist Press, 2000); and *New Wineskins: Re-Imagining Religious Life Today* (Mahwah, NJ: Paulist Press, 1986).

Chapter Nine

1. *Apostolicam Actuositatem*, 1–2. The decree's Latin title, taken from its first two words, refers to the imperative of the laity's "apostolic action."

2. Indeed, the opposite is more likely true, as poorly catechized and ill-formed Catholics have streamed into Congress and the state legislatures, often sowing further confusion about the teaching of the Church and its roots in moral reason. The 2004 presidential campaign of Senator John Kerry and the performance of Representative Nancy Pelosi as Speaker of the House, and later House Minority Leader, may stand as two representative examples of this sad phenomenon.

3. John Paul II, "Homily for the Inauguration of the Pontificate," October 22, 1978.

4. John Paul II, *Christifideles Laici*, 3.

5. Ibid., 15–17.

6. A fine evocation of this facet of the conversion of the Mediterranean world may be found in Evelyn Waugh's experimental novel *Helena* (Chicago: Loyola Classics, 2005).

7. See Rodney Stark, *The Rise of Christianity: A Sociologist Reconsiders History* (Princeton, NJ: Princeton University Press, 1996).

8. The full text may be found in *The Apostolic Fathers*, 2nd ed., trans. J. B. Lightfoot and J. R. Hammer, ed. and rev. by Michael W. Holmes (Grand Rapids: Baker, 1989), 296–306.

9. See *Catechism of the Catholic Church*, 1656.

10. See Allen M. Parkman, *Good Intentions Gone Awry: No-Fault Divorce and the American Family* (Lanham, MD: Rowman and Littlefield, 2000), and Judith S. Wallerstein, Julia M. Lewis, and Sandra Blakeslee, *The Unexpected Legacy of Divorce: A 25 Year Landmark Study* (New York: Hyperion, 2001).

11. *Catechism of the Catholic Church*, 1617.

12. John Paul developed this idea in his four-part *Theology of the Body*. In the first part, *Original Unity of Man and Woman*, the Pope taught that men and women are images of God, not only in their individual intellects and free wills, but, above all, "through the communion of persons which men and women form right from the beginning. . . . Man becomes the image of God . . . in the moment of communion." The idea of marriage as the primordial sacrament is developed in part three of the *Theology of the Body*, entitled *The Theology of Marriage and Celibacy*. See John Paul II, *Man and Woman He Created Them: A Theology of the Body*, edited and introduced by Michael Waldstein (Boston: Pauline Books and Media, 2006).

13. This increasing disjunction has led some evangelical Catholic priests to propose that the Church preemptively remove itself from the civil-marriage business, with its ministers declining to act as agents of the state for purposes of contracting civil-marriages. As the Church is likely to be forced out of the civil-marriage business in any case, the argument goes, why not make the prophetic move beforehand, announcing that, as the state's concept of marriage is utterly discordant with the Church's, it is impossible for deacons and priests to sign state marriage certificates any longer? Were the state to force the Church out of the civil-marriage business, the Church would be perceived (correctly) as having lost a political battle. Were the Church to preempt that exclusion by excluding itself from civil marriage, and doing so on the strongest evangelical and theological grounds, it might, it is argued, help bring the state to its senses. And even if it didn't, the Church would have reaffirmed its own integrity. Thus runs the argument, which is certain to intensify throughout the Western world.

14. The greatest challenge here would seem to be for the movement known as the Neo-Catechumenal Way, whose unique liturgical practices have created what many regard as a barrier between the movement and the rest of the Church.

A different kind of challenge is posed by the Community of Sant'Egidio, which played an important role in organizing the "Assisi Days" of John Paul II and has long practiced a kind of independent, "third-force" diplomacy in world affairs. Its work bore fruit in the negotiations that led to an end to internal violence in Mozambique. Yet the Community sometimes acts in ways that seem to undercut, or at least complicate, the Holy See's own diplomacy. Thus in September 2011, Sant'Egidio invited a Chinese bishop who had taken part in the illicit ordination of another Chinese bishop (i.e., an ordination without the authorization of the pope or the Holy See) to a Community-organized interreligious meeting in Munich, despite the fact that the invitation put the Community in the position of hosting a man who had sided with China's communist government, rather than the Vatican, on the basic issue at the center of conflict between Beijing and Rome.

15. John Paul II, "Annual Address to the Roman Curia," *L'Osservatore Romano* [English Weekly edition], January 11, 1988, 6–8.

Chapter Ten

1. Thomas Weinandy, O.F.M. Cap., "Faith and the Ecclesial Vocation of the Catholic Theologian," *Origins* 41, no. 10 (July 21, 2011): 162.

2. Although acknowledging that many scholars who helped make Vatican II possible "accepted the Chalcedonian symbol [i.e., definition] as a timely resolution of the historic Christological impasse" while seeking to develop an explication of Chalcedon appropriate in a modern intellectual context, Tilley put the matter far more stringently, arguing that "Chalcedon's 'solution' was hardly a solution." Thus he seemed to reject the idea that the Chalcedonian Christology of two natures in the one divine person of Christ was normative and binding within the Church, the baseline from which Christology ought to proceed. The full text of Dr. Tilley's address may be found at Terrence Tilley, "Three Impasses in Christology," *CTSA Proceedings* 64 (2009): 71–85, www.ctsa-online.org/Convention%202009/0071-0085.pdf.

3. David Tracy, "A Social Portrait of the Theologian: The Three Publics of Theology—Society, Academy, Church," in Tracy, *The Analogical Imagination: Christian Theology and the Culture of Pluralism* (New York: Crossroad, 1981), 3–46.

4. In "A New Generation of Theologians" (*First Things*, "On the Square," September 27, 2011), Ryan N.S. Topping reported on a September 2011 meeting of untenured theologians hosted by the U.S. bishops' conference on the subject, "The Intellectual Tasks of the New Evangelization." The contrast between such a gathering and the annual CTSA convention could not be more striking.

5. Blog post of the Cardinal Newman Society, May 23, 2011. This same post described similar "lavender commencements" or their equivalents at the University of San Francisco and St. Mary's College in the East Bay.

Catholic proabortion commencement speakers on Catholic campuses in 2011 included former New York governor George Pataki (Fordham University Law School) and Second Lady Jill Biden (Salve Regina University).

The graduation at Seton Hall's Whitehead School of Diplomacy featured former undersecretary of state Timothy Wirth; during his years in the Clinton administration, Wirth displayed a "condom tree" on his desk (the tree was removed for the visit of Vatican "foreign minister" Archbishop Jean-Louis Tauran in 1993, when Wirth refused to acknowledge that moral education had anything to do with "children having children," as he put it to Tauran). [See George Weigel, *Witness to Hope: The Biography of Pope John Paul II* (New York: HarperCollins, 1999), 716.]

6. Quoted in *Catholic Culture*, May 19, 2011.

7. The CTSA's statement may be found at "Resolutions: 2011 Annual Convention," Catholic Theological Society of America, www.ctsa-online.org/resolutions.html. Sister Elizabeth Johnson's response to the bishops' committee may be found in *Origins* 41, no. 9 (July 7, 2011): 128–147. A very different view of the theological vocation, one which is far more supportive of the Church's evangelical mission, may be found in Weinandy, "Faith and the Ecclesial Vocation of the Catholic Theologian," 154–163.

8. News Release, Catholic League for Religious and Civil Rights, September 27, 2011.

9. Cardinal Newman Society blog post, October 31, 2011.

10. See Father Wilson Miscamble, C.S.C., "Mr. Notebaert, *Ex Corde Ecclesiae*, and the Future of Notre Dame," *Irish Rover*, December 28, 2011.

11. The full text is available at "Apostolic Journey to the United States of America and Visit to the United Nations Organization Headquarters: Meeting with Catholic Educators.

Address of His Holiness Benedict XVI," Conference Hall of the Catholic University of America in Washington, D.C., April 17, 2008, Libreria Editrice Vaticana, www.vatican.va/holy_ father/benedict_xvi/speeches/2008/april/documents/hf_ben-xvi_spe_20080417_cath-univ -washington_en.html.

12. Tom Wolfe, *I Am Charlotte Simmons* (New York: Farrar, Straus, and Giroux, 2004).

13. Cited in *Seattle Times*, September 29, 1999.

14. Father Ryan Maher's comments and John Paul II's letter are cited in *First Things*, June–July 2011, 66.

15. It might also be described as an effort at consumer protection on the part of bishops, the consumers in question being students, their parents, and university donors.

Chapter Eleven

1. See George Weigel, *Witness to Hope: The Biography of Pope John Paul II* (New York: HarperCollins, 1999), and *The End and the Beginning: Pope John Paul II—The Victory of Free-dom, the Last Years, the Legacy* (New York: Doubleday, 2010). See also John Lewis Gaddis, *The Cold War: A New History* (New York: Penguin, 2006). On the distinctive contributions of John Paul II to the development of Catholic social doctrine, see "The Free and Virtuous Society" in George Weigel, *Against the Grain: Christianity and Democracy, War and Peace* (New York: Crossroad, 2008), 11–36.

2. Cf. *Centesimus Annus*, 38; *Caritas in Veritate*, 51. The title of *Centesimus Annus* [The Hundredth Year], as noted, referred to the centenary of Leo XIII's groundbreaking 1891 social encyclical, *Rerum Novarum*, and suggested that John Paul would analyze the "new things" of the post–Cold War world, as Leo had analyzed the "new things" of the world of the Industrial Revolution.

3. See, for example, Benedict XVI, "Address to the General Assembly of the United Nations," April 18, 2008.

4. For three compelling examples, see Benedict XVI's address to British civil society in West-minster Hall, London, on September 17, 2010, www.vatican.va/holy_father/benedict_xvi/ speeches/2010/september/documents/hf_ben-xvi_spe_20100917_societa-civile_en.html; his address to the civil and cultural leaders of Croatia in the National Theater of Zagreb on June 4, 2011, www.vatican.va/holy_father/ benedict_xvi/speeches/2011/june/documents/hf_ben -xvi_spe_20110604_cd-croazia_en.html; and his address to the German Bundestag on September 22, 2011, www.vatican.va/holy_father/benedict_xvi/speeches/2011/september/documents/ hf_ben-xvi_spe_20110922_reichstag-berlin_en.html.

5. John Paul II, *Evangelium Vitae*, 20.

6. Benedict XVI, *Caritas in Veritate*, 28, 51.

7. Arendt's three-volume work was *The Origins of Totalitarianism*; Kołakowski's masterpiece was the three-volume *Main Currents of Marxism*.

8. An older Catholic generation called these things the *res sacrae in temporalibus*, the "sacred things in temporal life," and understood them as "prior" to the state, both historically and on-tologically: that is, they existed before the state both in the course of history and in the order of being, such that a just state had to respect and protect them, not usurp their functions or re-define them. See John Courtney Murray, S.J., "Paul Blanshard and the New Nativism," *The Month* [new series] 5, no. 4 (April 1951): 224.

9. "Gay marriage" as mandated and witnessed by the state bears an eerie resemblance to state-confected marriages under communism, which were regarded as a farce by serious Chris-tians compelled by law to participate in them.

10. John Paul II, *Centesimus Annus*, 47, 43.

11. See John Paul II, *Sollicitudo Rei Socialis*, 41, and John Paul II, *Redemptoris Missio*, 58. Benedict XVI offered the same demurral on "technical solutions" in *Caritas in Veritate*, 9.

12. See "The Free and Virtuous Society" in Weigel, *Against the Grain*, for a discussion of these four principles and their relationship to the evolving social doctrine of the Church.

13. It has not always been well understood by various offices and officials of the Roman Curia, either, but that is a question for the next chapter.

14. See John Paul II, *Redemptoris Missio*, 37, and John Paul II, *Christifideles Laici*, 15.

15. Addressing the Fifth General Conference of the Bishops of Latin America and the Caribbean in 2007, Pope Benedict XVI summarized the institutional Church's distinct approach to the public policy arena in these lucid terms:

> The political task is not the immediate competence of the Church. Respect for a healthy secularity—including the pluralism of political opinions—is essential in the Christian tradition. If the Church were to start transforming herself into a directly political subject, she would do less, not more, for the poor and for justice, because she would love her independence and her moral authority, identifying herself with a single political path and with debatable partisan positions. The Church is an advocate of justice and of the poor, precisely because she does not identify with politicians or with partisan interests. Only by remaining independent can she teach the great criteria and inalienable values, guide consciences and offer a life choice that goes beyond the political sphere. To form consciences, to be the advocate of justice and truth, to educate in individual and political virtues: that is the fundamental vocation of the Church in this area. And lay Catholics must be aware of their responsibilities in public life; they must be present in the formation of the necessary consensus and in opposition to injustice.
>
> Just structures will never be complete in a definitive way. As history continues to evolve, they must be constantly renewed and updated; they must always be imbued with a political and humane ethos—and we have to work hard to ensure its presence and effectiveness. In other words, the presence of God, friendship with the Incarnate Son of God, the light of his word: these are always the fundamental conditions for the presence and efficacy of justice and love in our societies.

16. See John Paul II, *Centesimus Annus*, 5, 54.

17. On the controversy over "gay adoption" and the related imposition of political correctness in the academy, see Andrew Ferguson, "Revenge of the Sociologists," *Weekly Standard*, July 30–August 6, 2012, 24–28.

Chapter Twelve
1. Matthew 16.13–19.
2. John 21.15–19.
3. Excerpted in Adam Boniecki, M.I.C., *The Making of the Pope of the Millennium: Kalendarium of the Life of Karol Wojtyła* (Stockbridge, MA: Marian Press, 2000), 835–836.
4. Morris L. West, *The Shoes of the Fisherman* (New Milford, CT: The Toby Press, 2003), 23.
5. Morris L. West, *The Devil's Advocate* (Chicago: Loyola Classics, 2005), 25.
6. *Catechism of the Catholic Church*, 1831; see also 1808.
7. See George Weigel, *Witness to Hope: The Biography of Pope John Paul II* (New York: HarperCollins, 1999), 741–743.

8. Thus the bureaucrats in charge of St. Peter's Basilica erected barriers to keep the people of the Church at a distance from the tomb of John Paul II when it was relocated to the main floor of the basilica after his beatification. Men and women who had come from great distances to pray before the relics of the least clerical pope in centuries were brusquely told that the space for prayer directly in front of the tomb was for "priests only."

9. According to various informed sources, it was at the instigation of Cardinal Tarcisio Bertone, S.D.B., the secretary of state of the Holy See, that Bishop Rino Fisichella, then rector of the Pontifical Lateran University and president of the Pontifical Academy of Life, wrote a sharp critique in *L'Osservatore Romano* of the pastoral actions taken by a Brazilian bishop in dealing with the case of a girl who was pregnant with twins as a result of being raped. Fisichella wrote the article without any clear understanding of what the Brazilian bishop had done, and in condemning the bishop's alleged insensitivity, Fisichella also misrepresented the Church's settled teaching on abortion. Fisichella refused to acknowledge any error, even when confronted with his mistakes by the majority of the members of the Academy for Life. An anodyne "clarification" was printed in the back pages of *L'Osservatore Romano*, which also declined to acknowledge that it had printed an article misrepresenting Catholic teaching; that it had slandered a good bishop who was doing his duty under extremely difficult circumstances; and that, in doing all of this, it had given a weapon to proabortion advocates throughout Latin America. When it became clear that Fisichella could no longer function as president of the Pontifical Academy of Life, he was relieved of his position at the Lateran University and named the president of a new Pontifical Council dedicated to advancing the New Evangelization. None of the Italian principals in this tawdry affair suffered any consequences from it, and Fisichella was in fact promoted—outcomes that could hardly be considered an advance for either curial discipline or the New Evangelization.

10. For a critique of certain of these default positions, see Douglas Farrow, "Baking Bricks for Babel," *Nova et Vetera* 8, no. 4 (Fall 2010): 745–762.

11. In such a reconfiguration, the Church would be spared the embarrassment of public statements from Pontifical Councils that have little or nothing to do with the New Evangelization, and everything to do with the tendency of all bureaucracies to issue voluminous statements. One thinks here of the April 2011 statement from the president of the Pontifical Council for Migrants and Travelers, celebrating World Circus Day, which celebration, Archbishop Antonio Velio hoped, would remind governments of "their duty to safeguard the rights of circus workers, so that they, too, may feel they are a full-fledged part of society."

12. A similar process of self-examination ought to take place within the various Pontifical Academies. It was not clear to many, for example, why scientists such as David Baltimore and Paul Berg, who have taken positions in favor of abortion and embryo-destructive stem-cell research, should be members of the Pontifical Academy of Sciences, or why the Pontifical Council for the Social Sciences should mark the fiftieth anniversary of *Pacem in Terris* [Peace on Earth], John XXIII's encyclical on war and peace, with a conference that, while interesting in many other respects, studiously ignored the development of the just-war tradition, Catholicism's normative intellectual and moral framework for thinking about these difficult questions.

Epilogue

1. Matthew 26.58; Mark 14.54; Luke 22.54.
2. *Lumen Gentium*, 40.
3. John Paul II, *Redemptoris Missio*, 90, 91.
4. John Paul II, *Novo Millennio Ineunte*, 31.
5. Ibid., 59.

Index

Bishops, 55, 107, 111, 117, 119, 120, 162,
    171, 221, 226, 229, 243, 248
  age of, 124–125
  appointment of, 78–79, 97, 114, 121,
    126–127, 129, 130, 131, 135
  consultation and, 124
  criteria for selecting, 122–124
  Eucharistic discipline and, 70
  failed, 132–133
  making, 122–124, 126
  marriage and, 200
  meeting with, 129
  mission and, 61–62, 112, 113, 114, 121,
    122, 126
  previous experience of, 125–126
  priests and, 149–150
  public policy and, 223–224, 228
  replacing failed, 115, 132
  role of, 70, 79, 80, 112, 120, 131, 135,
    170, 230
  truth and, 215–216
Bishops' conferences, 113, 127–129, 199,
    201, 219, 231
Bismarck, Otto von, 5, 15, 21
Bloch, Ernst, 104
Body of Christ, 53, 54, 62, 63, 65, 93, 160,
    203
  breaking/sharing, 35
  Church as, 19
Borromeo, St. Charles, 79, 120, 125
Brave New World (Huxley), 45
Bridegroom, Christ as Church's, 54, 153,
    154, 178, 259
Brink, Laurie, 184

Campus ministry, 23, 24, 126, 190
Camus, Albert, 28, 104
Canon law, 37, 66–67, 102, 180
Caritas in Veritate (Benedict XVI), 219,
    220
Carmelites, sexual corruption and, 148
Carroll, John, 217
Catechesis, 74, 76, 84, 101, 157, 199
Catechism, 56, 57, 79, 169, 196
Catechism of the Catholic Church, 138,
    142, 167, 198, 199
Catherine of Siena, 106
Catholic Action, 153, 190
Catholic Family Movement, 200

Catholic identity, 36, 181, 215, 217, 231,
    232, 245
  crisis in, 10
  debate over, 66, 69
Catholic life, 15, 51, 127
  Evangelical Catholicism and, 71–74
  renaissance of, 200–201
Catholic Moment, The (Neuhaus), 52
Catholic Rural Life Movement, 200
Catholic Studies programs, 215, 216
Catholic Theological Society of America
    (CTSA), 206, 209
Catholic University of America, 212, 213
Catholic Youth Organization, 200
Catholicism, 23
  catechetical-devotional, 79, 102
  demographics of, 246
  twenty-first-century, 1–2, 2–3
Catholicism (film series), 143
Celebrant, 161–163, 164
Celibacy, 140–142, 148, 150
Centesimus Annus (John Paul II), 218,
    219, 224
Chanel, Peter, 15
Charity, 96, 128, 189, 194, 219, 237
  works of, 66–67, 153
Chastity, 172, 173, 176–177, 182, 199
Chesterton, G. K., 24
*Christ the Sacrament of the Encounter with
    God* (Schillebeeckx), 42
Christian Initiation programs, 196
Christifideles Laici [Christ's Faithful Laity]
    (John Paul II), 192–193, 226
Christology of the Council of Chalcedon,
    206
Christophobia, 5, 82, 83, 87–88, 103, 150,
    204
Christus Dominus, 97
Citizenship, 195, 218
Civil society, 223, 225, 228
Clement I, Pope St., 79
Clericalism, 80, 101, 139, 147–149, 191
Code of Canon Law (1983), 67, 98
College of Cardinals, 246–249, 255
Communion, 37, 50, 55, 66, 67, 81, 150,
    164, 171
  defective state of, 52, 70, 223
  full, 54, 61, 62, 70, 122, 187, 194
Communism, 173, 221, 258